1989

2 nd edition

# Special Education for the Early Childhood Years

**JANET LERNER**
*Northeastern Illinois University*

**CAROL MARDELL-CZUDNOWSKI**
*Northern Illinois University*

**DOROTHEA GOLDENBERG**
*Cooperative Association for Special Education*

*Prentice-Hall, Inc., Englewood Cliffs, New Jersey 07632*

Library of Congress Cataloging-in-Publication Data

Lerner, Janet W.
 Special education for the early childhood years.

 Bibliography:
  Includes index.
  1. Handicapped children—Education (Preschool)
 2. Child development.  I. Mardell-Czudnowski, Carol.
 II. Goldenberg, Dorothea.  III. Title.
 LC4019.2.L47 1987      371.9      86-16883
 ISBN 0-13-826470-8

Editorial/production supervision and
 interior design: **Marjorie Borden**
Cover design: **20/20 Services, Inc.**
Manufacturing buyer: **John Hall**

Photos on p. 143 and p. 171: Courtesy of Ken Karp

© 1987, 1981 by Prentice-Hall, Inc.
A Division of Simon & Schuster
Englewood Cliffs, New Jersey 07632

Printed in the United States of America

10  9  8  7  6  5  4  3  2  1

ISBN 0-13-826470-8     01

Prentice-Hall International (UK) Limited, *London*
Prentice-Hall of Australia Pty. Limited, *Sydney*
Prentice-Hall Canada Inc., *Toronto*
Prentice-Hall Hispanoamericana, S.A., *Mexico*
Prentice-Hall of India Private Limited, *New Delhi*
Prentice-Hall of Japan, Inc., *Tokyo*
Prentice-Hall of Southeast Asia Pte. Ltd., *Singapore*
Editora Prentice-Hall do Brasil, Ltda., *Rio de Janeiro*

# Contents

PART II    EARLY INTERVENTION: TEACHING AT-RISK AND
EXCEPTIONAL YOUNG CHILDREN

# Preface

This is an exciting time for the field of early childhood special education. Society is finally beginning to recognize that young children with special needs can be identified and helped. Professionals from many disciplines and governmental agencies are accepting the reality that the preschool years are critical. Moreover, it is during these years that essential prevention and intervention efforts are most effective. Further, early identification, assessment, planning, and intervention are essential services for young children and infants who are handicapped or at-risk for handicapping conditions. Research demonstrates conclusively that early intervention for children with special needs is highly beneficial.

This book is intended for teachers, prospective teachers, related professionals, parents and family members of young children with special needs. It includes current information about young children who have special needs because they are handicapped or at-risk for handicapping conditions and provides training for people who will be providing services for these children.

The book is organized into two major parts. Part I discusses topics related to young children who have special needs, and their families. It includes a description of the contributions of disciplines of early childhood education and that of special education to the new field of early childhood special education (Chapter 1); the characteristics of young children who are handicapped or at-risk for handicapping conditions (Chapter 2); the important role of parents and families (Chapter 3); methods of identifying, screening, and diagnosing young children (Chapter 4); and the various ways of providing early intervention services (Chapter 5).

Part II discusses specific intervention strategies. It includes a discussion of the curriculum and principles of teaching young children with special needs (Chapter 6); motor and perceptual intervention (Chapter 7); strategies to stimulate communication and language development (Chapter 8); methods to improve cognitive skills (Chapter 9); and strategies to help children develop social and affective skills (Chapter 10).

The Appendices provide helpful information. Appendix A is a chart of normal development in gross and fine motor skills and in understanding and expressing language. Appendix B is a description of screening and diagnostic tests for young children. Appendix C contains a listing of publishers who sell tests and materials for young children with special needs.

The book contains a number of pedagogical features to help the reader. Case examples that clarify the various concepts are included throughout the book. Each chapter begins with an advance organizer to help the reader prepare for the chapter. Each chapter ends with a summary, review questions, and references.

We wish to thank the many colleagues, students, and parents with whom we have worked over the years. In particular we wish to thank faculty of the Early Childhood Special Education program at Northeastern Illinois University, Chicago, for their many stimulating ideas and discussions: Dr. Rosemary Egan, Dr. Kenneth James, and Dr. Barbara Lowenthal. We also would like to acknowledge the faculty in the Department of Learning, Development and Special Education at Northern Illinois University, DeKalb; and colleagues at the Cooperative Association for Special Education, Lombard, Illinois. We also wish to thank our families for their unending encouragement and patience.

*Janet W. Lerner*
*Carol D. Mardell-Czudnowski*
*Dorothea S. Goldenberg*

# Foreword

Interest in the early education of handicapped children is not new, but the support of such programs is relatively new. The history of early intervention for handicapped children is a history of procrastination. It has been rationalized that early training of all children is the responsibility of the parents and not of a public agency. The activist parent movements in behalf of their handicapped children have challenged the rationalization and have rekindled the drive to organize early intervention programs for handicapped children.

In addition there is now a greater need for preschool education of handicapped and disadvantaged children. We have gone through and are going through a series of societal changes that are making it necessary to establish preschools. These include major changes in family life, more mothers working, and more females assuming the responsibilities for the family. No longer can one depend on "mama" taking care of the children while "papa" works. These and other societal changes are increasing the need for preschools, and increasing the need for early intervention.

In the late 1930s I attended a lecture by Harold Skeels, who then told us that he was obtaining phenomenal results by initiating early stimulation for young mentally handicapped children. He informed us that as a psychologist for the Board of Control in Iowa he was responsible for orphanages and institutions for mentally deficient individuals. At one visit, the superintendent of the orphanage requested Dr. Skeels to find placement for two young girls who appeared to be mentally defective at the age of 1½ and 2 years. These children were not talking or walking and, according to the superintendent, were developmentally delayed. The institution for the mentally deficient did not accept children below age 6, but upon the urging of Dr. Skeels, the superintendent accepted the two girls, placing each in a ward with older mentally deficient women. They became the babies of the ward and obtained a great deal of attention and stimulation from these women. Two years later Skeels was surprised to find these girls near normal in intelligence. They were tested, paroled, and placed in foster homes.

Dr. Skeels followed up this accidental experiment by bringing 12 babies (ages 1 to 2) who tested below average on intelligence tests, from the orphanage to the state institution and leaving 13 similar children in the orphanage. Two years later he found that the children in the state institution for the mentally deficient placed in wards with older mentally retarded women increased in IQ by 26 points, while those in the orphanage dropped 25 points in IQ during the same period.

The publication of the article by Skeels and Dye in 1939 met with a cold reception by psychologists and social workers. Critics felt that the data was faked. How could anything change the IQ when it had been "proven" that the IQ was constant and unchangeable beyond the probable error of measurement?

Since the 1930s there have been a series of experiments in the United States and in England that have confirmed Skeels' results. My own study on *The Early Education of the Mentally Retarded,* published in 1958, showed that early intervention of 4 year old mentally handicapped children accelerated their social and mental growth. Similar results were obtained in England by Lyle, and by Heber in Milwaukee, Wisconsin, and by Sue Gray with disadvantaged children. The results of these experiments lead to the conclusion that initiating preschool education at an early age tends to accelerate the social, mental, and physical development of handicapped children, and further, the greater the environmental change the more rapid the development of the child. A meta-analysis of 74 such studies by Casto and Mastorpieri (*Exceptional Children*, 1986) has confirmed these conclusions.

Today many states have provided for more preschools, and today we are concentrating not on whether we are producing results, but on what to teach and how to teach. This book by Lerner, Mardell-Czudnowski, and Goldenberg is aimed to meet this latter need.

*Samuel A. Kirk*

# ONE

# The Field of Early Childhood Special Education

## INTRODUCTION

This book examines the relatively new field of study, *early childhood special education*. With a growing concern in our society for young children who have special needs, this book focuses on children—ages birth to six years—who have identified handicaps or who are considered at-risk for handicapping conditions because of environmental, health, biological, or social/emotional factors. Early intervention programs for at-risk and exceptional preschool children are expanding rapidly. In fact, they increased more than programs for other groups who received special education services for the 1984–85 school year (U.S. Department of Education, 1985). Several types of services are provided in early intervention programs: special education, medical and physical treatment, and language, family, social/emotional therapies.

The first part of this book discusses topics related to young children who have special needs and their families: the field of early childhood special education (Chapter 1); characteristics of these children (Chapter 2); the important role of parents (Chapter 3); methods of assessing and evaluating handicapped preschoolers (Chapter 4); and ways of providing early intervention services (Chapter 5).

Specific intervention strategies are discussed later in the book: the curriculum and principles of teaching young children (Chapter 6); motor and perceptual intervention (Chapter 7); communication and language development (Chapter 8); cognitive learning (Chapter 9); and social and affective skills (Chapter 10). Appendix A is a chart of normal development

in gross                              s and in understanding and expressing
languag                               w of tests for young children, and Appendix C cc                              shers who sell tests and materials for these
children

Ch                                    e field of *early childhood special education*
through                               ) the need for early childhood special education;                               ildhood education; (3) the field of special
educatic                              ood special education as an integration of
these tw

## THE NEED FOR EARLY CHILDHOOD SPECIAL EDUCATION

The early childhood years are crucial for all children; but for the child who deviates from the norm in terms of physical, mental, behavioral, emotional, developmental, or learning characteristics, these years are especially critical. By the time such children reach school age, precious learning time has passed and opportunities for providing vital early intervention experiences are lost.

Early intervention programs serve young children, ages birth to six years, who have special needs or who are at-risk for special needs. Included are children with *established risk* (for example, medically diagnosed handicapping conditions); children with *biological risk* (for example, at-risk conditions indicated in their early medical and health history); and children with *environmental risk* (for example, high-risk environmental factors indicated in early life experiences). Descriptions of the characteristics of many of these specific conditions appear in Chapter 2.

*1. Established risk.*   This category includes children who have handicapping conditions that can be identified through a medical diagnosis early in life. The likely outcomes and probable implications of these conditions are well established. Examples of such conditions are cerebral palsy, spina bifida, and Down's syndrome. Also in this category are children who during their early years begin to manifest developmental delays or deviations, although the etiology often is unknown. Examples of such conditions are language delay and mental retardation.

*2. Biological risk.*   This category includes children with a history of prenatal, perinatal, postnatal, or early developmental events which increase the probability of later atypical development. Examples of such conditions are premature birth and certain genetic predispositions.

*3. Environmental risk.*   This category includes young children who are biologically sound but whose early life experiences, including maternal and family care, health care, nutrition, opportunities for expression of adaptive behaviors, and patterns of physical and social stimulation are so limiting that they impart a high probability for delayed development. For the "urban underclass," early childhood education provides the one key that will unlock the chain of poverty. It gives children of the urban underclass the motivation and stimulation that other children routinely get in their formative years. Early childhood education offers these children the resources to move up, the drive to use these resources, and the chance to develop their minds and their spirits (Wilson, Mulligan, and Turner, 1985).

Early detection makes it possible to provide the kinds of interventions that at-risk and handicapped young children need. Specific intervention services that are provided depend upon the individual child but could include special education, medical and physical treatments, social and emotional therapies, and services for the child's family system. With appropriate identification and treatment procedures during the early years, most handicapped children can learn to function at higher levels. For many children, the handicapping conditions can be remedied; for others, the problems can be overcome to a large extent. For the most severe cases, the children can be helped to live a better life. Early intervention programs can reduce the numbers of children needing restricted special education services and can increase the potentials of severely handicapped children who require long-range programming.

Research has demonstrated quite conclusively that early intervention for children with special needs is beneficial. Moreover, by initiating appropriate training at a very early age, the probability is that the child will be less handicapped in the years that follow (Strain, 1984; *A Tribute to Samuel A. Kirk*, 1984; DeWeerd, 1984; U.S. Department of Education, 1984b, 1985; Reynolds, Egan, and Lerner, 1983). In addition to the obvious benefits for children, there are also economic benefits to society for making a commitment to handicapped preschoolers. The U.S. Department of Education (1984a, p. 199) notes;

> Early intervention with handicapped children results in a significant decrease in services required later; in some cases it eliminates or reduces the services which would otherwise be needed to be provided when the child enters school, thereby resulting in notable cost savings.

The field of early childhood special education integrates concepts, information, and practices from two established disciplines: early childhood education and special education. The first discipline, *early childhood education*, concentrates on the development and growth of the young child along with the child-rearing practices that can enhance that development.

The second discipline, *special education,* deals with the location, identification, diagnosis, and treatment of exceptional or atypical children. The handicapping conditions (as identified in Public Law 94-142) are learning disabilities, speech impaired, mentally retarded, emotionally disturbed, deaf and hard-of-hearing, multihandicapped, orthopedically handicapped, other health impaired, visually handicapped, and deaf–blind. Special education also is concerned with the needs of gifted and talented children. Over the past thirty years, there has been a significant increase in special education programs and services for handicapped students at the preschool, elementary, and secondary school ages.

Although each of the two fields—early childhood education and special education—developed quite separately, they have a common interest in young children who have special needs. By integrating these two established areas of study, information, concepts, and practices from both disciplines contribute to a better understanding of young handicapped children and to ways to more effectively help them.

## EARLY CHILDHOOD EDUCATION: FOCUS ON YOUNG CHILDREN

The field of early childhood education includes the study of the normal developmental growth of young children and how child-rearing practices within the home and teaching procedures in the schools and child-care organizations affect that growth and development. Since the early work of Froebel (1896) in the nineteenth century, there has been a steady expansion of interest in young children. This interest is evident in the explosive increase in the establishment and enrollment in daycare centers, nursery schools, kindergartens, and Head Start programs. The historical evolution of the field reflects changes in the beliefs and values of society, changes in attitudes toward children, and added knowledge through research in child development. The impact of several of these forces is discussed in this section.

### Changes in Attitudes About Legal Responsibility

In the United States, young children occupy a unique and important place within each individual family, even though the child's role may be viewed somewhat differently among various cultural groups. By law, children below compulsory school age are the complete responsibility of the family.

There are, however, several exceptions to the law. Parents may not physically abuse their children, and laws are emerging that protect children from neglect and abuse. There also are a variety of state and federal laws that affect the young handicapped child. Because the range of services for the young handicapped child varies from state to state, each local school district abides by individual state guidelines. For children below school age who have several exceptional needs, the law is quite explicit. Specialized early intervention programs can include home intervention, and most programs include parent participation for meeting educational goals.

### Changes in Family Structure

Some changes in the care of young children have resulted from changes in the lifestyles of society. An early change was the release of the parents' supervision of young children. That came about with the outbreak of the Second World War. The political stress of the late thirties and early forties altered the pattern of family life in American communities. There was a heightened need for increased production of war materials, and the young men who normally would have filled such positions were joining the armed forces. Consequently, large factories sought women to fill the open assembly-line positions. The series of events that followed brought about a total family reorganization. Mothers who were caught up in the national effort found that overlapping work shifts forced them to seek alternative methods of providing competent care for their young children while they were working. The pressures of the times permitted little concern about the possible side effects of these child-care methods. National patriotism overrode the philosophical questions of early forced separation of mothers as primary caregivers. Daycare for young children became an important part of the factory and shipyard employment fringe benefits. In a few exemplary programs, children of employees were given attractive playrooms, meals, and often were provided with sleeping arrangements as well.

When the parents observed that their children not only survived but even enjoyed the daycare program, similar enriching experiences were sought for their children after the war years. Interest in preschool education also was encouraged by academic studies in child development theory. Thus, early childhood education was seen as cultural enrichment, and many of the developing models of early childhood education seemed to be directed at stimulating young middle-class children.

Although the benefits of early education were discussed in the literature, there was little hard research data to substantiate the effects of preschool programming. The extensive longitudinal studies of Shirley (1931), Gesell and Ames (1937), Bergman and Escalona (1949), and Bayley (1968) provided data for establishing the normative stages of child growth.

Today, the trend to leave young children in daycare homes, centers, or nursery schools is rapidly increasing with over 60 percent of all women part of the labor force. Many mothers no longer feel guilty about leaving their young children since most studies have emphasized that the *quality* of the time parents spend with their children is more significant than the *quantity* of time. With the spiraling cost of living, two incomes have become necessary to adequately support many households. In addition, many children are being reared in single-parent households, which necessitates that the parent work. Recognizing that their employees have young children, many large business establishments are opening suitable facilities so parents can see their preschool children at various times during the day.

### Changes in Educational Theory

Other events in society have affected the development of early childhood education. In the broader realm of general education, the progressive movement, begun in the thirties, instituted changes in attitudes toward formal school curricula. Dewey and Dewey (1962) had stressed the value of early experiences as well as environments that offered active learning, rather than static methods of rote learning and drill. In addition, Montessori (1967) demonstrated preschool program success with the use of her didactic materials. Private schools were the first to include these new practices in their general curriculum guides, and public schools also have assimilated many of the new ideas.

### Impact of Parent Education

Other events produced changes in the attitudes of parents and educators. Meetings, newspaper articles, and films focused attention on the significance of learning environments upon children's intellectual capacities. Books written by child psychologists and pediatricians, such as Dr. Benjamin Spock's widely used book (1946), popularized new views of child rearing and provided parents with practical suggestions for solving the day-to-day problems that all families were likely to face. With birth rates skyrocketing during this period, masses of parents were interested consumers of such literature and found that they were able to make immediate applications of educational findings and medical suggestions.

The permissive child-rearing attitudes of the thirties and forties may have resulted from limited parental instruction about child-rearing practices. However, over the past fifty years, there have been many changes in child-rearing styles. At one time, "mothering qualities" were thought to be instinctive. A good mother, it was assumed, possessed natural traits that provided a store of information that could easily be drawn from and that would naturally lead to positive results (White, 1975). Tidbits of necessary information were handed down verbally from one generation of mothers to the next. Today, however, there are major revisions of those preconceived notions. Current research conducted through observation and monitoring of mothering styles shows how important a positive interaction between mother and child is. The research shows that negative styles of mother–child interaction lead to adverse long-term effects and continuing relationship problems (Thomas and Chess, 1977).

### Approaches to Early Childhood Education

There is not just one theory of early childhood education. Rather, there are several theories—each differing in philosophy, pedagogy, and psychological orientation. Six basic theoretical approaches to studying and teaching the young child are briefly reviewed.

*Philosophical or moral approach.* This framework views early childhood education as an extension of parental child rearing. Its purpose is to prepare children to fit into a socialized role in society. An early advocate of this concept was Froebel (1896), who pioneered the first kindergarten in Germany.

*Developmental or normative approach.* This is a psychological view of child development. Research within this framework focuses upon the description of sequential stages of growth for the average, or normal, child. The recommendation of this view is that educational instruction be provided only when the child is developmentally ready for that learning. Teachers and parents are advised to wait until the child reaches the appropriate developmental stage before trying to teach a certain task. The research of Gesell (1940) and his colleagues at Yale University, in which extensive developmental data on large numbers of children were collected, contributes much to this perspective. The research also provides the basis for much of our knowledge about young children. One of the most apparent applications of this position concerns the teaching of reading to preschool children. The proponents of the normative perspective of early childhood education argue that most preschoolers are not developmentally ready for formal reading instruction.

*Psychoanalytic approach.* This perspective of the young child focuses on the development of the child's personality or psychodynamic structure. The position is based on the theories of Sigmund Freud (1938) and his followers and disciples. Current early childhood programs within this perspective frequently follow the teachings of Erikson (1950). The approach postulates that human personality unfolds through the development and satisfaction of stages of psychosocial behavior. Fixations, or arrested development at an early stage, can thwart or distort development in the child and create problems for both the child and adults. The emphasis in child rearing is to help the child go through the various psychodynamic stages in as healthy a fashion as possible to prevent a fixation at any developmental psychodynamic stage and to encourage and permit the child to follow natural responses.

*Compensatory education approach.* This approach suggests that there are crucial inadequacies in the culture, family, or environment in which certain children live. Formal training is needed to help such children compensate for these deficits in their background. An early advocate of compensatory education in the field of early childhood education was Margaret Macmillan (1919), who began the first nursery school in England. In the United States, the early *Head Start* program was based upon the compensatory education approach to early childhood education.

*Behavioral approach.* Behavioral psychology has contributed another view of early childhood education. According to the concepts underlying reinforcement learning theory, the child's environment can be planned and arranged to bring about the desired behavior within the child. B. F. Skinner (1953) is often considered a pioneer of the behavioral approach to learning. Reinforcements, rewards, careful tracking of observable behavior, and the baseline measurement of skills to be learned all are important to this approach. The early childhood programs developed by Bereiter and Engelmann (1966) are based upon this method of education.

*Cognitive psychology approach.* One of the most recent approaches to child development concentrates on the child's maturing thinking abilities and the changing ways children view and understand the world about them. Jean Piaget's (1952) significant work was an in-depth comprehensive analysis of the growth of the young child's intellectual structures and abilities. His research into the cognitive development of young children has been continued and expanded upon by present-day scholars (Elkind, 1976; Kamii and DeVries, 1978; Schweinhart and Weikart, 1980; and Berrueta-Clement, Schweinhart, Barnett, Epstein, and Weikart, 1984).

Applications of these various approaches to teaching young handicapped and at-risk children are discussed later in the book. The types of experiences young children encounter depend upon many factors, such as family size, financial conditions, and educational background of the primary caregivers. There is a growing conviction that *all* children benefit from a generalized early education program. A basic assumption of early childhood education is that a stimulating environment and appropriate instruction can greatly influence a child's ability and improve the likelihood of school success. Indeed, research shows that early and continuing education can dramatically improve the academic performance of at-risk children (Ramey, 1985). Early childhood education is still a young and growing field of study. As interest in the young child expands and as our knowledge increases, we can expect many advances in early childhood education.

## SPECIAL EDUCATION: FOCUS ON HANDICAPPED CHILDREN

The field of special education is concerned with atypical children; that is, children who deviate from the norm to such a marked degree that special kinds of educational services are needed.

Special education began with programs and services to assist children with severe sensory and intellectual deficits, such as blindness, deafness, and mental retardation. Later, other areas of special need were recognized. As the field developed, additional categories of exceptionality were established. Each category became a field within itself, with its own research, professional personnel, and literature to study the specific symptoms as well as to design instructional procedures for that category.

### Categories of Exceptionality in Special Education

What areas of exceptionality make up the field of special education? The exceptional child deviates from the average or normal child in (1) mental characteristics; (2) sensory abilities; (3) neuromuscular or physical characteristics; (4) social or emotional behavior; (5) communication abilities; or (6) multiple handicaps to such an extent that he or she requires a modification of school practices or special education services in order to develop to maximum capacity.

Federal legislation known as Public Law 94–142 defines "handicapped children" as children evaluated as being deaf, deaf–blind, hard-of-hearing, mentally retarded, multihandicapped, orthopedically handicapped, other health impaired, seriously emotionally disturbed, with specific learning disabilities, speech impaired, or visually handicapped who because of those impairments need special education and related services (*Federal Register*, 1977). The term *exceptional children* is a little broader and includes the category of gifted and talented children as well. P.L. 94–142 defines the categories of handicapped children as follows (U.S. Dept. of Education, 1983):

> *Deaf* means a hearing impairement which is so severe that the child is impaired in processing linguistic information through hearing, with or without amplification, which adversely affects educational performance;
> *Deaf–blind* means a concomitant hearing and visual impairment, the combination of which causes such severe communication and other developmental and educational problems that such children cannot be accommodated in special education programs solely for deaf or blind children;
> *Hard-of-hearing* means a hearing impairment, whether permanent or fluctuating, which adversely affects a child's educational performance but is not included under the definition of "deaf" in this section;
> *Mentally retarded* means significantly subaverage general intellectual function existing concurrently with deficits in adaptive behavior and manifested during the developmental period, which adversely affects a child's educational performance;
> *Multihandicapped* means concomitant impairments (such as mentally retarded–blind, mentally retarded–orthopedically impaired, and so on), the combination of which causes such severe educational problems that these children cannot be accommodated in special education programs solely for one of the impairments. The term does not include deaf–blind children.
> *Orthopedically impaired* means a severe orthopedic impairment which adversely affects a child's educational performance. The term includes impairments caused by congenital anomaly (for example, clubfoot, absence of some

member, and so on), impairments caused by disease (for example, poliomyelitis, bone tuberculosis, and so on), and impairments from other causes (for example, cerebral palsy, amputations and fractures, or burns which cause contractures).

*Other health impaired* means (a) having an autistic condition which is manifested by severe communication and other developmental and educational problems; or (b) having limited strength, vitality, or alertness, due to chronic or acute health problems, such as a heart condition, tuberculosis, rheumatic fever, nephritis, asthma, sickle cell anemia, hemophilia, epilepsy, lead poisoning, leukemia, or diabetes, which adversely affects a child's educational performance.

*Seriously emotionally disturbed* means a condition which exhibits one or more of the following characteristics over a long period of time and to a marked degree which adversely affects educational performance: (a) an inability to learn which cannot be explained by intellectual, sensory, or health factors, (b) an inability to build or maintain satisfactory interpersonal relationships with peers and teachers, (c) inappropriate types of behavior or feelings under normal circumstances, (d) a general pervasive mood of unhappiness or depression, or (e) a tendency to develop physical symptoms or fears associated with personal or school problems. The term includes children who are schizophrenic. The term does not include children who are socially maladjusted, unless it is determined that they are seriously emotionally disturbed.

*Specific learning disability* means a disorder in one or more of the basic psychological processes involved in understanding or using language, spoken or written, which may manifest itself in an imperfect ability to listen, think, speak, read, write, spell, or do mathematical calculations. The term includes such conditions as perceptual handicaps, brain injury, minimal brain dysfunction, dyslexia, and developmental aphasia. The term does not include children who have learning problems which are primarily the result of visual, hearing, or motor handicaps; or mental retardation; or of environmental, culture, or economic disadvantage. [In addition, the child shows a severe discrepancy between achievement and intellectual ability in one or more of the following areas: (1) oral expression, (2) listening comprehension, (3) written expression, (4) basic reading skill, (5) reading comprehension, (6) mathematics calculation, or (7) mathematics reasoning.]

*Speech impaired* means a communication disorder, such as stuttering, impaired articulation, language impairment, or a voice impairment, which adversely affects a child's educational performance.

*Visually handicapped* means a visual impairment which, even with correction, adversely affects a child's educational performance. The term includes both partially seeing and blind children.

In addition, *gifted and talented* means performance in any valuable line of human activity which is consistently or repeatedly remarkable. It includes unusual performance in any of the following: general intellectual ability, specific academic aptitude, creative and productive thinking, leadership ability, visual and performing arts, or psychomotor ability. (This category is not included in PL94-142.)

### Historical Roots in Special Education

Tremendous changes have taken place over the years in society's attitude toward the exceptional individual. Three stages in the development of attitudes toward the handicapped child and adult are recognized. The first was one of persecution, neglect, and mistreatment; the second stage was one of pity and protection; the third and current stage is marked by greater acceptance of the handicapped person and integration into society to the fullest extent possible (Kirk and Gallagher, 1986). Current legislation for the handicapped in the United States accepts this latter position and recognizes the "civil rights" of the handicapped.

The public school movement in special education began quite slowly in the early 1900s, but in the past 30 years there has been rapid growth. Today, special education programs of almost all types and degrees of exceptionality can be found in public and private school programs. As noted earlier, current federal and state legislation supports the concept that handicapped children have the right to a free, appropriate public education. School projects provide exceptional children with programs designed to meet their specialized needs. After many years of relative administrative indifference, school budgets have been updated to include increases in special services and staff for added testing and guidance components.

### Prevalence of Exceptional Children

How many children in the general population are considered exceptional? Giving specific prevalence figures has been difficult because various studies use different criteria to specify an area of exceptionality, thereby coming up with different estimates. The Department of Education reports the number of handicapped children receiving services by category of handicap (Table 1.1).

**TABLE 1.1   Percentage Of Students Receiving Special Education Services, Ages 3–21, by Handicapping Condition**

| HANDICAPPING CONDITION | PERCENTAGE OF TOTAL SCHOOL POPULATION* |
|---|---|
| Learning disabled | 4.57 |
| Speech impaired | 2.86 |
| Mentally retarded | 1.84 |
| Emotionally disturbed | .91 |
| Hard-of-hearing/deaf | .18 |
| Orthopedically handicapped | .14 |
| Other health impaired | .13 |
| Multihandicapped | .07 |
| Visually handicapped | .07 |
| Deaf–blind | less than  .01 |
| Total | 10.89 |

*The percentages are based on school enrollment for preschool through twelfth-grade children and handicapped enrollment for children aged 3 through 21.

**Source:** U.S. Office of Education. *To Assure the Free Appropriate Public Education of All Handicapped Children.* Seventh Annual Report to Congress on the Implementation of P.L. 94-142: The Education of All Handicapped Children Act. Washington, DC: Government Printing Office, 1985, p. 2.

Public Law 94–142 specifies that a state may not count more than 12 percent of the number of children between ages five through seventeen as handicapped. This count or identification becomes the criterion for reimbursement purposes from the federal government. However, the federal law also specifies that services must be provided for handicapped children ages three to twenty-one. The three- to five-year-old age group must be served unless state guidelines limit such services.

### Recent Trends in Special Education

In a field developing as rapidly as special education has in the past few years, changes, modifications, and new directions are inevitable. Some of the trends have occurred as a natural extension of ongoing programs; others result from shortcomings experienced in earlier programs; still others have come about because of outside pressures. The passage of P.L. 94–142 revolutionized the field in terms of identification, evaluation, and the provision of services. Teachers working with young handicapped children should be familiar with the features of the federal law and state compliance to implement the law (see Chapter 5). Many of the following trends in special education have particular impact on programs for young handicapped children.

*Cross-categorical placement.*    The cross-categorical (often referred to as multicategorical or noncategorical) movement reverses an earlier direction in special education to classify and place children by specific areas of exceptionality; that is, mental retardation, learning disabilities, emotional disturbance, and so on. Rather than perceiving each category of handicap as clearly differentiated from the others, the common characteristics across catgories are emphasized. There are common techniques and methods for diagnosing and treating children, whatever specific label they are given. Morever, often it is difficult to determine the specific special education category for an indivdual child if the child exhibits characteristics of several handicapping conditions.

The problem of determining a handicapping category is especially difficult with young children. Because their performance during a diagnostic assessment may be erratic, testing results are often tenuous. Moreover, young children can change dramatically through maturation over a short period of time. However, the law requires that to be eligible for services, the child must be identified by a category of handicap at the multidisciplinary conference. Many early childhood special educators believe this requirement to be an inhibiting factor in the evaluation process. A formal recommendation was sent to the Department of Education by the professional organization, the Division for Early Childhood (DEC), a unit of the Council for Exceptional Children (CEC), to permit the use of noncategorical identification procedures for young children (*DEC Communicator,* 1985). In practice, most early childhood programs are cross-categorical programs and include youngsters with many types of handicapping labels.

*Expanded age range.*   While the first programs in special education concentrated on the children in the elementary grades, the field is now expanding the ages at both ends of the continuum. Programs for the secondary school student and the adolescent are growing at the same time that better programs for the preschool handicapped child are being provided. As noted earlier, federal and state legislation mandates services beginning with three-year-olds in many states. Some states and some private programs offer diagnostic and treatment services from birth to three years of age for those suspected of having problems identifiable at birth, as well as counseling and training for the parents of these babies.

*Degree or severity of exceptionality.*   Children differ in the severity of exceptionality as well as in their type of exceptionality. In mental retardation, for example, the degrees of retardation are specified as four levels: mild, moderate, severe, and profound. Similar levels of severity can be determined for the other areas of handicapping conditions. Some schools offer programs for the mildly handicapped and other programs for the severely handicapped. Prevalence rates also are related to the degree or intensity of the handicap. Thus, mild handicaps often are termed *high incidence handicaps* because they occur more frequently than severe handicaps, known as *low incidence handicaps*. The Department of Education has set a priority on the severely handicapped because they are the children who have often been most neglected in the past. The preschool population, of course, will have youngsters who are mildly handicapped as well as those who must be considered within the realm of the severely handicapped.

*Other new directions.*   Several other new directions in special education that affect preschool children should be mentioned. They include special concerns with language disorders, mainstreaming, legislation, medical research and treatments, and use of the microcomputer. These topics are discussed further in relevant chapters.

## EARLY CHILDHOOD SPECIAL EDUCATION: A MERGING OF TWO DISCIPLINES

The goal of the field of early childhood special education is to prevent or reduce the effects of a handicapping condition in young children and to help these preschoolers function better in school and in life. To meet this goal, it is imperative that appropriate services be provided to meet the needs of handicapped and at-risk children, ages birth to six. The early formative years are the most important periods of development in a child's life. The child's learning experiences during these years are critical for later success. Research in child development shows that these five or six years are periods of the highest potential growth in physical, perceptual, language, cognitive, and affective areas. Moreover, environmental experiences during these crucial years have a major impact on the child's development in these areas (Erikson, 1950; Piaget, 1952; Bloom, 1964, 1976; Kagen, 1976).

The early years of rapid growth, development, and learning are even more important for the handicapped child than for the normal child. Early intervention has proved to be the most promising system for dealing with special learning needs. When handicapped and at-risk children are identified early, their chances for academic success increase and the long-range effects of their handicap decrease. One of the strongest arguments for early childhood special education is that it can eliminate many problems that may become entrenched if they persist into later years. It serves as a preventive program for many children who are likely to need special education support and enables the handicapped child to function at higher levels than would be possible without early intervention (Ramey, 1985; Edmiaston and Mowder, 1985; Strain, 1984; Reynolds, Egan, and Lerner, 1983; Bailey and Trohanis, 1982).

A number of forces and programs have shaped the emerging early childhood movement for handicapped and at-risk children, ages birth to six. Discussed in this section are P.L. 94-142, P.L. 98-199, HCEEP, Head Start, the Developmental Disabilities Act, infant/toddler birth-to-three programs, and the increasing prevalence of handicapped preschoolers.

### Public Law 94-142

As noted earlier, Public Law 94-142, The Education for All Handicapped Children Act, passed by Congress in 1975, has been a major force in providing educational services to young handicapped children. Although P.L. 94-142 does state that it applies to all ages three through twenty-one, the individual states do not have to comply with the federal law for youngsters within the three- to five-year-old group. If an individual state does not require special education for handicapped three- to five-year-olds within its state law, then the federal law cannot supersede the state legislation. However, the number of states requiring services for this age group is rapidly increasing. A recent study showed that 42 states mandate services to some portion of handicapped preschool children from birth to age five (U.S. Department of Education, 1985).

P.L. 94-142 also contains an *incentive grant program* that enables states to apply for a grant to provide preschool programs for handicapped three- to five-year-olds. These special funds are designed to encourage the states to develop early childhood special education programs.

P.L. 94-142 does not specify any requirements or recommendations for children from birth to three years of age.

### Public Law 98-199

Passed by Congress in 1983, P.L. 98-199 addresses the needs of handicapped children ages birth to three. This law encouraged the development of programs for children below the age of three by granting permission to use federal funds under the preschool incentive grant program to serve handicapped children under age three. Also, under this law each state could apply for a grant to develop and implement a comprehensive plan for educating all handicapped children beginning at birth.

### Handicapped Children's Early Education Program (HCEEP)

The great majority of programs for preschool handicapped children today are the direct result of the implementation of a federal law passed in 1968, the *Children's Early Assistance Act.* The act spawned the collection of demonstration projects known as HCEEP (Handicapped Children's Early Education Programs). These projects, which represent a wide variety of curriculum approaches and many different types of handicaps, were placed in a variety of rural and urban settings. The HCEEP projects have proved to be remarkably successful. Most of the projects started under this grant have continued without federal funding. The demonstration projects have been replicated at many sites and have served over 100,000 children. A follow-up study of the children who had received services in HCEEP projects showed that 55 percent of the children were placed in mainstreamed settings in their schools and 67 percent performed at average to above-average levels when they entered school after the HCEEP training (DeWeerd, 1984).

HCEEP has five complementary components (DeWeerd, 1984):

1. *Demonstration Programs* This is the core of HCEEP; these projects develop and demonstrate effective models of early childhood special education. The projects, which are initially funded for a three-year period, are located in a wide array of settings and environments.

2. *Outreach* This component is for projects that have completed a three-year demonstration phase. Funding is provided to replicate the demonstration program at other sites.

3. *State Implementation Grant* This component supports states to develop statewide plans for early childhood special education.

4. *Technical Assistance* This component provides help and assistance to demonstration and outreach projects. Technical assistance includes guidance, a communication systems network, and needed training for project staff personnel. The Frank Porter Graham Child Development Center at the University of North Carolina at Chapel Hill has been serving as the Technical Assistance Development System (TADS) for the HCEEP projects.

5. *Early Childhood Research Institutes* This component proivdes the opportunity to conduct research on various aspects of early childhood special education programs.

### Head Start

The Head Start program, first launched in 1964, was intended to provide preschool education to the nation's disadvantaged children. Project Head Start has become one of the most influential and massive federal social experiments in the history of early education. In 1972, Head Start legislation was amended to include handicapped children. Ten percent of the total enrollment in Head Start is to be reserved for handicapped children.

Head Start created the opportunity to investigate the impact of early intervention on cognitive growth and later adjustment. Several longitudinal studies show impressive long-term effects of early intervention for high-risk children. Two follow-up studies of the children who were in Head Start or similar programs some fifteen to twenty years later provide impressive and very encouraging information. One follow-up study is the Head Start longitudinal study (Lazar and Darlington, 1979). The other is the Perry Preschool Program study (Schweinhart and Weikart, 1980; Clements, Schweinhart, Barnett, Epstein, and Weikert, 1984). The longitudinal evidence from these studies demonstrates that early intervention for handicapped and high-risk preschoolers is very successful. It results in significant improvement in children's cognitive skills, behavior, attitude toward school, and academic achievement. In terms of cost/benefit analysis, society gets its money back with interest. There is less need for special education services for these children and a decrease in the retention rate, thereby reducing the time that children spend in public school. Further, upon completion of schooling, the students are more likely to be gainfully employed—to be taxpayers rather than tax receivers—and to be citizens who contribute to society.

### Developmental Disabilities Act

Handicapped children from birth through twenty-one years of age are covered by the Developmental Disabilities Act (Public Law 95-602). This population includes youngsters with severe chronic disabilities. Since infants and toddlers ages birth through age two are not covered by P.L. 94-142, they might be eligible for services through the Developmental Disabilities Act. The condition of "developmental disabilities" is discussed further in Chapter 2.

### Infant/toddler Programs: Birth to Three

With the realization that the needs of handicapped young children and their families begin before age three, there has been an extension of services to children beginning at birth. Groups of children in this age group include infants and toddlers who (1) are medically vulnerable; (2) are severely and/or multiply handicapped; (3) have mild to moderate developmental delays, often of unknown etiology and prognosis; and (4) live in high-risk environments likely to compromise their development. The U.S. Department of Education (1985) reported that the number of infants from birth through age two receiving special education and related services is increasing. In 1984, five states had passed mandated legislation requiring services for handicapped children from birth and other states were considering such legislation.

Programs for infants and toddlers are different from those serving three- to six-year-olds. Parents of handicapped babies are desperately in need of services. They often are confused, distraught, and guilt-ridden. Yet they must learn to become the baby's first teacher, and they need help and training for this difficult task. Child-care givers must be sensitive to the parents' emotional stress and the parents' stage of acceptance of their child's problem. It also is important to consider the needs of the entire family. Interagency cooperation is another important aspect of the birth-to-three program. One profession or agency cannot provide all the knowledge, skill, and expertise needed by handicapped infants and toddlers.

### Prevalence of Handicapped Preschoolers

The number of handicapped preschool children receiving services has increased substantially since the implementation of Public Law 94-142. The increase from the 1976–77 school year to the 1983–84 school year was over 24 percent (U.S. Department of Education, 1985). The increase was due to a greater awareness of the value of programs for handicapped young children and an increase in the number of states and communities providing services for young children.

Of the total population of 3- to 6-year-olds in the nation, more than 2½ percent received special education services during the school year 1983–84. It is estimated that this is far less than the number of preschool children who are in need of special education services. More than 240,000 children ages 3 to 6 received special education services during the 1983–84 school year. Of these children, the percentage in each category of handicap is shown in Table 1.2. Table 1.2 indicates (1) the total number of 3- to 6-year-old children receiving special education services in each of the categories specified in P.L. 94-142; (2) the percentage of children from each category in the *general* population of 3- to 6-year-olds; and (3) the percentage of each category in the total *handicapped* 3- to 6-year-old population. Overall, about 2.7 percent of the general 3- to 6-year-old population in the United States received special education services.

Classifying the category of handicapping condition for young children has been a troublesome issue. For many preschoolers it is very difficult to know with certainty the nature of the handicap. For example, if the

**TABLE 1.2   Handicapped Children, Ages 3–6 Served Under P.L. 94-142 School Year 1983–84**

| CATEGORY OF HANDICAP | NUMBER OF CHILDREN | PERCENTAGE OF GENERAL POPULATION | PERCENTAGE OF HANDICAPPED POPULATION, AGES 3–5 |
|---|---|---|---|
| Speech & language impaired | 168,176 | 1.8 percent | 69.2 percent |
| Learning disabled | 19,204 | .2 | 7.9 |
| Mentally retarded | 19,052 | .2 | 7.8 |
| Emotionally disturbed | 5,860 | .06 | 2.4 |
| Hard-of-hearing & deaf | 5,374 | .06 | 2.2 |
| Multihandicapped | 12,500 | .13 | 5.1 |
| Orthopedically impaired | 7,031 | .07 | 2.9 |
| Other health impaired | 4,015 | .04 | 1.7 |
| Visually handicapped | 1,736 | .02 | .7 |
| Deaf–blind | 139 | .002 | .06 |
| Total | 243,087 | 2.7 percent | 100 percent |

**Source:** U.S. Department of Education. *To Assure the Free Appropriate Public Education of All Handicapped Children.* Seventh Annual Report to Congress on the Implementation of Education of the Handicapped Children Act. Washington D.C.: Government Printing Office, 1985, p. 201.

child exhibits limited language development, the handicap could have one of several causes: delayed language and speech impairment, learning disability, mental retardation, deaf or hard-of-hearing, orthopedically impaired, or multihandicapped. Early childhood special educators therefore are reluctant to categorize and label a very young child, preferring instead to work with and observe the child for a period of time. The nature of the handicapping condition becomes more clearly defined after a more extensive diagnostic teaching period. Yet the law (P.L. 94-142) requires that a diagnostic label be determined at the time the child is identified and placed for special education services and the individualized education program (IEP) is written. This issue of classification presents a problem yet to be resolved. As noted earlier, the Council for Exceptional Children (CEC) has recommended to the U.S. Office of Special Education Programs that identification and child-count procedures allow states and localities to use noncategorical identification procedures for young children if they so choose (*DEC Communicator*, 1985).

## SUMMARY

The need for special education intervention for young handicapped children is becoming more evident. The early childhood years are critical learning years for all children. For the handicapped preschool child, however, these early years are especially important. Early childhood special education serves to alleviate the handicapping conditions for some children, helps some children overcome their problems and prevents later failure, and helps others to live a better life.

The field of early childhood special education integrates concepts, information, and practices from the established fields of early childhood education and special education.

The field of early childhood education concentrates on the development and growth of young children, as well as on child-rearing practices that can enhance that development. Many changes are taking place in this field, including changes in attitudes about the responsibility for young children, a drastic change in family structure, changes in educational theory about learning, and changes about the parenting role.

Six basic approaches to early childhood education include (1) the philosophical or moral approach; (2) the developmental or normative approach; (3) the psychoanalytic approach; (4) the compensatory education approach; (5) the behavioral approach; and (6) the cognitive psychology approach. Each suggests a different approach to teaching.

The field of special education consists of a collection of categories of atypical children. In the federal legislation, P.L.

94-142, these categories of handicap include deaf, deaf–blind, hard-of-hearing, mentally retarded, multihandicapped, orthopedically impaired, other health impaired, seriously emotionally disturbed, specific learning disability, speech impaired, and visually handicapped. The gifted and talented also are considered exceptional. The young handicapped child could display characteristics from several of these categories.

Recent trends in special education affecting young handicapped children include cross-categorical placements, the expanding age range in special education, and the categorization of children according to the degree or severity of exceptionality.

The field of early childhood special education results from a merging of the two disciplines: early childhood and special education. The goal of this field is to prevent or reduce the effects of a handicapping condition in young children and to help these children function better in school and in life. Among the events and trends affecting this field are: P.L. 94-142, P.L. 98-199, the HCEEP projects, Head Start, Developmental Disabilities Act, and Infant/Toddler programs. The number of handicapped preschoolers identified and served has increased substantially in recent years.

## REVIEW QUESTIONS

### Terms to Know

exceptional children
prevalence
early childhood education
special education
Public Law 94-142
Head Start
HCEEP

cross-categorical
early intervention
primary caregiver
developmental approach
cognitive approach
psychoanalytic approach

1. What is the historical evolution of the field of early childhood special education?
2. Define each of the twelve categories of handicapped children in your own terms.

3. Six approaches to early childhood special education are discussed in this chapter. Describe the differences among them.

4. The field of early childhood education and the field of special education have been integrated into early childhood special education. List three major concepts from each of the two disciplines. How are they similar and how are they different?

5. What is the behavioral approach? Give an example of its use in a special education setting for a three-year-old who is not toilet trained.

6. Cross-categorical placement often is used in early childhood special education programs. What is it? How does it differ from a self-contained categorical placement? Why is it growing?

7. Check your own state law regarding mandatory legislation for three- to five-year-olds. Does your state law require special education for this age group? What provisions are there for ages birth to three in your state?

8. Why are early childhood special educators reluctant to label handicapped preschoolers?


## REFERENCES

"A TRIBUTE TO SAMUEL A. KIRK" (1984) *Journal of the Division for Early Childhood*, 9 (1), 2–3.

BAILEY, P. and P. TROHANIS (1982) *Benefits of Early Intervention for Special Children* (ED 222-008) TAD Script-5. Arlington, VA: ERIC Document Reproduction Services, 1–83.

BAYLEY, N. (1968) "Behavioral Correlates of Mental Growth: Birth to Thirty-six Years." *American Psychologist*, 23, 1–17.

BEREITER, C. and S. ENGELMANN (1966) *Teaching Disadvantaged Children in the Preschool.* Englewood Cliffs, NJ: Prentice-Hall.

BERGMAN, P. and S. ESCALONA (1949) "Unusual Sensitivities in Young Children." *Psychoanalytic Studies of Children*, 332–52.

BERRUETA-CLEMENT J., L. SCHWEINHART, S. BARNETT, A. EPSTEIN, and D. WEIKERT (1984) *Changed Lives.* Ypsilanti, MI: High/Scope Educational Research Foundation.

BLOOM, B. (1964) *Stability and Change in Human Characteristics.* NY: John Wiley.

BLOOM, B. (1976) *Human Characteristics and School Learning.* NY: McGraw-Hill.

*DEC COMMUNICATOR* (1985) Division for Early Childhood, The Council for Exceptional Children, Vol. 12 (1), 2.

DEWEERD, J. (1984) Introduction. D. Assael (ed.) *Handicapped Children's Early Education Program: 1982–83 Overview and Directory.* Technical Assistance Development System of Special Education Programs. U.S. Department of Education. Washington, DC: Government Printing Office, vii–xvii.

DEWEY, J. and E. DEWEY (1962) *Schools of Tomorrow.* NY: Dutton.

EDMIASTON, R. and B. MOWDER (1985) "Early Intervention for Handicapped Children: Efficacy Issues and Data for School Psychologists." *Psychology in the Schools*, 22, 171–78.

ELKIND, D. (1976) *Child Development and Education: A Piagetian Perspective.* NY: Oxford University Press.

ERIKSON, E. (1950) *Childhood and Society.* NY: W.W. Norton.

*Federal Register.* Department of Health, Education, and Welfare, Office of Education, Education of Handicapped Children, August 23, 1977.

FREUD, S. (1938) *The Basic Writings of Sigmund Freud.* New York: Modern Library.

FROEBEL, F. (1896) *The Education of Man.* NY: Appleton and Co.

GESELL, A. and L. AMES (1937) "Early Evidences of Individuality in the Human Infant." *Scientific Monthly*, 45, 217–25.

GESELL, A., et al. (1940) *The First Five Years of Life: A Guide to the Study of the Preschool Child.* NY: Harper & Row.

KAGAN, J. (1976) "Emergent Themes in Human Development." *American Scientist,* Mar–April, 186–96.

KAMII, C. and R. DEVRIES (1978) *Physical Knowledge in Preschool Education: Implications of Piaget's Theory.* Englewood Cliffs, NJ: Prentice-Hall.

KIRK, S. and J. GALLAGHER (1986) *Educating Exceptional Children.* Boston: Houghton Mifflin.

LAZAR, I. and R. DARLINGTON (1979) *Lasting Effects After Preschool.* Publication No. (OHDD) 80-30179. Washington, DC: Government Printing Office. U.S. Department of Health and Human Services. Office of Human Development Services. Administration for Children, Youth, and Family.

MACMILLAN, M. (1919) *The Nursery School.* London: J.M. Dent & Sons.

MONTESSORI, M. (1967) *The Absorbent Mind.* NY: Holt, Rinehart & Winston.

PIAGET, J. (1952) *The Origins of Intelligence in Children.* NY: International University Press.

RAMEY, C. (1985) *Do Early Interventions Make a Difference? If So, How?* (Paper presented at the National Early Childhood Conference on Children with Special Needs, Denver, CO, October 7, 1985).

REYNOLDS, L., R. EGAN, and J. LERNER (1983) "The Efficacy of Early Intervention on Pre-Academic Deficits: Review of the Literature." *Topics in Early Childhood Special Education,* 3, 47–76.

SCHWEINHART, L. and D. WEIKART (1980) *Young Children Grow Up: The Effects of the Perry Preschool Program on Youths Through Age 15.* Ypsilanti, MI: The High/Scope Press.

SHIRLEY, M. (1931) *The First Two Years: A Study of 25 Babies.* Institute for Child Welfare Monographs. Minneapolis: University of Minnesota Press, I, 6.

SKINNER, B. (1953) *Science and Human Behavior.* NY: Macmillan.

SPOCK, B. (1946) *Baby and Child Care.* NY: Pocket Books.

STRAIN, P. (1984) "Efficacy Research With Young Handicapped Children: A Critique of the Status Quo." *Journal of the Division for Early Childhood,* 9 (1), 4–10.

THOMAS, A. and S. CHESS (1977) *Temperament and Development.* NY: Bruner/Mazel.

U.S. DEPARTMENT OF EDUCATION (1984a) "Executive Summary." Sixth Annual Report to Congress on the Implementation of Public Law 94-142: The Education of All Handicapped Children Act. *Exceptional Children* 51 (3), 199–202.

U.S. DEPARTMENT OF EDUCATION (1984b) *To Assure the Free Appropriate Public Education of All Handicapped Children.* Sixth Annual Report to Congress on the Implementaton of Public Law 94-142. The Education of All Handicapped Children Act. Washington, DC: Government Printing Office.

U.S. DEPARTMENT OF EDUCATION (1985) *To Assure the Free Appropriate Public Education of All Handicapped Children.* Seventh Annual Report to Congress on the Implementation of the Education of All Handicapped Children Act. Washington, DC: Government Printing Office.

WHITE, B. (1975) *The First Three Years of Life.* Englewood Cliffs, NJ: Prentice-Hall.

WILSON, R., M. MULLIGAN, and R. TURNER (1985) "Early Childhood Intervention in an Urban Setting." *Teaching Exceptional Children,* 17 (2), 134–39.

# TWO

# Characteristics of Exceptional Preschool Children

## INTRODUCTION

This chapter reviews the categories of exceptionalities in young children. After reviewing high-risk factors, the chapter discusses the exceptionalities of speech and language impairments, mental retardation, learning disabilities, behavioral and emotional disorders, hearing impairments, visual impairments, physical handicaps, other health impairments, multiple handicaps, and the gifted and talented.

In special education, the term *category* means a specific area of atypical development. Public Law 94-142 requires that during the evaluation of a handicapped child, the child's category of exceptionality be identified. However, a few states have elected to identify children on the basis of needed services instead of the category of handicap. (U.S. Department of Education, 1985). It is important for teachers of young handicapped children to be familiar with the characteristics associated with the various categories of handicapping conditions. Classifying exceptional children by category can be useful: It helps in identifying the problem and communicating with others about certain types of children; it provides a structure for mobilizing an advocacy force for a specific category of children; and it stimulates research to find the causes and treatment of specific conditions. In Chapter 1, Table 1.2 indicates by category the percentage of handicap-

pe⋯⋯ ⋯ served in special education programs.
th⋯⋯ ⋯ category of handicap does not always provide
yo⋯⋯ ⋯n for making decisions about the placement of
m⋯⋯ ⋯ning their instruction. For these decisions, it is
se⋯⋯ ⋯he child's educational needs. Moreover, because
so⋯⋯ ⋯f exceptionality have overlapping symptoms, it
T⋯⋯ ⋯agnose, with certainty, the category of handicap.
ta⋯⋯ ⋯en with special needs usually are placed and
g⋯⋯ ⋯al grouping. That is, children from several cate-
t⋯⋯ ⋯well as nonhandicapped children, are placed
⋯⋯ ⋯The latter part of this book is organized cross-
categorically; that is, according to the educational needs of special education preschoolers.

## HIGH-RISK FACTORS

In many cases, the cause of the handicapping condition in young children is unknown. There are, however, a number of conditions that are considered high-risk factors. These high-risk conditions may occur during the *prenatal* stage (before birth), the *perinatal* stage (during birth), or the *postnatal* stage (after birth). This section reviews some of the high-risk conditions that can lead to a number of handicapping conditions, including physical handicaps, mental retardation, sensory deficits, emotional disorders, multiple handicaps, or learning problems.

### Prenatal Factors

*The health of the mother.* The mother's general health during the pregnancy is an important element for the developing baby. There are a number of conditions that have been found to adversely affect the developing baby.

*Malnutrition* of the mother during the pregnancy has a direct effect on the development of the fetus. Recent studies indicate that even the eating patterns of teenage girls will later influence the growth and development of their unborn children (Gibson, 1978). Undernourished mothers tend to have fragile babies who are more likely to have developmental problems (Bergan and Henderson, 1979). Rickets, a bone malformation that occurs in early childhood, is a condition caused by a vitamin deficiency in the diet of the mother during pregnancy. This deficiency also can cause mental defects or general physical weakness in newborns (Goldenson, 1970). Other conditions attributable to poor maternal diet include anemia, toxemia, brain damage, and prematurity (Gibson, 1978).

The *mother's health and physical condition* during pregnancy is associated with a number of handicapping conditions. Mothers from poor

*131,509*

socioeconomic environments who lack pre          to have
babies with birth defects. The disease of r          ) during
the first three months of pregnancy can          icapping
conditions in the baby. Gonorrhea can r          ness; and
syphilis can lead to natural abortion, i          maturity.
Chronic anemia can cause cleft palate          of of the
mouth) or hair lip; and diabetes in the          related to
congenital abnormalities and infant inf          The use of
alcohol, drugs, and tobacco by the pre          t in miscarriage, decreased birth weight, prema          l problems,
lack of coordination, and/or developmental retardation         an and Henderson, 1979 Wallis, 1986). Drug- or alcohol-dependent mothers often
produce drug-dependent infants (Bergan and Henderson, 1979 Wallis,
1986). According to Furey (1982), Fetal Alcohol syndrome may be the
third most common cause of mental retardation.

How the *emotional condition* of the mother affects the fetus is not as
readily documented. However, it is thought that stress and tension can
cause hormonal or metabolic imbalances which can result in obstetrical
complications.

*Maternal age* is another factor related to the health of the baby. Babies
born to very young women (under 16) or older women (over 40) have a
greater risk of being handicapped than those born to mothers in their
twenties or thirties (Nortman, 1974).

*Radiation* is another cause of birth defects. X-rays, ionizing radiation,
and atomic radiation can affect fetal development and should be avoided
during pregnancy (Sisson, Clatworthy, and Zadroga, 1975). One result of
radiation is microcephaly, a condition in which the sutures of the skull close
before they should. This causes the skull and brain to stop growing and
results in severe mental retardation.

*Congenital, genetic, and chromosomal factors.* Through medical research, scientists are discovering that certain handicapping conditions have
congenital, genetic, and chromosomal causes. Three categories of genetic
defects have been identified in humans: the solitary mutant gene, chromosomal abnormalities, and multifactoral inheritance traits (Nelson, 1983).
Some congenital defects can be explained by the pattern of dominant or
recessive genes or chromosomal abnormalities. Several genetic disorders
are described here.

The *Rh factor* is a genetically determined difference between the
blood types of the mother and fetus, making them incompatible. This can
cause miscarriage, still birth, or defects such as brain damage and anemia.
Fortunately, there are ways to deal with this problem today by giving
immunizations to Rh-negative mothers.

*Phenylketonuria* is a genetic condition that can lead to mental retardation. This genetic anomaly can be readily diagnosed through a simple test

of the newborn's urine or blood and counteracted immediately by strict dietary regulation.

*Down's syndrome* is the most common chromosomal cause of retardation, affecting one in 660 births. Children with this syndrome have a slow rate of learning and other physical symptoms. Down's syndrome is the result of an oddity of genes of the twenty-first chromosome. The risk factor for this condition increases with the mother's age. A mother aged forty has a thirty times greater chance of having a child with Down's syndrome than a mother under twenty years of age (Reed, 1975). Of all Down's syndrome children, 65 percent are born to women over thirty. While not eradicating the handicap, home and infant stimulation have reduced the rate of decline from that once seen in institutionalized Down's syndrome children.

*Turner's syndrome* and *Klinefelter's syndrome* are two conditions that are the result of irregularity of sex chromosomes. In *Turner's syndrome,* which affects females, there is only one $X$ chromosome and no $Y$ chromosomes. Children with Turner's syndrome are not mentally retarded on a generalized scale, but they do experience space and form perception difficulties. *Klinefelter's syndrome* affects males and is a form of male hypogonadism, with the addition of an extra $X$ chromosome ($XXY$). Sexual development and delayed onset of secondary sex characteristics require the application of hormonal therapy.

### Perinatal Factors

*Premature birth.* *Prematurity* is commonly defined as a gestation period of less than 37 weeks or a birth weight of less than 2500 grams (5½ pounds). Premature babies are at-risk for many developmental problems. In general, the lower the birth weight or the shorter the gestation period, the greater the chance that the child will have a handicap. Premature babies more often have serious respiratory difficulties than full-term infants. Moreover, premature birth reduces the effectiveness of the infant's life-support systems. Thus, low-birth-weight infants often have greater difficulty in performing independent survival tasks, since their immature physiological structures cannot operate independently. If the respiratory system is not functioning adequately, then oxygen does not flow to meet the needs of the organs and the brain cells. Any reducton of oxygen supply can have irreversible results. Oxygen imbalance can also result in metabolic and chemical imbalances which lead to more generalized cell damage, jaundice, intracranial bleeding, and apraxia (motor problems).

*Difficulty during the birth process.* A number of handicapping conditions are related to difficulties that occur during the birth process. One of these conditions is *anoxia,* a condition in which the infant is deprived of oxygen during the birth process. Anoxia can be caused by a number of factors, including abnormality in the fetal position, hemorrhaging or severe bleeding by the mother, ineffective uterine contractions, a birth canal too small for the size of the baby, or an interference with the flow of blood through the umbilical cord. The longer the deprivation of oxygen, the more serious the problem. It can lead to mental retardation, neurological dysfunction, or language disorders (Gibson, 1978).

### Postnatal Factors

*Injuries.* Injuries due to accidents occur quite frequently with young children. The more serious injuries can result in handicapping conditions. Bicycle and automobile accidents cause the greatest number of cases of paralysis.

*Illness.* Illness and treatment effects of childhood illness can lead to handicapping conditions; for example, polio or meningitis. Research findings show long-term survivors of childhood leukemia who received treatment with radiation and chemotherapy may suffer from neuropsychological defects and learning disabilities (Brouwers, Riccardi, Fedio, and Poplach, 1985).

*Environment.* Poor environmental conditions can be a contributing factor in producing high-risk babies. Research shows that factors contributing to an impoverished environment include lack of intellectual stimulation, neglect, teenage parents, child abuse, and lack of home teaching. These children are likely to be unprepared for school learning and consequently do poorly in school.

## SPEECH AND LANGUAGE IMPAIRMENTS

As shown in Table 1.2 (in Chapter 1), speech and language impairments are the most frequently reported category of handicap for 3- to 6-year-olds. Speech and language problems comprise about 1.8 percent of the general 3- to 6-year-old population and more than 69 percent of all handicapped 3- to 6-year-olds. The ability to use speech and language in a functional way is an essential aspect of human development. Although other animal forms are able to communicate, only human beings have the ability to use speech and language as a means of transferring information.

### Causes

There are numerous causes of speech and language disorders. Moreover, children in many of the categories of exceptionality are likely to have some form of speech and language difficulty. Because neurological dysfunction can delay the development of language abilities, these children may be late in their acquisition of speech and language. Mentally retarded children are slow in general development, including speech and language; they may have speech problems due to motor difficulties and language problems related to memory deficits. Deaf children always have speech and language problems, and hearing-impaired children sometimes have difficulty. Emotional problems can inhibit the quality of language production, and traumatic emotional events also can interrupt language development. Since most young handicapped children in all of the categories of handicap also have speech and language problems, this classification becomes a kind of cross-categorical classification.

### Characteristics

It is necessary to differentiate between a speech disorder and a language disorder. The first refers to the production of speech sounds; the latter to the understanding and use of the language process.

*Speech disorders.* Children with *speech disorders* have difficulty in producing and articulating the sounds of language. Their speaking patterns deviate so markedly that attention is drawn to the impairment and this interferes with communication. Young children learning to talk normally make many types of developmental speech errors, such as consonant substitution errors (for example, "wabbit" for "rabbit" or "widdle" for "little"). The child with a speech disorder, however, continues to have articulation errors long beyond the normal developmental age for learning to produce these sounds.

Speech disorders include problems of articulation, voice, and rhythm. *Articulation errors* include additions of speech sounds, distortions, substitutions, and sound omissions. *Voice defects* include marked deviations in pitch, quality, and intensity. These children speak in a voice that is pitched too high, too low, or in a nonmelodious monotone. Children with cleft palates may have a nasal quality to their speech. Growths or polyps on the vocal cords may produce a hoarseness of the voice. *Rhythm-defects,* another type of speech difficulty, include stuttering, blocking, cluttering, or echolalic repetition of sounds, words, and phrases. The frustraton of stuttering may create emotional problems, and emotional problems can be one cause of stuttering.

*Language disorders.* A *language disorder* is much broader, entailing the entire spectrum of communication and verbal behavior. Language disorders include a poor understanding of the meanings of words and the way words are put together into sentences. The child with a language disorder might be delayed in talking, be unable to understand the language of others or be unable to string words together to create sentences. A language disorder is the marked inability to use language, or to communicate verbally. The problem of delayed language is one in which the child does not develop language skills at the appropriate age, has a limited vocabulary, and uses a skeletal construction of sentences. Severely language-delayed children will show little to no use of verbal communication and often rely upon nonverbal gestures to communicate their needs.

### Impact On The Young Child

The power of having language at one's command is great. Being unable to communicate to express one's wants is very frustrating for a child. Without verbal communication skills, children must use gestures, pointing, and temper outbursts. The dramatic illustration of the power of language comes from the well-known story of Helen Keller. Possessing language transformed her from behaving in an animallike fashion to normal human behavior. Teachers and parents must be sensitive to the problems of communication disorders and be knowledgeable about alternative methods for helping children improve speech and language skills. (A more in-depth discussion of communication problems and methods for instruction are presented in Chapter 8.)

## MENTAL RETARDATION

### Definition and Levels

Defining mental retardation is not an easy task. No *one* set of criteria seems inclusive enough to meet the many diverse behaviors seen in children with varying degrees of retardation. The definition suggested by the American Association of Mental Deficiency (AAMD) is one that is generally accepted:

> Mental retardation refers to significantly subaverage general intellectual functioning existing concurrently with deficits in adaptive behavior and manifested during the developmental period. (Grossman, 1983, p. 1).

Crucial to the AAMD definition is the inclusion of *both* low intellectual functioning (an IQ of less than 70) and deficits in adaptive behavior measures. Intellectual functioning is usually measured through the use of an intelligence test. Adaptive behavior means the degree to which the child can meet age-level standards of self-sufficiency and social responsibility. In early childhood, adaptive behavior includes sensory-motor, communication, self-help, and socialization skills.

The AAMD definition categorizes four functional levels of mental retardation: mild, moderate, severe, and profound. The IQ scores for each of these levels are shown in Table 2.1.

**TABLE 2.1 Levels of Mental Retardation**

| LEVEL OF SEVERITY | IQ SCORE |
| --- | --- |
| Mild | 50–55 to 70 |
| Moderate | 35–40 to 50–55 |
| Severe | 20–25 to 35–40 |
| Profound | below 20–25 |

Adapted from H. J. Grossman, ed., *Classification in Mental Retardation*. Washington, DC: American Association on Mental Deficiency, 1983.

Prior to the AAMD classification of retardation, mentally retarded children were categorized as *educable mentally handicapped* (EMH) or *trainable mentally handicapped* (TMH). Many schools have retained this classification because it is helpful for educational purposes.

### Characteristics

Mentally retarded children have a generalized or global delay in all areas of development. Perception does not develop at a normal rate, resulting in slow development in body control and hand–eye integration skills. Speech and language skills are acquired at a slower rate, which affects communication abilities. Social and emotional behaviors also show slow development. The characteristics of severe and profound mentally retarded children are fairly obvious, and those children can be readily identified in the preschool years. The more subtle symptoms of mild and moderate retardation are not as obvious, and accurate identification may take a longer period of time.

### Causes

Determining the cause of mental retardation is difficult. In fact, in only about 15 percent of cases of mental retardation can the cause be determined. When the cause can be identified, the degree of retardation is likely to be rather severe. Most mentally retarded children, however, fall within the mild level, where often little is known about the causation.

Two general origins of mental retardation are brain damage and the broad category of cultural–familial causes. Brain damage is caused by specific diseases, infections, traumas, and chromosomal abnormalities; and these cases are likely to be severe. For most mild cases of retardation the cause is unknown, and these cases often are thought to have cultural–familial causes (due to environmental or inherited factors).

Most authorities agree, today, that one's level of intellectual functioning is not a question of selecting *either* environment or heredity. Intellectual functioning and the ability to learn are at least partly the product of home and school training. Children need stimulation and nurturance if they are to develop intellectually. Research evidence from the longitudinal Head Start studies and other research with young children from impoverished environments show that these children do improve in intellectual functioning when provided with a stimulating preschool experience (see Chapter 9).

Thus, there is an interactive relationship between the two factors of environment and heredity. Heredity is a component in one's intellectual capacity, but environmental experiences and educational interventions can significantly raise an individual's intellectual functioning. Moreover, it is during the early years that educational interventions are most effective in increasing cognitive growth and the ability to learn.

### Impact on the Young Child

Teachers working with mentally retarded preschool children should be aware of the impact of these characteristics in a learning situation. Parents should be given realistic and practical information concerning the educational limitations and reasonable expectations for their child's future.

Mentally retarded children need extensive drill, a highly structured environment, and individualized teaching. They need many repetitions of a single task in order to learn it. The teacher cannot assume that the child knows the task until the child can perform it consistently over a reasonable period of time. Instruction should be closely related to daily experiences. For example, to teach the concepts of inside and outside, the teacher could physically open the door and walk to the *outside* environment and then physically open the door and come *inside*. Along with the physical movement should be a verbal description of going outside and inside. Instructional experiences should be concrete rather than abstract. For example, in learning to count, it is more helpful for the child to use concrete objects that can be held and manipulated rather than to learn the concepts from abstract symbols on a printed page.

## LEARNING DISABILITIES

Preschool children with learning disabilities have not yet encountered academic failure in school. Yet they can be identified as high-risk children as preschoolers through behavior and development delays in areas such as motor, language, and attentional behaviors. Young children with learning disabilities are considered at-risk: that is, they are predicted to have future difficulty with academic learning. By identifying them before they do fail in school, measures can be taken so that learning failure can be prevented or lessened.

## Definition and Characteristics

Children with learning disabilities have difficulties in learning specific skills, such as speaking, reading, arithmetic, or writing. These children do not have a sensory impairment, they are not mentally retarded, and they do not have a primary emotional disorder. Yet they have difficulty in acquiring certain skills. They often are identified through a severe discrepancy between their potential for learning and their actual achievement. Some of the characteristics of learning disabilities follow (Lerner, 1985).

*Neurological dysfunction.* This implies that the child's learning problem is brain-related. Much is still unknown about the relationship between brain function and learning. It is presumed that for the child with learning disabilities, the nervous system is not processing information in a normal fashion.

*Attentional deficit disorders.* These hyperactive behaviors in the preschool learning-disabled child are highly visible. These children have difficulty in focusing and attending to a task. They often exhibit extremely impulsive and distractible behaviors.

*Uneven growth patterns.* Children with learning disabilities are not developing in an even fashion; they may excel in some skills and seriously lag in others. For example, they may be poor in tasks requiring auditory perception and memory, such as language, but do well in certain tasks requiring visual skills, such as number learning.

*Difficulty in learning and academic tasks.* Since preschool children have not yet failed in academic school tasks, such as reading, writing, and/or arithmetic, learning disabled preschoolers often have difficulty in motor skills and language skills.

As noted earlier, since the preschool child has not yet encountered school failure, the academic learning disability is often predicted for these children. The areas in which the learning disability would be evident for preschoolers is in preacademic areas: motor and perceptual skills, language, and in the ability to attend to tasks (Lerner, 1985).

## Impact on the Young Child

To reduce the negative effects of detrimental labeling, the preschool child is viewed as a high-risk child—one who has a delay in maturation and needs careful monitoring and assistance. Early identification and individualized programs of intervention offer ways of preventing a school learning disability from occurring or reducing the effects of this condition.

## BEHAVIORAL AND EMOTIONAL DISORDERS

### Definition

Children with emotional and behavioral disorders are in conflict with themselves or with others. Their behavior deviates significantly from that of the normal child over a substantial period of time. Their coping skills are poor or nonexistent. For some children, the behavior problems appear during the preschool years; for others, the problem becomes evident in later years. Very severe emotional disorders include *childhood schizophrenia* and *autism*.

### Characteristics

Symptoms of behavioral and emotional disorders include hostility, unhappiness, and a general unsuccessful pattern of social development or academic progress. Usually, these children do not or cannot comply with the controls and expectations of their parents, teachers, or peers. Their behavior is characterized by uncontrolled and disruptive activity, bizarre behavior, or complete withdrawal from social interactions. Their social behaviors may become inappropriate, extreme, and offensive. They are unusually inflexible and difficult to manage. Changes of any established routines or schedules often result in anger and behavior tantrums. Generally, there is a poor fit between the child's temperament and the environmental expectations (Thomas and Chess, 1977).

Types of emotional disorders found among preschool children are: (1) aggressive, acting out behavior, and (2) immature, withdrawn behavior.

*Aggressive behavior* occurs when children act out because of a lack of inner controls. Often their energy patterns are spasmodic, with activity spurts. They need and demand great amounts of physical contact. They will initiate situations that will guarantee that attention is drawn to them.

In *withdrawn behavior*, children are unusually quiet, having few emotional highs or lows. Preferring to be alone, they will avoid group activities. Their body posture is unusually tight and strained. These children will not spontaneously initiate conversation. Often they will try to avoid verbal contacts.

### Impact on the Young Child

In the natural course of growth and development, all young children experience some emotional upheavals and socialization problems. It is appropriate for a very young child to be agreeable at one stage of development and negative at another. However, when the emotional mood swings erratically from one extreme to another, with bizarre, inappropriate coping mechanisms, these may be symptoms of deeper emotional problems. These children cannot develop normal social interactions and are deprived of normal kinds of approval and satisfaction from others. Their emotional problems also can impede learning.

Early identification of emotional difficulties is important for both the family and child. Once there is an acceptance of the problem by the family, a generalized plan can be developed to work toward a solution. Teaching social and affective skills are discussed in Chapter 10, and structured play activities are discussed in Chapter 9.

## HEARING IMPAIRMENTS

The ability to hear is crucial to learning, and normal growth patterns require adequate hearing skills. Yet auditory problems are often over-looked as a possible reason for developmental difficulties.

### Development of Auditory Skills

The auditory mechanism consists of the outer ear, the middle ear, the inner ear, and the nerves that carry the transmission of sound to areas of the brain where they are interpreted and remembered. Sound vibrations from the environment are scooped up through the outer structure of the ear and transmitted through the ear canal to the inner ear. Sound waves are then transmitted to the inner ear, which leads to the stimulation of nerve endings. Messages are then transmitted through the auditory nerve to various brain centers (Davis and Silverman, 1978).

Babies have the capacity to hear at birth. Even newborn infants respond to sound, having an intact auditory system that can be immediately organized to respond to auditory stimuli (Eisenberg, 1976). With maturation and experience, children acquire more sophisticated auditory behaviors. They learn to attend to a variety of sounds and to link sounds with meaning.

### Deaf and Hard-of-Hearing Children

In terms of severity of hearing loss, there are two groups of children with hearing impairments: *hard-of-hearing* and *deaf*. *Hard-of-hearing* children have a deficit in auditory acuity but possess some functional hearing. Their ability to hear may or may not be improved through the use of a hearing aid.

*Deaf* children have a severe to profound auditory loss and do not possess functional hearing. Many of these children are deaf from birth; others acquire deafness as young children, usually through an illness (such as meningitis). For educational purposes, it is useful to divide deaf children into two groups: *prelanguage deaf*, which includes those whose deafness came before their language developed, and *postlanguage deaf*, those who lost their hearing after they had developed language.

### Causes

Three types of hearing loss are (1) conductive impairment; (2) sensorineural impairment; and (3) central impairment. *Conductive impairment* is a loss of ability to hear due to an outer or middle ear problem. *Sensorineural impairment* is a nerve or nerve pathway disorder resulting in a lack of tonal clarity. *Central impairment* is a term that describes the interference of sound perception due to pathway, brain system, and cerebral cortex involvement.

*Otitis media,* a middle ear disease caused by infection, is a common cause of conductive hearing impairment in young children. Since 25 to 65 percent of children under the age of two have had at least one ear infection involving some hearing loss, infants and young children with colds should be watched closely for signs of otitis media. Although ear infections respond well to antibiotic medication, fluid may persist for months following the infection. The resulting temporary or fluctuating hearing loss can interfere with language learning.

### Characteristics

The severity of hearing impairment is assessed through the use of pure tone hearing tests and a language assessment. The hearing specialist must determine the degree of hearing loss, whether the condition is temporary or permanent, and the disease or condition causing the problem. The degree of hearing loss is measured by assessing hearing thresholds in decibel levels (dB) at varying frequencies. *Decibel levels* refer to the loudness of the sound. *Frequency* refers to pitch (highness and lowness of the sound).

The ability to understand speech is related to the amount of hearing loss (Davis and Silverman, 1978). As shown in Table 2.2, with each successive level of decibel loss, there is a greater severity of the auditory handicap and less of an ability to understand speech. If the child loses hearing prior to the development of speech and language, this loss can significantly delay and distort the young child's ability to express ideas verbally.

Parents, teachers, and other caregivers of young children should be alert to the symptoms of auditory deficits. The following are signals of hearing difficulty. The child:

1. does not respond to sound
2. does not talk or even attempt to talk
3. uses indistinct speech
4. is unusually attentive to facial expressions and lip movements
5. is unduly sensitive to movement and visual clues
6. has a perpetual cold or runny nose, frequent earaches, or is a mouth breather
7. has recently recovered from scarlet fever, measles, meningitis, or from a severe head injury

**TABLE 2.2  Classes of Hearing Handicap**

| Class | Degree of handicap | AVERAGE HEARING THRESHOLD LEVEL FOR 500, 1000, AND 2000 Hz IN THE BETTER EAR | | Ability to understand speech |
|---|---|---|---|---|
| | | More than | Not more than | |
| A | Not significant | | 25 dB (ISO) | No significant difficulty with faint speech |
| B | Slight handicap | 25 dB (ISO) | 40 dB | Difficulty only with faint speech |
| C | Mild handicap | 40 dB | 55 dB | Frequent difficulty with normal speech |
| D | Marked handicap | 55 dB | 70 dB | Frequent difficulty with loud speech |
| E | Severe handicap | 70 dB | 90 dB | Can understand only shouted or amplified speech |
| F | Extreme handicap | 90 dB | | Usually cannot understand even amplified speech |

From H. Davis and S. R. Silverman, eds. *Hearing and Deafness*, 3rd ed. Copyright © 1970 by Holt, Rinehart and Winston, Inc. Reprinted by permission of Holt, Rinehart and Winston.

8.  needs much repetition before demonstrating understanding
9.  is unusually active, running about and touching things
10. does not respond to being called in a normal voice when out of sight
11. requires many activities and visual cues before responding
12. uses a voice that has a nonmelodious quality
13. does not moderate his or her own voice and either talks too loudly or too softly

No child is too young for a formal hearing evaluation. Even the hearing acuity of newborn babies can be measured, although often a definitive diagnosis is delayed for infants until the child is older and more stable responses can be obtained. New ways of measuring the infant's response to sound are being used and include infant cardiac patterns and overt behaviors (such as cessation of sucking, widening of the eyes, blinking and turning of the head to sounds). As can be seen in Table 2.3, levels and states differ even at neonatal ages. Parents need to be informed about the importance of an infant's responses to sounds, as they are the most reliable early screeners of potential hearing impairments.

**TABLE 2.3   Stimulus Variables as a Determinant of Neonatal Responses to Sound**

| Input | Processing Level | MOST FREQUENTLY OBSERVED OUTPUTS | |
|---|---|---|---|
| | | Overt Behavior | Cardiac Pattern |
| High frequency tones and noisebands | I | Freezing; startle | Very shortlasting: accelerative |
| Low frequency tones and noisebands | II | Undifferentiated movements | Relatively shortlasting; accelerative |
| Tonal sequences and other nonspeech ensembles | III | Differentiated movements; utterance | Somewhat prolonged; diphasic |
| Speech and speech-like sounds | IV | Differentiated movements; utterance | Very prolonged; decelerative |

From R. B. Eisenberg, *Auditory Competence in Early Life*. Baltimore: University Park Press, 1976, p. 140.

### Impact on the Young Child

Children suffering from auditory impairments are handicapped in many ways. The most obvious delay is seen in their development of speech and language.

Deaf children often experience isolation which in turn can lead to excessive unresolvable frustration and behavior problems. Intelligence and cognitive abilities are not impaired in the young deaf child. However, because of their lack of language experience, deaf children may perform poorly on cognitive items when measured with standard intelligence tests.

Children with severe auditory impairments may have some remaining intact hearing, which is called *residual hearing*. This residual hearing can be used and assisted with a sound amplifier or a hearing aid. Audiologists suggest fitting the child with a hearing aid as soon as possible because it encourages the child to make use of the residual hearing at the time that language is developing. A hearing aid is actually a kind of miniature mobile public address system that increases the intensity of sound for both desirable and undesirable noises. The hearing aid does not clarify sound perception. If a hearing aid is recommended for a young child, it is important to make sure that there is a proper fit, that the batteries are operating, that the cords are not worn out or broken, and that the child can operate the aid. If the ear is sore or becomes infected, the child should see a physician.

Means of communication for the deaf include lip-reading, finger-spelling, and the use of sign language. *Total communication* is the system in which speech, finger-spelling, signing, and lip-reading are combined. Deaf children *do* learn to speak. However, the quality of their speech is different and requires patience and attentiveness on the part of the listener. The more severe the impairment, the less intelligible is the speech. Therefore, the earlier children can benefit from sound amplification, the better will be their chance to develop understandable speech.

## VISUAL IMPAIRMENTS

Children with visual impairments have some type of limitation in seeing. The visual impairment affects how children learn and their performance, both in and out of the classroom.

### Development of Visual Skills

The process of seeing is complex. In order to see, light and images are received through the cornea and lens of the eye. The visual information is then sent to the brain, where it is coded and stored. This process enables the individual to understand what is seen and to recall from memory specific images when necessary.

The normal visual system of the child develops gradually. At birth, infants can distinguish patterns of light and dark but objects are blurred. From birth through four months of age, a baby begins to follow and reach for slowly moving objects. By four to six months, the baby will turn from one side to the other to reach moving objects using arms and legs as an assist. By six to eight months, both eyes generally focus equally, and the baby begins to transfer objects from one hand (side) to the other. By eight to twelve months, visual judgment of distance becomes important, and the child throws and retrieves objects using crawling and stepping actions (Blackman, 1984). Throughout the first three years, the child develops greater visual acuity and visual motor coordination, allowing more extensive visual explorations. Preschoolers are normally nearsighted (myopic); 20/20 (normal) vision is not reached until six years of age (Nelson, 1983). (A normal measurement of 20/20 means that the individual can see at 20 feet what the normal person sees at 20 feet.).

### Blind and Partially Sighted Children

Depending upon the degree of visual loss, visually handicapped children are classified as either *blind* or *partially sighted.*

*Blind children* have the most severe form of visual impairment. Legal blindness is defined as central visual acuity of 20/200 or less in the best eye or with corrected lenses. The visual measurement of 20/200 means that the visually impaired person can see an image or object from a distance of 20 feet what the normal-seeing person can see with clarity at a distance of 200 feet.

Blind children need to be taught through special methods that do not require sight. They learn to read Braille, a method in which the sense of touch is used to identify letter symbols impressed, or raised, on a paper surface. The microcomputer with peripherals that read print, speech synthesizers that convert print to spoken words, and printers that print output in braille, provide another learning tool for people with visual impairment.

*Partially sighted* children have some usable vision, but they need special provisions. For example, to read they need magnification and large print. Partially sighted children have visual acuity between 20/200 and 20/70 in the best eye with possible correction.

### Causes

*Central vision and acuity problems.*   Two common types of visual difficulties are nearsightedness and farsightedness. *Nearsightedness* (myopia) is the inability to see objects or print at a distance. *Farsightedness* (hyperopia) is the inability to see objects and print at close range.

*Strabismus* is a muscle coordination problem. The eyes do not move together. One or both eyes may move outward or inward independent of the other. Early detection of strabismus is critical for young children and it should be corrected before age seven. If treated early, the prognosis for correction is good, but if the condition goes untreated, further loss of vision can be expected due to amblyopia. Strabismus affects about 3 percent of the population.

*Amblyopia* (lazy eye) is condition that usually affects only one eye and results in a loss of near or distant visual acuity. Since it occurs in only one eye, the stronger eye "takes over" and does the majority of the work. Early diagnosis and treatment with corrective lenses, prisms, contact lenses, or patching improves the functional clarity of vision in the weaker eye. Correction becomes more difficult as the less able eye becomes weaker. In some cases cosmetic surgery is performed to correct the alignment (Buncic, 1980).

*Other causes.*   The child's visual system may not function properly for a number of reasons: (1) the retina of the eye does not receive light; (2) the retina of the eye does not receive a clearly focused image; (3) nerve impulses do not reach the vision center of the brain; or (4) information from the eye is not processed by the brain (Blackman, 1984). Any one of these difficulties can be caused by abnormalities in the visual system or structure, creating visual impairments ranging from mild to severe. Damage to the visual system may be congenital, the result of infections, the aftermath of a severe accidental injury, or a condition associated with premature birth.

*Retrolental fibroplasia* is a condition in which fibrous scar tissue forms a film or curtain behind the lens of the eye, cutting off light, which may lead to blindness. It can occur in premature babies who receive an excess of oxygen while in incubators. During the 1950s, many premature infants suffered from this malady until medical scientists discovered its cause. A more careful monitoring of the oxygen supply in incubators dramatically reduced the number of cases of blindness in children.

*Rubella* (German measles) contracted by the mother during the pregnancy is another cause of visual impairment. The rubella epidemic of 1964 resulted in a substantial increase in the number of visually impaired children.

Visual ability may be affected by other conditions, diseases, or damage to the retina or optic nerve. Vision conditions such as *optic atrophy, retinal detachment,* or *Retinis pigmentosa,* can cause a loss of visual function.

### Characteristics

Early vision screening for preschool children is an essential component of the assessment process. The Society for the Prevention of Blindness recommends visual screening for all children between the ages of three and five. In addition, teachers should be alert to symptoms of general visual difficulty, such as frequent rubbing of eyes; sensitivity to light; tears produced by close work; difficulty playing games requiring judgment of distance; headache, nausea, or dizziness; squinting; crusty, watery, or red eyes; eyes turning inward or outward; difficulty keeping a place when reading; covering of one eye to see an object; double vision; turning or tilting of the head to one side; and excessive blinking behavior. Children with suspected visual problems should be referred for a thorough visual examination.

It would be advantageous to diagnose congenital eye problems at birth. Research shows that the newborn *does* attend to visual stimuli and even scans in a totally dark room (Mendelson and Haith, 1976). The effects of visual damage to young children are not easily followed in longitudinal studies because the total number of cases is small and there are so many different kinds of visual damage.

### Impact on the Young Child

The young child's environment is normally filled with a constant bombardment of visual stimulations which shape the child's ability to form relationships between objects and people. Activities such as moving a toy car, grasping a block, or watching a fish swim in a bowl of water involve seeing and integrating those sights. Children with impaired visual capacity are deprived of such experiences. They miss glimpses of facial expressions; they see indistinct shades of color and configurations. They need sensory stimulation through other sensing systems. The more limited a child is visually, the greater is the need to use tactile and auditory senses to experience the world. Young children with limited visual experiences should be encouraged to practice using other intact senses during the early stages of development.

Blindness, in itself, does not alter many aspects of general patterns of growth and development in young children. However, blind children tend to be delayed in body posture movements and self-awareness (Millar, 1976). They tend to move toward sounds rather than objects and engage in manipulative play significantly more often than children with normal sight (Olson, 1983). Blind children, as would be expected, demonstrate greater use of their hands in manipulative explorations.

Occasionally, visually impaired children engage in self-stimulating activities, a behavior known as *blindism*. These activities include rocking, finger poking, spinning about, and the imitation of strange noises. The child should be distracted when such behaviors occur. The behaviors can be eliminated or reduced if they are replaced with more positive activities.

Sometimes parental concerns can lead to overprotection. It is important for visually impaired children to be encouraged to explore the world around them. Falling down or getting a small bump here and there are part of that learning experience. Once the environment is made safe for experimentation, there is usually less reason for a parent to fear for the child's safety. Blind children should learn to *trail*, a way of exploring and touching things around them to determine pathways and general organization for safe movement (Wilson et al., 1976).

Finally, it is important to remember that visually impaired children are, first of all, children. They need continuous and consistent interactions with both their parents and their peers (Donlon and Burton, 1976). The more severe the handicap, the more the child tends to depend upon the caregiver. Educational programs that integrate visually impaired children with sighted children increase their opportunities for more normalized social interactions.

## PHYSICAL DISABILITIES AND OTHER HEALTH IMPAIRMENTS

This section discusses the conditions of (1) orthopedic impairments and (2) other health impairments.

### Orthopedic Impairments

There are a number of conditions that result in orthopedic impairments in children. These children may require wheelchairs and other adaptive devices (Umbreit, 1983).

*Cerebral palsy* affects the largest number of children with physical handicaps in the schools. Cerebral palsy is a permanent nonprogressive neurological disability caused by injury or disease to the central nervous system. Causes include birth process injuries, trauma to the head, brain or spinal cord infections, lead poisoning, jaundice, and reduction of oxygen during delivery. The damage within the brain is lifelong.

The severity of the condition ranges from barely noticeable clumsiness to crippling muscle spasms, and many children with cerebral palsy need to use a wheelchair. Some children have developmental deficits. The motor disorders can result in problems of muscle action, posture, and balance (Bobath and Bobath, 1975). The lack of coordination varies with the severity of the condition and the number of extremities affected. If muscles of the oral cavity are involved, the child's speech can be affected.

There are three types of cerebral palsy: (1) *Hypertonia,* which involves spasticity of body movements and is present in about 60 percent of all cases; (2) *Dyskinesia,* which involves unwanted involuntary movement of wrist, fingers, trunk, or legs and is present in roughly 24 percent of all cases; and (3) *Ataxia,* which involves a lunging gait with balance difficulties and is present in about 1 percent of all cases. Most cases of cerebral palsy can be detected by eighteen months of age (Bigge and Sirvis, 1978; Blackman, 1984).

*Spina bifida* is a congenital disorder related to abnormal development of the spinal column. There is a failure of the bones in the spinal column to close completely during fetal development. As a result, the spinal cord (nerve fibers) may protrude, resulting in damage to the nervous system and lack of function or paralysis to the lower extremities. Thus, these children are physically disabled, needing braces, crutches, or a wheelchair. When surgery to correct this defect is performed in early infancy, the lives of many children can be saved. In addition to the physical disabilities, many children with spina bifida lack bladder and bowel control.

Children with spina bifida may also have *hydrocephalus,* which is the retention of intracranial fluid within the brain and is an outcome of an incomplete spinal cord. Lack of proper drainage creates cranial pressure and possible infection. Most children with this condition have difficulty with bowel and bladder control. Intermittent catherization can help prevent urinary infections. A surgical procedure, known as shunting, helps with the drainage of fluid.

*Muscular dystrophy* is a hereditary sex-linked disease that affects the skeletal muscles. Mobility decreases with increased muscle weakness, and the disease is progressive and terminal, resulting in death. Females are rarely afflicted with this condition, but they can pass it on to their male children.

*Spinal atrophy* is a hereditary neuromuscular disability. It is a progressive condition that usually causes the child's death before school age is reached.

*Traumatic injuries* are also quite common with young children. Some of the more serious accidents result in spinal damage and possible paralysis. Bicycle and automobile accidents cause the largest numbers of paralysis cases. The residual effects of the damage are dependent upon the number of extremities affected and the resultant loss of mobility. A child with paraplegia has paralysis of both lower extremities. As the mobility decreases, the potential side effects of urinary and respiratory problems increase. Slow circulation and pressure sores also can be problems. The more debilitating the damage, the more adaptive aides are necessary to assist the child toward personal independence.

### Other Health Impaired

There are a number of handicapping conditions that are not easy to classify and are generally categorized as "other health impaired" (Umbreit, 1983).

*Autism* is a severe behavior disorder seen in young children. In a recent revision of the regulations of PL94-142, autism was reclassified under the category "other health impaired." Autism is a rare condition in which the child is almost void of human interactions. Autistic children are unable to establish relationships with other people, avoiding eye contact and resisting physical contact. Even gentle handling causes the child's body to stiffen and leads to visible physical withdrawal. Autistic children are also characterized by lack of communication skills. Although autism may be suspected during infancy, it usually is not diagnosed until two to four years of age. Because autism is difficult to diagnose with certainty, the behaviors often are referred to as "autistic-like" behaviors.

*Epilepsy* is a condition that involves convulsive seizures due to abnormal patterns of brain activity. The seizures can be severe or mild; and they can be generalized, partial, or miscellaneous seizures. Partial and miscellaneous seizures affect both motor control and behavior.

Childhood epilepsy occurs in about 2 to 3 percent of the population. The generalized seizures (*major motor* and *grand mal*) are the most frequent types of convulsive disorders in infancy and childhood. The onset of a seizure may be a cry and then a pale face, with pupils dilated and rolling, body tension, and rigidity, followed by loss of consciousness. If ambulatory, the infant or young child will fall, and the body will experience short jerking motions for a brief period of time. Since the grand mal seizures create uncontrolled movements, there is potential bladder and bowel release, excessive salivation, and possible choking. *Petit mal* seizures are not as noticeable as grand mal because behavior states may not change drastically. Children may exhibit five-to ten-second attention interruptions which are seen as staring, blinking, and an overall disorientation. The true petit mal seizure rarely occurs below four years of age and over 13 years of age.

The most useful laboratory test for diagnosing epilepsy is the electroencephalogram (EEG). The EEG is a recording of electrical signals from the brain, measuring brain wave activity. Anticonvulsant medications commonly used to control seizures are Phenobarbital and Dilantin. Differences in the size and ages of children necessitate a careful monitoring of dosage reactions to the medication. Dosage requirements should be regulated under the direct supervision of the child's personal physician.

*Asthma* is difficult to categorize. Many leading medical experts consider it an allergic condition of the lungs. The symptoms include labored breathing, wheezing, and coughing. Medication relieves the constriction of the bronchial tubes and provides relief for the shortness of breath. Some experts think that asthma also can be brought about by emotional stress.

*Hemophilia*, often called "bleeders disease," is a blood condition that results in poor blood-clotting ability. The normal bumps and bruises of young active children can create mortal danger. Possible hemorrhage and internal bleeding are serious effects of even a minor jolt. Medical treatment includes the use of the missing clotting medication and a reduction of the activities that can lead to bleeding. Hemophilia usually affects only males.

## MULTIPLE HANDICAPS

Recent advances in medical science have increased the survival rate of high-risk infants. However, along with the increased survival rate is a greater likelihood of long-term multiple impairment. These children may have several handicapping conditions, and the handicaps are severe.

### Deaf-Blind Children

One of the severe multiple handicaps is the dual sensory impairment of a deaf-blind condition. The deaf-blind child has both auditory and visual impairments. This combination causes such severe communication and educational problems that these children cannot properly be accommodated in special education programs for either the hearing handicapped or the visually handicapped.

Although deaf-blind children have dual impairments of visual and auditory systems, they do not necessarily have total or complete loss of both sensory channels. Generally, one of the systems will continue to have some residual strength which may be used for educational instruction. However, the sense of touch remains a major channel for instruction for these children.

Public awareness of deaf-blind children came about through the popularity of the Helen Keller story—as a book, play, and movie. The unrelenting dedication and persistent efforts of her teacher, Anne Sullivan, enabled Helen Keller finally to cope successfully with the dual handicaps of deafness and blindness.

Early educational programs for deaf-blind children were conducted through private tutoring or in private residential schools. In 1968, the federal government established ten model centers for deaf-blind children. These centers offered related services, such as family counseling, itinerant home services, remedial and educational diagnosis, and programs for teaching children and preparing teachers.

### Developmental Disabilities

The term *developmental disabilities* frequently is used in reference to young children with severe handicaps or who are debilitated with severe or multiple handicaps. The legislation for developmental disabilities (P.L. 95-602) supplements that of P.L. 94-142 by including handicapped children starting at birth. According to this law, *developmental disability* means a severe chronic disability of a person that

1. is attributable to a mental or physical impairment or combination of mental and physical impairments;
2. is manifested before the person attains age twenty-two;
3. is likely to continue indefinitely;
4. results in substantial functional limitations in three or more of the following areas of major life activity:
   self-care
   receptive and expressive language
   learning
   mobility
   self-direction
   capacity for independent living
   economic self-sufficiency
5. reflects the person's need for a combination and sequence of special inter-disciplinary or generic care, treatment, or other services that are individually planned and coordinated.

Children not covered under P.L. 94-142 below the age of three might be covered by the Developmental Disabilities Act. The continuing needs of children with developmental disabilities as they grow and experience new handicapping difficulties require a combination and sequence of specialized treatment and generic care. Since it is quite plausible that a child could have some but not necessarily all of the features associated with a handicapping syndrome, it is important that each child be evaluted individually (Blackman, 1984).

## GIFTED AND TALENTED

*Gifted and talented* children are another category of exceptional children. These children are considered exceptional, even though they are not handicapped, because they deviate markedly from the normal population and require special kinds of education. Gifted and talented children need an explorative environment and opportunities for creative experiences to further develop their talents.

### Characteristics

Gifted children demonstrate unusual abilities and talents. Their giftedness takes many forms—superior intellectual capacity, creativity, artistic or musical talents, verbal or mathematical aptitude, and/or problem-solving abilities. Methods for identifying gifted and talented children include standardized measures of mental ability and teacher referral. Gifted and talented children are found in all cultures and socioeconomic groups.

### Impact on the Young Child

A major question in working with gifted children is whether to accelerate their education or to provide enriched experiences without speeding up the instructional levels of the educational process. Although many research studies found acceleration resulted in good achievement, adjustment, and vocational success, this approach has not been accepted as a general practice. There is still concern about mixing of chronological ages and the unique differences that each developmental stage contains. One way to accelerate gifted children is to begin their formal education earlier. Some gifted children apply for early entrance to school, beginning their formal education prior to the age of five. Also, gifted children often are involved with socialized group experiences early due to daycare and nursery school placements prior to kindergarten.

Another issue is whether to place gifted children in separate ability-ranked groups. Advocates of ability grouping think that grouping provides bright children with the opportunity to stimulate and challenge each other. Moreover, by removing gifted children from the regular group, a new set of leaders has the opportunity to emerge and take leadership roles. Critics of ability grouping claim that such programs are elitist. They cite the need for all students to develop democratic principles gained from working among all levels of academic ability.

Today's programs for the gifted and talented tend to have flexible grouping plans with greater emphasis on specialized independent activities. A group of gifted children may meet for limited specific activities—to study an academic problem of interest or for general social purposes. Students learn to set their own pace for work and attain a performance level that they can accept or change. Programs provide more independent activities early in the school experience which promote self-directed behavior.

Academically bright children often are taken for granted. Without special identification and special provision, they may not recognize their own talents and never reach their potential. They may be pressured to increase the quantity of work, without concern for its quality. Young gifted and talented children should be allowed to practice and experiment in environments that are open and stimulating.

## SUMMARY

Exceptional preschool children are classified by their "category" of exceptionality. All areas of atypical development and behavior are included in the term *exceptional children*, both handicapped and gifted.

There are a number of high-risk factors that are related to handicapped conditions. These factors can be divided into prenatal conditions, perinatal conditions, or postnatal conditions.

Speech and language disorders characterize many children in early childhood special education programs. Speech refers to the production of language (articulation and voice). Language is the cognitive foundation underlying speech. Disorders can occur in one or both areas.

The concept of mental retardation has changed much in the past few years. The definition now includes both low performance on intelligence measures and poor adaptive behavior.

Young children with learning disabilities are at-risk for later school failure. For the preschool child, this handicap is likely to be evident in poor motor skills, delayed language development, perceptual disorders, or inattentive behavior.

Behavioral disorders describe children who display inappropriate social and emotional behavior. These children can be aggressive or withdrawn.

Auditory impairments include both children who are hard-of-hearing and children who are deaf. The deaf child has the more severe hearing loss, which drastically affects language learning. The impact on learning depends upon the degree of hearing loss and the child's age when the loss of hearing occurred.

Visual impairments include both blind children and partially sighted children. Children with visual impairments require special techniques for learning, particularly for reading.

Causes of physical impairments include congenital factors, birth injuries, diseases, and accidents. Physically handicapped children may need adaptive devices for school learning.

The term *other health impaired* includes a number of conditions, such as autism, epilepsy, asthma, and other maladies. Children with these handicaps may require special consideration in school.

The term *multiple handicaps* refers to children who have several handicaps. One of these conditions is the child who is deaf-blind.

Gifted and talented children have unusual abilities and require special educational services to enable them to reach their full potential.

## REVIEW QUESTIONS

**Terms to Know**

visual impairment
auditory impairment
mental retardation

gifted and talented
postnatal factors
autism

high-risk children
speech and language impairments
learning disabilities
behavior disorders

epilepsy
prenatal factors
decibel level
Downs syndrome

1. What are some symptoms of learning disabilities during the preschool years?
2. What does the term *category* mean in special education? What are some of the limitations of using "categories" in planning preschool instruction?
3. What are the differences between a deaf child and the child who is hard-of-hearing?
4. What is the difference between a speech disorder and a language disorder?
5. Name three areas in which a child could be gifted.
6. Why are so many handicapped preschoolers identified as having speech and language impairments?

## REFERENCES

BERGAN, J. and R. HENDERSON (1979) *Child Development.* Columbus: Charles E. Merrill.

BIGGE, J. and B. SIRVIS (1978) "Children with Physical and Multiple Disabilities." In G. Haring (ed.) *Behavior of Exceptional Children.* Columbus: Charles E. Merrill.

BLACKMAN, J. (1984) *Medical Aspects of Developmental Disabilities in Children Birth to Three.* Rockville, MD: Aspen.

BOBATH, K. and B. BOBATH (1975) "Cerebral Palsy." In P. Pearson and C. Williams (eds.) *Physical Therapy Services in the Developmental Disabilities.* Springfield, IL: Chas. C. Thomas.

BROUWERS, P., R. RICCARDI, P. FEDIO, and D. POPLACH (1985) "Long-term Neuropsychologic Sequelae of Childhood Leukemia: Correlations with CT Brain Scan Abnormalities." *The Journal of Pediatrics,* 106 (5), 723–28.

BUNCIC, J. (1980) "Disorders of Vision." In S. Gabel and M. Erikson (eds.) *Childhood Development and Developmental Disabilities.* Boston: Little, Brown.

DAVIS, H. and S. SILVERMAN (eds.) (1978) *Hearing and Deafness,* (4th ed.) NY: Holt, Rinehart & Winston.

DONLON, E and L. BURTON (1976) *The Severely and Profoundly Handicapped: A Practical Approach to Teaching.* NY: Grune & Stratton.

EISENBERG, R. (1976) *Auditory Competence in Early Life.* Baltimore, MD: University Park Press.

FUREY, E. (1982) "The Effects of Alcohol on the Fetus." *Exceptional Children,* 49, 1.

GIBSON, J. (1978) *Growing Up: A Study of Children.* Reading, MA: Addison–Wesley.

GOLDENSON, R. (1970) *The Encyclopedia of Human Behavior.* Garden City, NY: Doubleday.

GROSSMAN, H. (ed.) (1983) *Classification in Mental Retardation.* Washington, DC: American Association on Mental Deficiency.

LERNER, J. (1985) *Learning Disabilities: Theories, Diagnosis, and Teaching Strategies,* (4th ed.) Boston: Houghton Mifflin.

MENDELSON, M. and M. HAITH (1976) *The Relationship Between Audition and Vision in the Human Newborn.* Monograph for the Society for Research in Child Development, 41, 4, 167.

MILLAR, S. (1976) "Spatial Representation of Blind–Sighted Children." *Journal of Experimental Child Psychology,* 21, 460–79.

NELSON, W., R. BEHRMAN, and V. VAUGHAN (eds.) (1983) *Textbook of Pediatrics.* Philadelphia: W.B. Saunders.

NORTMAN, D. (1974) *Parental Age as a Factor in Pregnancy Outcome and Child Development.* Reports on Population/Family Planning, No. 16.

OLSON, M. (1983) "A Study of Exploratory Behavior of Legally Blind and Sighted Preschoolers." *Exceptional Children*, 50, 2.

REED, E. (1975) "Genetic Anomalies in Development." In F. Horowitz (ed.) *Review of Child Development Research*, 4:59–100. Chicago: University of Chicago Press.

SISSON, R., S. CLATWORTH and J. ZADROGA (1975) "The Nervous System." In G. Scipien, M. Barnard, M. Chard, J. Howe, and P. Phillips (eds.) *Comprehensive Pediatric Nursing.* NY: McGraw-Hill.

THOMAS, A. and S. CHESS (1977) *Temperament and Development.* NY: Brunner–Mazel.

UMBREIT, J. (ed.) (1983) *Physical Disabilities and Health Impairment: An Introduction.* Columbus: Merrill Publishing Co.

U.S. DEPARTMENT OF EDUCATION (1985) *To Assure the Free Appropriate Public Education of All Handicapped Children*: Seventh Annual Report to Congress on the Implementaion of the Education of all Handicapped Children Act. Washington, DC: Government Printing Office.

WALLIS, C. (1986) Cocaine Babies: Addicts bear ailing infants. *Time*, January 20, 50.

WILSON, J., et al. (1976) "Early Intervention: The Right to Sight." *Education for the Visually Handicapped*, 8, 83–90.

# THREE

# The Parent–Professional Partnership

## INTRODUCTION

The focus of this chapter is parents: What is their reaction to having an atypical child? How can parents manage and teach their child at home? How can programs involve parents and coordinate the parents' activities with other professional services? What rights do parents have under the law? Effective early intervention programs for handicapped and at-risk young children include parents as full participants, start intervention at a very early age, and involve a multidisciplinary team (Allen, 1980; Hayden, 1978).

## PARENT INVOLVEMENT

The child's first teachers are his or her parents. All children benefit when their parents are actively involved in their development and education. Parents can help their youngster feel competent, loved, whole, and better able to cope with the world (Scarr, 1984).

For preschool children with special needs, however, active parent involvement is especially important. Critical to the success of any intervention program is what parents and the family do to shape the growth and

development of their young handicapped child. Research shows that the family is the most effective, as well as the most economical, system for fostering and sustaining the development of the child (Bronfenbrenner, 1974). Parents and others responsible for the child must work at establishing a cooperative relationship and developing a coordinated plan for teaching the child. Stiles, Cole, and Gardner (1979) point out that in programs for young handicapped children:

> *Parents are in strategic positions* because they know their children better than anyone else and spend more time wiith their youngster over an extended period.
>
> *Parents can compensate* for shortages of professional services or personnel, such as the lack of one-to-one services.
>
> *Parents can reduce costs* of instruction and other services.
>
> *Parents can solve time and distance problems,* particularly in rural areas.

### Stages Of Adjustment

Parents of young handicapped children face many difficult problems of adjustment. A major challenge for them is recognizing and accepting the reality that their child has an impairment. Whether the impairment is short-term or lifelong, this fact is a staggering blow from which parents recover slowly and seldom totally (Cansler, Martin, and Valand, 1975). Acceptance of their child's problem has a profound effect on the functioning of the total family unit (Dunlap, 1979). Unfortunately, sometimes there is a tendency on the part of professionals to judge parents as rejecting, overprotective, unrealistic, or unaccepting when, in fact, the parents are merely exhibiting normal reactions to this difficult and stressful situation. Such reactions actually are useful coping behaviors that give parents time to adjust and strengthen their inner reserves, reestablish balance, and look for alternative actions.

The process of adjusting to a child with a disability is similar to the stages that have been observed in the mourning process. Three broad phases have been identified (as shown in Table 3.1): (1) denial; (2) intellectual awareness; and (3) intellectual and emotional adjustment (Cansler et al., 1975). The first stage, *denial,* is characterized by a disbelief and rejection of reality. The second stage, *intellectual awareness,* is characterized by the person's emotional reaction to reality. The third stage, *intellectual and emotional adjustment,* is a positive response, characterized by the taking of actions to constructively work with the problem. It often takes people a long time to work through these phases of adjustment.

Sometimes home problems intensify because the two parents are at different stages of adjustment. Moreover, the process of parent adjustment cannot be hastened. Professionals should try to understand and be aware of the painful parent and family adjustment process. By doing so they can better accept the behaviors and reactions of the various family members

**TABLE 3.1   Stages of Adjustment for Families of Handicapped Children**

| STAGE | TYPICAL BEHAVIOR(S) |
| --- | --- |
| 1. Denial | Shock<br>Flatly disregards the diagnosis<br>Pretends diagnosis never occurred<br>Diagnostic "shopping" for cause or cure<br>Continuous training of child to disprove diagnosis |
| 2. Intellectual awareness | Anger<br>Guilt<br>Depression (anger turned inward)<br>Grief; sorrow<br>Disappointment<br>Bitterness and shame<br>Blame |
| 3. Intellectual and emotional<br>    adjustment (acceptance) | Organizes time and energy constructively<br>Demonstrates realistic expectations for the child<br>Advocates child program<br>Cooperates and interacts appropriately |

Adapted from D. Cansler, G. Martin, & M. Valand. *Working with Families.* Winston-Salem, NC: Kaplan Press, 1975, p. 11–13.

and extend an attitude of patience and understanding, rather than one of intolerance or disapproval.

Three factors that can influence parents' adjustments to their child's handicap are (Schell,1981): (1) the severity of the child's handicap; (2) the support system within the family; and (3) the external support systems. These factors are interdependent. Although the impact varies from family to family and within a family at any given time, each contributes to the family's adjustment.

Four major components of parent programs serve to help parents in the adjustment process (Lillie, Trohanis, and Goin, 1976): (1) getting parents to participate in the program; (2) supporting parents emotionally; (3) exchanging information with parents; and (4) improving parent-child interactions. Each of these components is discussed in the following sections.

### Developing Parent Participation

The most successful way to obtain parent participation and commitment is to offer programs that meet the needs of parents as well as the needs of children. Good parenting is not something one knows instinctively but is an aggregate of many learned skills. Parents should recognize that parenting skills are well worth learning. Skillful parenting has been shown to be the most effective and economical means for fostering the optimum development of any child (Bromwich, 1981). When the emphasis is on how to promote the child's development, regardless of the level of functioning, such training is helpful to parents of all children—handicapped, normal, or gifted.

While parent training should be made available to *all* parents of young children, parents of a handicapped child have even more need for assistance in learning how to interact appropriately with their child (Karnes and Shwedel, 1983; Kelly, 1982; Welsh and Odum, 1981). Successful application of parenting skills increases the parents' feelings of satisfaction (Wiegerink, Hocutt, Posante-Loro, and Bristol, 1980).

Three obstacles that can interfere with the development of good parenting skills may be overwhelming when involving a young child with special needs (White, 1975):

1. *Ignorance* Most, if not all, parents are unprepared for the responsibility of parenting. With little sound, legitimate information to share, parents do not know how to do their job—how to deal with a baby's curiosity or social development, to recognize developmental milestones, or to provide appropriate experiences. Parents need to learn the nature of their role in caregiving.
2. *Stress* The 8- to 24-month period is one of the most dangerous periods in life due to the child's intense curiosity, poor control of the body, lack of awareness of common dangers and the value of objects, and the child's ignorance about the rights of others. There is resentment between siblings, extra work from a toddler, and possible tension between the parents over the neatness of the house. Parents need to learn how to cope with this stress.
3. *Lack of assistance* Due to the small nuclear family, prevalence of single-parent families, and the mobility of Americans, parents may have no nearby relatives or friends to offer physical and/or psychological relief. Parents need to learn how to overcome this obstacle within their financial constraints, such as cooperative baby-sitting arrangements.

These obstacles can be overcome in parent programs if parents are motivated, involved, and accept their responsibility regarding the development of their child (Turnbull and Turnbull, 1985). However, there are many factors that can interfere with parent participation, no matter how well a program is designed to meet the general needs of parents. Some of these factors are

The child is living in a single-parent household or with a parent who is remarried.

The child is living in a multigenerational family under one roof.

The child is living with working parent (s).

The child has transferred from a different preschool program that had other goals and/or procedures.

The parents lack transportation or baby-sitting services.

These and other factors require modification in the content and timing of parental participation.

Parent involvement has been the focus of several of the model early education demonstration programs. These programs showed that successful programs (1) recognize parents as the child's primary teacher; (2)

define the parents' role with stated objectives for parent involvement; and (3) are flexible and individualized to meet the needs of specific parents (Karnes and Lee, 1978; DeBerry, Ristau, and Galland, 1984).

The involvement of fathers as well as mothers should be promoted. Parenting roles in our society appear to be changing regarding appropriate gender behavior. The conventional nuclear family, with father employed and mother at home, is no longer the predominant family unit. As a result, fathers are beginning to accept a greater role in parenting and more responsibility for child care, even though mothers usually continue to be the primary person in early intervention programs. Programs can encourage the participation of fathers and working mothers by providing activities for working parents and their child on Saturdays, late afernoons, or during early evening hours. To further encourage father participation, teaching sessions can be videotaped for fathers to view at home, more male staff can be used, and fathers can be contacted by phone or mail to obtain the father's input when needs assessments and program evaluations are conducted (Linder and Chitwood, 1984; Vadasy, Fewell, Meyer, Schell, and Greenberg, 1984; Markowitz, 1984).

### Supporting Parents Emotionally

All parents experience stress in providing care for their young children. Parents of exceptional children, however, suffer additional feelings of guilt and inadequacy. They may need help in deriving satisfaction from daily interactions with their child and in developing feelings of personal worth. Although teachers are not therapists, they can take on the important role of being an active listener. Parents are encouraged to express feelings and attitudes, which is important in the process of adjusting. Many parents receive sufficient emotional support by using the teacher as a sounding board. Other parents, however, will need the help of a professional counselor.

Often parents can be effective in providing other parents of handicapped preschoolers with emotional support. If parents are given the opportunity to interact with each other through local parent education groups and parent support groups, they have an opportunity to discuss mutual problems and concerns. These groups serve to ease the burden and help dispel the feelings of isolation often experienced by parents of exceptional children. In many cases, lifelong friendships are developed through the contacts made in these parent groups (Keefe, 1984).

Parents, however, have the right to limit their participation in the program without the risk of feeling guilty or losing the necessary services for their child. Either family demands or lack of interest is sufficient reason for not participating. Professionals should accept parent decisions not to participate, and program models should have a flexible approach to meet the needs of the various types and degrees of parent involvement.

### Exchanging Information With Parents

Parents can receive valuable information from professionals about the ways that young children learn and the parent role in this learning process, but parents and professionals also should exchange information. Parents have many insights and knowledge that can help the professional better understand the child; for example, information about a child's developmental history, the family's social history, and how the child acts and interacts on a daily basis. If a healthy two-way communication system is established as the needs of the child and parent(s) change and new objectives are formulated, parent input readily becomes an integral part of the process. It is also beneficial for the child when both teacher and parents have similar expectations for the child. Information can be exchanged informally through parents' verbal comments or more formally through a needs-assessment questionnaire and a parent advisory council. The ultimate parent-information exchange occurs when parents become active participants in policy making (Karnes and Lee, 1978).

### Improving Parent-Child Interactions

Parents can be helped to grow in their caregiving role by learning new ways of behaving as they tackle the daily management of their child. Parents can learn new techniques by observing as the teacher works with their child. These observation–teaching sessions can occur during home visits (which is more typical in programs serving 0- to-3-year-olds), or in the classroom (which is more typical in programs serving 3- to-6-year-olds). Parents also can learn new behaviors by observing another parent working with a child. They can practice behaviors and receive systematic feedback on their performance by trying out a new procedure with another child, not their own. To improve parent–child interactions, parents need encouragement and support. They also need to develop competence in problem solving–to perceive a problem situation and discover the best solution for them and their child at a particular time (Bromwich, 1981).

As they participate in an intervention program, parents assume the role of the learner as they are taught how to work with their child. They learn to present tasks in a clear, understandable manner and at a level geared to their child's ability. In addition, their relationship with their child changes because of involvement in the formative stage of the educational process.

### Other Guidelines for Parent Involvement

Several other guidelines are helpful in encouraging parent involvement. Professionals have to tread the fine line between cool objectivity and emotional subjectivity. That is, although professionals need to be objective, neutral, and somewhat detached in dealing with the problem, they should not withdraw behind a cool facade which comes across as intellectual but uncaring. On the other hand, if professionals become so involved that they allow their emotions to control or intrude, their actions become counterproductive. Obviously, the professional who bursts into sympathetic tears cannot be an effective counselor.

Parents should recognize that they are the managers responsible for their child's educational program until that youngster reaches adulthood. To manage well, parents need to learn how to be effective advocates for their child. This is true for all children: the gifted, normal, or handicapped (Karnes and Shwedel, 1983).

In summary, to foster a constructive and cooperative parent–professional relationship, the following guidelines are suggested (Fallen and Umansky. 1985):

> Parents should participate fully as members of the educational team rather than playing a subordinate or supplementary role.
>
> Professionals need to accept parents where they are in the adjustment process and learn to listen. Communicating with parents begins with listening.
>
> All relevant information should be shared with parents.
>
> Parents should have the principle responsibility for selecting goals and objectives; professionals should have the principle responsibility for selecting methodology and technology.
>
> Professional jargon should be eliminated or at least minimized.

Support and encouragement should be given to parents as they struggle to cope with the frustration and practical problems of raising a handicapped child on a day-to-day basis.

## PROGRAMS FOR PARENTS

### Service for Families

Some programs focus on the entire family rather than just the child or the child and a parent. When the multidisciplinary team and family are seen as a cooperative team with common goals, it becomes necessary to determine the particular needs for each child–family unit and then provide the appropriate services (Berger and Fowlkes, 1980). The following services could be offered to families (Cansler et al., 1975):

1. Training in teaching methods
2. Interpretation of test scores
3. Counseling for family problems (group and/or individual therapy)
4. Coordination of other community resources
5. Help with behavior management
6. Transportation
7. Suggestions for home activities
8. Suggestions for inexpensive or homemade materials
9. Training for siblings
10. Meetings and workshops for parents and family groups. Parents also can develop objectives for their own involvement by indicating their needs, which could range from medical and transportation services to individualized home visits.

### Models for Delivering Services

There are several systems for delivering services to parents:(1) home-based parent-training programs, in which parents are trained in their own homes; (2) center-based programs in which parents are trained at a center; and (3) combination home/center programs and even parent-implemented preschool programs where the parents are responsible for the delivery of services and evaluation rather than professionals (Lillie et al., 1976). These models are described more fully in Chapter 5.

An exemplary home-based program that provides services to parents is the Portage Project (Shearer and Shearer, 1976). The Portage Project program covers five developmental areas: language, cognition, self-help, motor, and socialization. Reasons for having this program in the home include:

Learning occurs in the child's natural environment (the home).
Skills generalize when taught by parent(s).

Parents determine what and how the child will be taught.
The entire family is more likely to be involved.
Self-help skills are more accessible.
Instructional goals are individualized.
There are economic advantages because there is no need for a center or transportation.

An exemplary center-based program providing service to parents is PEECH (Precise Early Education for Children with Handicaps) (Karnes and Zehrbach, 1977). The program integrates nonhandicapped children with children who have a wide range of handicapping conditions. A variety of opportunities, such as observing in the classroom, group meetings, home visits, and conferences, are available to parents.

Another type of parent service is providing newsletters about local programs—baby-sitting referral agencies and social service agencies, and resources such as helpful books and publications. Some communities provide a library or resource room with toys, materials, and reading information. The informational materials can deal with topics such as parent roles, the needs or interests of mothers and/or fathers, and the child's needs.

Regardless of the type of program, successful parent programs have certain features (Cartwright, 1981):

> The program is structured so objectives for both parents and children are clear and procedures and responsibilities are precisely described
>
> The intervention occurs early and is well coordinated between parental and professional roles.
>
> Programs are individualized for the parent as well as for the child
>
> The family is dealt with as a unit, and emphasis is placed on the reciprocity between parent and child.
>
> The ultimate goal for parents is preparing them to become advocates on behalf of their child throughout the child's life span.

### Materials for Parents

There is considerable diversity among programs for young handicapped children in the curriculum of parent involvement (White, Mastropieri, and Casto, 1984). However, most programs stress parent involvement in the development of the child's *self-help skills* and *language*. A number of materials are designed specifically for parent use. Weiss and Lillywhite's (1976) *101 Ways to Help the Child Learn to Talk* can be implemented by parents. Hatten and Hatten (1975) give parents of language-delayed children a precise step-by-step guide to teach their child. Karnes (1977) has a kit of 200 lesson cards, *Learning Language at Home,* to be utilized by parents. These lessons are sequenced according to difficulty in four areas of development: motor, auditory, visual, and verbal. *Parent Cards* (Mardell-Czudnowski and Goldenberg, 1985b) guide parents in developing their child's motor, conceptual, and language skills with materials available in most homes. The *Activity Card System* (Mardell-Czudnowski and Goldenberg, 1985a) also is geared for parents. One component of this system, called "Activities for the Child at Home," allows the teacher to send parents a list of activities that can be done at home which correspond with the motoric, conceptual, or language skills being taught at school, saving teachers hours of work coordinating the home and school experiences.

Excellent materials also are available through the Portage Project. In the *Portage Guide to Early Education* (Bluma, Shearer, Frohman, and Hilliard, 1976), parents learn how to teach 580 sequential behaviors, what to reinforce, and how to observe and record behavior. Other products for parents developed by the Portage Project present practical suggestions for helping parents assist their children to become successful and independent in kindergarten (Portage Project, 1984).

### Useful Books for Parents

The following books are useful resources for the parents of preschool children with special needs.

*Let's Play to Grow Kit. A Program of Family Fun.* Special Olympics, Inc., 1350 New York Avenue, N.W.; Washington, DC 20005. ($5.00) An idea kit for the whole family, with sports activities especially designed for early childhood (0—5 years).

*New Directions for Parents of Persons Who Are Retarded* by R. Perske. Abington Press; 201 8th Ave., So.; Nashville, TN 37202 ($1.95) A short book for parents on different kinds of feelings they may be experiencing and ways of coping.

*Parents Speak Out: Views from the Other Side of the Two-Way Mirror* by A. Turnbull and H. Turnbull. Charles E. Merrill; Columbus OH 43216.

*Helping the Handicapped Through Parent/Professional Partnerships.* DLM Teaching Resources; One DLM Park; Allen, TX 75002 ($5.50) A concise overview of the services provided by professionals who work with handicapped children. It assists parents in interpreting professional reports and provides guidance in coordinating clinical and educational information.

*A Basic Guide to Language Development* and *A Basic Guide to Language Problems* by P. Newcomer. DLM Teaching Resources; One DLM Park; Allen, TX 75002 ($4.00 each) Basic overview and description of the process and possible problems in the development of language, written in nontechnical language.

*Changing the Behavior of Handicapped Children* by N. Ketchel and S. March. DLM Teaching Rescources; One DLM Park, TX 75002 ($45.00 for a teacher's guide and 10 each of 7 booklets for parents) This set of materials offers practical assistance to teachers and parents of behavior-disordered children. It focuses on developing a collaborative relationship between teachers and parents and provides strategies for use in the classroom and at home.

Helpful books and printed materials also are available through national organizations that offer information and other forms of assistance. In addition, many of these national organizations have state and local chapters that provide local contacts for parents. Table 3.2 lists some of the national organizations of special interest to parents.

**TABLE 3.2   National Organizations of Special Interest to Parents**

| NAME | ADDRESS | SERVICE |
| --- | --- | --- |
| Alexander Graham Bell Association for the Deaf | 3417 Volta Pl., N.W. Washington, DC 20007 202/337-5220 | National organization for parents and teachers interested in hearing impaired children; provides information on home training, amplification, and has a large library on deafness. |
| Allergy Foundation of America | 801 2nd Ave. New York, NY 10017 212/876-8875 | Provides a listing of allergy clinics available across the country as well as informational pamphlets describing different allergies (pamphlets cost 50¢ each). |
| Amer. Association for the Severely-Profoundly Handicapped | 1600 W. Armory Way Seattle, WA 98119 206/543-4011 | A new national organization; publishes a monthly newsletter for parents and professionals concerned with children having great needs for special assistance. |
| American Foundation for the Blind | 15 West 11th St. New York, NY 10011 212/924-0420 | Private agency that provides information and referral services for the public. |
| American Speech and Hearing Association | 1801 Rockville Pike Rockville, MD 20852 301/897-5700 | An educational and professional organization for speech, language, and audiology. Provides clinical referral services for those seeking clinical services. Free public information literature is available on request from the association. |
| Association for Children and Adults with Learning Disabilities (ACLD) | 4156 Library Rd. Pittsburgh, PA 15234 412/881-1191 | National organization within every state; provides information on advocacy, publications, and new developments related to children with learning disabilities. |
| Closer Look | Box 1942 Washington, DC 20013 202/833-4160 | National information center to help parents find out about rights, how to get services, and locate a local group. Publishes a free newsletter, The Closer Report, with much helpful information. |
| Down's Syndrome Congress | Ms. Betty Buczynski 16470 Ronnies Dr. Misawaka, IN 46544 | National information service for and by parents of Down's syndrome retarded children; publishes a monthly newsletter on new information of special interest ($5 a year). |

**TABLE 3.2  (Cont.)**

| NAME | ADDRESS | SERVICE |
| --- | --- | --- |
| Epilepsy Foundation of America | 1828 L St., N.W. Washington, DC 20036 202/293-2930 | A national agency for people with epilepsy. Provides free information on epilepsy and its consequences and educational materials to individuals and groups dealing with seizures/ disorders. Provides referral service, monitors related legislative activity, and is a strong advocate to help obtain needed services and rights for those with epilepsy. |
| Mental Health Association, National Headquarters | 1800 North Kent St. Arlington, VA 22209 703/524-3352 703/524-4230 | Provides referral services for parents as well as delivering workshops and seminars on the various aspects of mental health. Makes available to the public a large collection of free literature. |
| National Association for Retarded Citizens | 2709 Ave. E East P.O. Box 6109 Arlington, TX 76011 817/261-4961 | Has over 1900 state and local chapters; promotes programs for retarded children and their families. |
| National Association for Visually Handicapped | 305 East 24th St. New York, NY 10010 212/889-3141 | Provides free learning materials for parents to help their children, including large print books and a monthly newsletter to keep families informed on the new techniques used with the visually handicapped. |
| National Easter Seal Society for Crippled Children and Adults | 2023 West Ogden Ave. Chicago, IL 60612 312/243-8400 | National organization to provide rehabilitation services to persons with physical handicaps; has local societies throughout the country. |
| National Hemophilia Foundation | 25 West 39th St. New York, NY 10018 212/869-9740 | Provides free literature on Hemophilia and the handicapping conditions that can result from this disease. Provides referral services and was directly responsible for the establishment of 23 diagnostic centers for Hemophilia across the country that provide training and rehabilitation. |
| National Multiple Sclerosis Society | 205 East 42nd St. New York, NY 10017 212/986-3240 | A voluntary health agency. Provides literature, counseling, training, referral, group recreational activities, loans of special equipment, and financial support of Multiple Sclerosis clinics in local hospitals. Local chapters can be found throughout the country. |
| National Society for Autistic Children | 169 Tampa Ave. Albany, NY 12208 518/489-7375 | National organization with information on the education and welfare of children with severe needs in communication and behavior. |

**TABLE 3.2   (Cont.)**

| NAME | ADDRESS | SERVICE |
|------|---------|---------|
| Spina Bifida Association of America | 343 S. Dearborn Chicago, IL 60604 312/662-1562 | National association to distribute information to parents and professionals; has local chapters throughout the country. |
| United Cerebral Palsy Association, Inc. | 66 East 34th St. New York, NY 10016 212/481-6300 | National association for information and service needs to families with a child with cerebral palsy. |

From Division for Exceptional Children. *Hand in Hand: Parents and Educators Planning Special Education for the Child.* Raleigh, NC: State Department of Public Instruction, 1979.

## PARENT RIGHTS

Parents are usually aware of their responsibilities to their exceptional child, but they rarely are aware of their rights as parents of an exceptional child. According to P.L.94 -142, parents of children with exceptional needs have the following rights:

Public schools must *inform parents* that their child is entitled to specific services.

Parents have the right to obtain an independent evaluation at public expense if the public school's assessment is in error.

Parents have the right to study the data and decide whether to share the information with the school.

Public schools must *ask parents to participate* in making decisions and developing the educational program for their child.

Public schools must provide education to special-needs children at *no cost to parents.*

*Parents may request a due-process hearing* if they feel their child's current educational needs are not being met by the public school. However, the right to repayment of attorney's fees if the case goes to court is not recoupable.

Thus, parents participate in three ways in their child's education according to law:

1. They give permission for assessment and for beginning or changing any special education programming for their child.
2. They attend and participate in meetings that develop the special education and learning goals for their child.
3. They agree to the written special education program and annual learning goals for their child.

The Family Education Rights and Privacy Act (P.L.93-380) also gives rights to parents (Martin,1982). Parents may see all information that affects the evaluation, placement, or programming of their child. This includes all personally indentifiable educational records collected, maintained, and used by the school. Futhermore, parents can demand a change in any record they find inaccurate, misleading, or in violation of their privacy.

In addition, parents of exceptional children should realize that they have the following rights (Gordon, 1975):

> Freedom to feel that they have done the best they could.
>
> Freedom to enjoy life as intensely as possible, even though they have an exceptional child.
>
> Freedom to let their handicapped child have his or her own privacy.
>
> Freedom to have hostile thoughts once in a while without feeling guilty.
>
> Freedom to enjoy solitude at times.
>
> Freedom to tell people about their child's progress and achievements with a real sense of pride.
>
> Freedom to have their own hobbies and interests.
>
> Freedom to tell teachers and other professionals what they really feel about the job the professionals are doing and demand that their opinions be respected.
>
> Freedom to devote as much time as they want to the handicap cause and to get away from it for a while and return if they want.
>
> Freedom to tell their child if he or she displeases them even though their child has a handicap.
>
> Freedom to refrain from praising their child gratuitously, even though they have been told to offer much praise.
>
> Freedom to lie once in a while and say everything is fine; not to feel compelled to tell the truth to everyone who asks.
>
> Freedom to say at times that they do not want to talk about their problems or their handicapped child.
>
> Freedom to have an annual vacation without the children; have dates, celebrations, weekends away, time together to enhance their marriage.
>
> Freedom to spend a little extra money on themselves, even if they feel they can't afford it.

Gordon warns that parents who do not enjoy almost all of these freedoms are in trouble because martyred parents seldom are appreciated by anybody, least of all by their exceptional child.

## SUMMARY

Involving parents in their child's educational program is critical for the improvement of the child and the success of the program. However, the foundation of the parent–professional partnership must be based on mutual trust and respect. Professionals must recognize each parent as a unique individual, with a past, present, and future unlike any other. Parents are simply people— not a category called "parents of exceptional children" who have stereotyped reactions to having a child with special needs. Yet there is little question that parents of exceptional children experience stages of adjustment: denial, intellectual awareness, and finally, intellectual and emotional adjustment.

Most parents' programs have four major but overlapping dimensions: developing parent participation, supporting parents emotionally, exchanging information with parents, and improving parent–child interactions.

Services to families include parent intervention programs, available publications, and national organizations of special interest to parents. Most parent intervention programs stress the language and self-help areas of development.

Finally, the rights of parents, both legally and personally, should be considered and respected by parents and professionals alike.

## REVIEW QUESTIONS

**Terms to Know**

parenting
denial
diagnostic "shopping"
child advocacy

active listening
depression
acceptance
mourning process

1. Describe the three stages of adjustment that parents of handicapped children generally go through, along with typical behavior in each stage.
2. What obstacles interfere in the parenting of most children?
3. The four major dimensions of parents' programs are developing parent participation, supporting parents emotionally, exchanging information with parents, and improving parent–child interactions. List one appropriate activity for each dimension.
4. Discuss in depth three different services that can be provided for families of handicapped preschoolers.
5. Parent-training programs generally follow one of four models; name each.
6. What is "Closer Look"?
7. Complete the following chart:

**Rights of a Handicapped Child's Parents**

| Personal | Legal |
| --- | --- |
| 1. | 1. |
| 2. | 2. |
| 3. | 3. |
| 4. | 4. |

## REFERENCES

ALLEN, K.E. (1980) *Mainstreaming in Early Childhood Education.* Albany, NY: Delmar.
BERGER, M. and M. FOWLKES (1980) "Family Intervention Project: A Family Network Model for Serving Young Handicapped Children." *Young Children,* 35 (4), 22–31.

BLUMA, S., M. SHEARER, A. FROHMAN, and J. HILLIARD (1976) *Portage Guide to Early Education.* Portage, WI: Cooperation Education Service Agency, No. 12.

BRONFENBRENNER, U. (1974) *A Report on Longitudinal Evaluations of Preschool Programs,* Vol. 2, *Is Early Intervention Effective?* Washington, DC: U.S. Department of Health, Education and Welfare.

BROMWICH, R. (1981) *Working with Parents and Infants.* Baltimore: University Park Press.

CANSLER, D., G. MARTIN, and M. VALAND (1975) *Working with Families.* Winston–Salem, NC: Kaplan Press.

CARTWRIGHT, C. (1981) "Effective Programs for Parents of Young Handicapped Children." *Topics in Early Childhood Special Education,* 1 (3), 1–9.

DEBERRY, J., S. RISTAU, and H. GALLAND (1984) "Parent Involvement Programs: Local Level Status and Influences." *Journal of the Division for Early Childhood,* 8 (2), 173–85.

DIVISION FOR EXCEPTIONAL CHILDREN (1979) *Hand in Hand: Parents and Educators Planning Special Education for the Child.* Raleigh, NC: State Department of Public Instruction.

DUNLAP, W. (1979) "How Do Parents of Handicapped Children View Their Needs?" *Journal of the Division of Early Childood.* 1 (1), 1–10.

FALLEN, N. and W. UMANSKY (1985) *Young Children with Special Needs,* (2nd ed.) Columbus: Charles E. Merrill.

GORDON, S. (1975) *Living Fully: A Guide for Young People with a Handicap, Their Parents, Their Teachers, and Professionals.* New York: John Day.

HATTEN, J. and P. HATTEN (1975) *Natural Language: A Clinician-Guided Program for Parents of Language-Delayed Children* (rev. ed.) Tucson, AZ: Communication Skill Builders.

HAYDEN, A. (1978) "Early Childhood Education," in K.E. Allen et al. (eds.) *Early Intervention— A Team Approach.* Baltimore: University Park Press.

KARNES, M. (1977) *Learning Language at Home.* Reston, VA: Council for Exceptional Children.

KARNES, M. and R. LEE (1978) *What Research and Experience Say to the Teacher of Exceptional Children.* U.S. Department of Health, Education and Welfare, Publication Number 78-60985. Washington, DC: Government Printing Office.

KARNES, M. and A. SHWEDEL (1983) "Assessment of Preschool Giftedness," in K. Paget and B. Bracken (eds.) *Psychoeducational Assessment of Preschool Children.* NY: Grune and Stratton.

KARNES, M., and R. ZEHRBACH (1977) "Alternative Models for Delivering Services to Young Handicapped Children." In J. Jordan, A. Hayden, M. Karnes, and M. Wood (eds.) *Early Childhood Education for Exceptional Children: A Handbook of Ideas and Exemplary Practices.* Reston, VA: Council for Exceptional Children.

KEEFE, S. (1984) "Parents Are People, Too." *Teaching Exceptional Children,* Fall, 59–61.

KELLY, J. (1982) "Effects of Intervention on Caregiver–Infant Interaction When the Infant Is Handicapped." *Journal of the Division for Early Childhood,* 5, 53–64.

LILLIE, D., P. TROHANIS, and K. GOIN (eds.) (1976) *Teaching Parents to Teach: A Guide for Working with the Special Child.* NY: Walker.

LINDER, T. and D. CHITWOOD (1984) "The Needs of Fathers of Young Handicapped Children." *Journal of the Division for Early Childhood,* 8, 2, 133–39.

MARDELL-CZUDNOWSKI, C. and D. GOLDENBERG (1985a). *Activity Card System.* Edison, NJ: Childcraft Education Corporation.

MARDELL-CZUDNOWSKI, C. and D. GOLDENBERG (1985b) *Parent Cards.* Edison, NJ: Childcraft Education Corporation.

MARKOWITZ, J. (1984) "Participation of Fathers in Early Childhood Special Education Programs: An Exploratory Study." *Journal of the Division for Early Childhood,* 8, 2, 119–31.

MARTIN, R. (1982) "Legal Issues in Assessment for Special Education." In J. Neisworth (ed.) *Assessment in Special Education.* Rockville, MD: Aspen Systems.

PORTAGE PROJECT (1984) *Get a Jump on Kindergarten.* Portage, WI: Portage Project Materials.

SCARR, S. (1984) *Mother Care, Other Care.* NY: Basic Books.

SCHELL, G. (1981) "The Young Handicapped Child: A Family Perspective." *Topics in Early Childhood Special Education,* 1, 3, 21–27.

SHEARER, D. and M. SHEARER (1976) "The Portage Project: A Model for Early Childhood Intervention." In R. Tjossem (ed.) *Intervention Strategies for High Risk Infants and Young Children*. Baltimore: University Park Press.

STILES, S., J. COLE, and A. GARDNER (1979) "Maximizing Parental Involvement in Programs for Exceptional Children." *Journal of the Division for Early Childhood*, 1, 1, 68–82.

TURNBULL, A. and H. TURNBULL (1985) *Parents Speak Out*. Columbus, OH: Charles E. Merrill.

VADASY, P., R. FEWELL, D. MEYER, G. SCHELL, and M. GREENBERG (1984) "Involved Parents; Characteristics and Resources of Fathers and Mothers of Young Handicapped Children." *Journal of the Division for Early Childhood*, 8, 1, 13–25.

WEISS, C. and H. LILLYWHITE (1976) *Communication Disorders: A Handbook for Prevention and Early Intervention*. St. Louis: C.V. Mosby.

WELSH, M. and C. ODUM (1981) "Parent Involvement in the Education of the Handicapped Child: A Review of the Literature." *Journal of the Division for Early Childhood*, 3 15–25.

WHITE, B. (1975) *The First Three Years of Life*. Englewood Cliffs, NJ: Prentice-Hall.

WHITE, K., M. MASTROPIERI, and G. CASTO (1984) "An Analysis of Special Education Early Childhood Projects Approved by the Joint Dissemination Review Panel." *Journal of the Division for Early Childhood*, 9, 1, 11–26.

WIEGERINK, R., A. HOCUTT, R. POSANTE-LORO, and M. BRISTOL (1980). "Parent Involvement in the Early Education Programs for Handicapped Children." *New Directions for Exceptional Children*, 1, 67–86.

# FOUR

# Assessment: Locating, Screening, Diagnosing, and Evaluating the Child

## INTRODUCTION

This chapter provides an overview of assessment and discusses four different sequential phases of assessment: the locating process, the screening process, the diagnostic process, and the evaluative process. Although it is acknowledged that the younger the child, the less valid and reliable are test predictions across all areas of measurement, there is general agreement that early identification and intervention does lead to improved functioning of the young child with special needs. Evaluating the behaviors and abilities of young children serves to alert professionals and parents to potential problems, to eliminate or lessen the severity of future problems, to decrease the formation of undesirable patterns of behavior, and to prevent the development of emotional problems caused by the frustration of failure. It is more productive to prevent medical and educational problems from developing than to attempt to cure, correct, or remediate debilitating conditions after they have occurred.

A case example, which includes all four elements of assessment (locating, screening, diagnosing, and evaluating), is presented at the end of the chapter.

## OVERVIEW OF ASSESSMENT

*Assessment* pertains to the total system of selecting and evaluating those children whose unique characteristics and needs in specific areas of behavior indicate that they should receive special services. The key purpose for assessing young children is to improve our ability to anticipate their needs so that problems can be remediated as soon as possible. Assessment is a complex task, particularly when trying to assess subtle types of handicapping conditions that cannot easily be observed.

The medical examination is an important area of assessment. It is recommended that all children receive a comprehensive health examination at regular intervals during the preschool years to detect and treat any medical problems as early as possible. However, surveys indicate that less than half of American children receive regular systematic health care before they go to school. Moreover, the children most likely to have developmental problems are often the ones who do not receive a medical assessment. To remedy this situation, a federal program known as *Early and Periodic Screening, Diagnosis, and Treatment* (EPSDT) was established in 1967 to provide medical examinations for children from medicaid-eligible families. Although approximately 12 million children from birth to twenty-one years of age received medical examinations under this program, EPSDT has not been viewed as successful in fulfilling its mission. According to Meisels (1985), the program lacks a systematic evaluation system to demonstrate the effectiveness of EPSDT.

There are four separate but related phases of assessment: (1) locating, (2) screening, (3) diagnosing, and (4) evaluating. As shown in Table 4.1, each phase of assessment serves a different purpose. *Locating* refers to ways of finding handicapped children in the community; *screening* refers to ways of quickly surveying many children to identify those who may be in need of special services; *diagnosing* refers to methods of providing a comprehensive in-depth examination of an individual child; and *evaluating* refers to ways of determining a child's progress within a program. Each of these types of assessment is described further in the balance of this chapter.

**TABLE 4.1   An Overview Of Assessment**

| | LOCATING | SCREENING | DIAGNOSING | EVALUATING |
|---|---|---|---|---|
| Purpose | To make initial contact and increase the public's awareness of services. | To sort out children who need further study. | To determine extent of medical and developmental –educational impairments; to determine treatment and program placement. | To determine entrance and exit criteria for special programs; to determine which children remain in special programs; to determine which programs have reached predetermined objectives. |
| Responsible Person(s) | Program staff, volunteers, community members | Volunteers, professionals, paraprofessionals | Multidisciplinary team of professionals | Multidisciplinary team of professionals |

Adapted from L. Cross and K. Goin (eds.), *Identifying Handicapped Children*. NY: Walker & Co., 1977, p. 5.

## THE LOCATING PROCESS

Since preschool children are not usually placed in a formal setting, educators need to make a concerted effort to search out preschoolers in need of special services. Locating such children requires a systematic procedure. The locating process is the first stage in total assessment and includes any or all of the following activities:

1. Defining the target population
2. Increasing the public's awareness of services

3. Encouraging referrals
4. Canvassing the community for children in need of services

*Child Find* is a program established to locate handicapped children in each community. The program is based on a federal law that mandates that the states actively seek out handicapped children who are currently unserved, underserved, or inappropriately served (P.L. 94-142). This process of locating handicapped children also is called *casefinding* (Barnes, 1982) or *outreach* (Lichtenstein and Ireton, 1984).

### Defining the Target Population

The initial activity is the process of locating all handicapped preschool children, ages birth through five years old, who can profit from early intervention services because they have a disability or delay of some type. The concern is to locate all preschool children who because of physical, social, intellectual, emotional, or communicative problems need additional and special assistance in order to succeed in school and/or society. The target population of the locating program is every eligible handicapped child in the community. Some communities include gifted children in their search for children with special needs.

### Increasing the Public's Awareness of Services

The success of the locating process is dependent upon informing the community of the importance of early identification. Methods that have been used to inform the community include press releases, bulletins, brochures, bumper stickers, radio and television spot announcements, posters placed in key locations such as supermarkets and doctors' waiting rooms, and flyers sent home with school children. Other means that have been used to distribute the message include referral postcards that have been included with utility bills, welfare checks, bank statements, school mailings, and payroll checks. Federal and state agencies have developed many innovative and effective "child find" systems to increase public awareness.

The responsibility of recognizing developmental problems cannot be left to parents alone. Free vision, hearing, and developmental checkups should be encouraged for all children, not just those children whose parents may suspect a problem.

The strategies for increasing the public's awareness vary throughout the country. A specific technique that is successful in one community, with a certain type of population, might not be effective in an area across town. Variables that affect the success of an awareness strategy include local customs, size of the target population, literacy and economic levels of the community, and availability and type of transportation.

Certain principles seem important to address regardless of the particular population. These should be used in planning a public awareness campaign:

1. *Understand the nature and intricacies of the community.* Any community, regardless of size, is a series of small groups that need to be treated separately in terms of locating potentially handicapped children.
2. *Communicate key concepts to the community.* This includes milestones of normal child development, the nature of exceptional developmental patterns and their early signs, the need for early intervention, the available services, and the right to a free and appropriate education.
3. *Develop a broad-based, multidimensional system.* This will ensure overlapping contact and will increase chances of finding all handicapped children. This effort need not be more expensive if planned well.
4. *Determine prior to the effort what "success" will be and how it will be measured.* Variables to consider are cost, time, percentage of children found in the effort, creation of public atmosphere (either positive or negative), and general spin-off effect to other agencies in the community. Evaluation need not be complex, just consistent and thorough.

The most important aspect of the public awareness effort is to make sure the parents view the activity positively. Schools need to create the feeling of *helping* in a cooperative way if this portion of identification is to succeed.

### Encouraging Referrals

Agencies that serve both handicapped and nonhandicapped children, daycare centers, nursery schools, and pediatricians all are excellent contacts to establish awareness of services and also as referral sources. Other private practitioners—such as psychiatrists, psychologists, dentists, orthopedists, optometrists, neurologists, and therapists—should be informed of the population sought and the range of services offered. In addition, coordination is necessary with the public health department, the welfare department, mental health clinics, family services, the state department of education, local colleges and universities with training programs in early childhood and/or special education, hospitals, medical schools, civic organizations, and religious groups. Parents are also an important potential referral source. One study reported that one of every two parents who suspected a potential learning problem was found to be correct by actual clinical follow-up. However, this does not mean that parents can *always* recognize that their child needs special services.

A door-to-door census designed to locate and register all children below school age is often one of the most effective child-find procedures for some communities. However, in large metropolitan areas actually knocking on doors may not be successful because few people are at home during the daytime hours. As more mothers join the labor force, this is an increasing problem. A telephone survey also can be part of this canvassing procedure if most families in the community have telephones. Both door-to-door canvassing and telephoning are time consuming and costly, requiring the use of volunteers and ample funding to be effective.

## THE SCREENING PROCESS

*Screening* is the second phase of the total assessment system. Screening provides an efficient way to sort out preschool children who *may* need special education services from the general population of preschoolers. Through screening procedures, about 10 to 12 percent of a total preschool population are identified as children at-risk or as young children who have handicaps or potential handicaps. With the implementation of P.L. 94-142, developmental screening has become an on-going procedure throughout the country. Thus, the screening process sorts out children in the general population who need a closer look, and the suspicion of a problem is later confirmed or denied through the next phase of assessment—the comprehensive diagnosis.

Screening enables children with problems to be identified earlier and therefore to have needed treatment begin earlier. The screening process is effective in finding mild handicapping conditions, but it is not as important for finding severe handicapping conditions. Since severe handicapping conditions are usually more obvious, children with severe handicaps usually are identified during the locating process and proceed directly to the diagnosis. The method of screening should be appropriate and reasonable in terms of time, money, and resources for dealing with large numbers of children. Medical and educational screening might be combined, but there are only two health-related conditions that are both relatively common and relevant to school functioning—vision and hearing impairment.

There are three major approaches to screening: (1) the mass screening, or the "round-up"; (2) screening an entire existing group (such as a nursery school population or a Head Start class); or (3) screening children who have been referred.

The screening process includes the following activities:

Selecting conditions to be screened
Choosing screening tests
Training staff
Planning for screening
Reporting results

Each of these activities is described in this section.

## Selecting Conditions to be Screened

Although there are many factors that can affect a child's success in school, it is unrealistic to expect to screen for all of them. In part, a child's school success is related to the school curriculum, the classroom environment, and the teacher. Even though the child's earlier functioning and experience may be contributing factors to school success or failure, the primary focus of the screening process is to assess the child's current status of functioning. The screening assessment typically gathers information about the child's functioning in the following areas:

Vision and hearing
Cognition
Speech and language
Gross-motor and fine-motor skills
Visual and auditory perception
Self-help skills
Social–emotional status

## Choosing Screening Tests

An acceptable screening test for identifying young children who may need special services should have certain qualities. The screening test should be able to be routinely administered by an examiner or technician with special but limited training; it should be capable of being administered to a large number of children in a relatively short period of time at a modest cost; and it should require little professional time of the qualified examiner for its interpretation. We caution that screening tests are not intended to be used alone, nor are they intended to be used for purposes of intervention, placement, or treatment. The screening test does not provide specific information to pinpoint the precise nature of atypical development or deficiencies. The purpose of the screening test is to identify those children in need of a full assessment or diagnostic evaluation. An example of a medical screening instrument is the clinical thermometer. The thermometer serves to sort out people who have a fever from those who do not; it does not give the cause of a fever (etiology), nor does it provide the needed treatment of the problem.

Many early childhood screening tests have been developed in recent years. Some of the tests stress certain aspects of development (such as language) while other tests provide a more comprehensive assessment. Tests should be selected according to predetermined criteria established by those responsible for the screening process. Some possible questions that should be considered in the test selection are

1. *What are the problems being screened?* Availability of services and agencies should be a consideraton.

2.  *Is the screening test valid or accurate?* The success of screening ultimately depends on the accuracy of the screening test in predicting how a child will progress at a later time. Therefore, predictive validity is the most important factor for a screening test. Supporting data in the test manual should report on the test's content, concurrent, and predictive validity (Salvia and Ysseldyke, 1985).

3.  *Can the test be administered in a short period of time?* Screening procedures should be short because (1) the young child has a short attention span and (2) a short test will reduce the cost of screening large numbers of children. The test should have a well-organized score sheet, be clear, and have specific directions and explicit scoring standards.

4.  *Is the test scored objectively so results are reliable?* Objective scoring is of particular importance when using people other than professionals in the administration so that results are reliable regardless of the tester (inter-rater reliability). There should also be test–retest reliability reported in the test manual. This should be a correlation coefficient of .80 or higher (Salvia and Ysseldyke, 1985).

5.  *Are the costs of screening reasonable?* This is dependent on the budget. Costs include the initial cost of the test; the need for consumable items (such as forms); and expenses for maintenance, depreciation, and the utilization of volunteers and paraprofessionals. The cost of screening should be compared to the cost of treatment after the usual time of diagnosis and to the human grief spared by early intervention.

6.  *Is the test physically and psychologically harmless and nonthreatening to both child and parent?* A good roundup screening procedure, whether at a well-baby clinic, a local church, school, or park district building can establish good will and strong positive public relations if it is seen as a good use of funds and time by the general public. Gamelike procedures and materials and a relaxed atmosphere where coffee is available and socializing can take place aid in establishing such a feeling. Parents and children should not be separated from each other, for this only produces unnecessary anxiety.

7.  *Is the screening test accepted by the specialists who will conduct the diagnosis?* The easiest way to accomplish this acceptance is to involve these specialists in the selection of the screening test(s) whenever possible.

8.  *Who will administer the screening test?* It is important to determine whether trained paraprofessionals, volunteers, and parents can administer the test, saving the professional staff for the diagnostic process. Service organizations—such as Kiwanis, Junior Women's League, parent–teacher associations, and retired-citizen groups—can play important roles in this process. Students in testing courses are another source of people who can help. One cautionary note regards confidentiality. All screening staff should be reminded that parent and child rights of privacy must be respected as a matter of human ethics and law.

9.  *Was the test normed on children similar to those in the population to be screened?* The test manual should state the age range, sex, race, socioeconomic status, and other demographic characteristics of the population on which the test was standardized. This may avoid the use of standards derived from the performances of white, middle-class children as the comparison basis for the performance of minority children.

10. *Is the test recommending correct decisions?* That is, does the test identify most of the children who should be identified and not overidentify too many children who should not go through diagnostic procedures. It is better to use a test that

tends to overidentify (sends more children for further evaluation) than one that tends to under-identify (misses children with problems) (Leigh, 1983).

Tests must be selected with extreme care. In a study of forty-four preschool assessment tests that are available nationally, only five met the American Psychological Association (APA) guidelines for educational and psychological tests (Berman, 1977). Meisels (1985) noted that only five screening tests met essential criteria for developmental screening. Further information on tests may be found in mental measurement yearbooks (Buros, 1978; Mitchell, 1985).

It is the user's responsibility to select a technically adequate test. A number of books have been written about preschool testing instruments (Lichtenstein and Ireton, 1984; Barnes, 1982; Southworth et al., 1981; Srangler et al., 1980; Goodwin and Driscoll, 1980; Johnson, 1979). These books discuss preschool tests in terms of age range, time needed for administration, training level of the person administering the test, developmental skills or domains covered, and whether the test is for purposes of screening or diagnosis. A description of more than thirty widely used screening tests for young children is presented in Appendix B.

### Screening Tests for Newborn Infants

Infants who exhibit serious developmental problems may be identified at birth or shortly thereafter. According to Beck (1977), 6.8 percent of handicapped children could or should be identified at or shortly after birth.

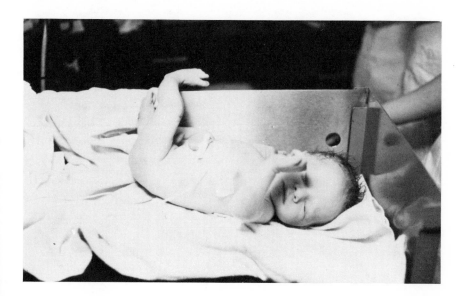

Two scales that assist workers in the field in such early identification are the *Apgar Rating Scale* (Apgar, 1953) and the *Neonatal Behavioral Assessment Scale* (Brazelton, 1973). The *Apgar Rating Scale* is used routinely in many hospitals across the United States to screen newborn infants. The test is given one minute after delivery and then repeated at five minutes after delivery. Five easily observed signs—*heart rate, respiratory effort, muscle tone, reflex response,* and *color* are scored on a scale from 0 (poor) to 2 (good). These signs are listed in Table 4.2 with their corresponding scores. Total scores in the 0 to 3 range suggest extremely poor physical condition and the need for resuscitation. A fair condition is indicated by a score of 4 to 6, and a score of 7 to 10 implies a good condition.

The *Neonatal Behavior Assessment Scale* (Brazelton, 1973) is a more detailed examination designed to identify abnormalities in the central nervous system and sensory abilities. The scale is a 47-item behavioral evaluation that measures the infant's responses to the environment. Designed initially for use with normal newborn infants, it takes approximately 30 minutes to administer. Published studies on test–retest reliability report correlation coefficients ranging from 0.83 to 1.00.

Recent studies suggest that the analysis of cry sounds could be a useful part of standard neonatal examinations. Abnormal cry patterns at birth may identify even full-term infants who are at risk for later problems because of poor central nervous system development.

**TABLE 4.2  Apgar Rating Scale**

| SIGN | SCORE | | |
|---|---|---|---|
| | 0 | 1 | 2 |
| Heart Rate | Absent | Slow (less than 100 beats per minute) | Over 100 beats |
| Respiratory effect | Absent | Slow, irregular | Good, crying |
| Muscle tone | Flaccid | Some flexion of extremities | Active motion |
| Reflex irritability | No response | Cry | Cry |
| Color | Blue, pale | Body pink, extremities blue | Completely pink |

From V. Apgar "Proposal for a New Method of Evaluating the Newborn Infant." *Anesthesia and Analgesia* 1953, *32*, 260–267.

## Examples of Comprehensive Screening Tests

Screening instruments that assess each specific developmental domain will be discussed later in this chapter. The trend, however, has been to use comprehensive screening systems that screen many different areas of development.

Some research indicates that medical complications during later infancy are better predictors of developmental outcome than are obstetric and neonatal events (Littman and Parmalee, 1978). Thus, the screening of babies between one and twenty-four months to detect developmental delays is highly recommended. Instruments commonly used by pediatricians that stress a medical, developmental emphasis include *The Neurological Screening Examination of the Newborn Infant* (Prechtl and Beintema, 1964; *Wheel Guide in Normal Milestones of Development* (Haynes, 1978); *Developmental Diagnosis* (Knobloch, Steven, and Malone, 1980), and the *Denver Developmental Screening Test—Revised* (DDST-R) (Frankenburg, Fandal, Sciarillo, and Burgess, 1981). These tests compare young children's current development with well-established normative data.

The *Denver Developmental Screening Test—Revised* (DDST-R) is probably the most widely used of these developmental preschool screening tests. It is administered individually and used with children two weeks to six years of age. The test consists of 105 tasks that are grouped into four areas: (1) personal–social; (2) fine motor–adaptive; (3) language; and (4) gross-motor. Children will usually be required to complete only about twenty of the test items. Norms indicate the age at which 25, 50, 75, and 90 percent of boys, girls, and all children successfully complete each task. Cutoff points are given for suspected developmental lags that require further testing.

Preschool screening tests that emphasize an educational model include the *Comprehensive Identification Process* (CIP) (Zehrbach, 1976); *Early Screening Inventory* (ESI) (Meisels and Wiske, 1983); and *Developmental Indicators for the Assessment of Learning—Revised* (DIAL-R) (Mardell-Czudnowski and Goldenberg, 1983).

*Developmental Indicators for the Assessment of Learning—Revised* (DIAL-R), one of the most widely used of these tests, is a revised and restandardized version of DIAL (Mardell-Czudnowski and Goldenberg, 1984a). The DIAL-R tasks were selected to reflect school behavior found in standard classroom situations. The test covers the developmental areas of motor, concepts, and language skills. Social and emotional factors also are considered but are scored separately from scores obtained in the screening process. Norms are given for typical behavior for each of the twenty-four items according to five age ranges. Cutoff points indicate the lowest 6 percent and the highest 6 percent of the nationally normed sample. The DIAL-R score sheet is shown in Figure 4.1.

**FIGURE 4.1**

# DIAL-R
## SCORESHEET

Child's Name _____ LAST _____ FIRST _____ NICKNAME _____

Address _____ NUMBER _____ STREET _____ CITY/STATE/ZIP

Phone Number ( _____ ) AREA CODE _____

Parents' Names
1  2  3
MOTHER _____ FATHER _____ Language _____

School _____ Today's Date _____

Class _____ Birth Date _____

C.A. _____

Hearing  +  –

Vision  +  –

YEAR  MONTH  DAY

Boy _____  Girl _____

## MOTOR (red)

| | SCALED SCORE | | | |
|---|---|---|---|---|
| | 0 under 2 yrs | 1 2-3 yrs | 2 3-4 yrs 4-5 yrs | 3 4-5 yrs | 4 5-8 yrs |

1. Catching — 0 | – | 1 | 2 | 3
2. Jumping, Hopping, and Skipping — 0 | 1-2 | 3-8 | 9-12 | 13-16
   jumps:  0  1
   + hops: (right) 0 1 2 3 4 5 6
           (left) 0 1 2 3 4 5 6
   + skip:  0-any 1-slide 2-step/hop 3-skip
3. Building — 0 | 1 | 2 | 3 | 4
4. Touching Fingers — 0 | 0-1 | 1 | 2 | 3 | 4
5. Cutting — 0 | 2 | 3 | 4
6. Matching — 0 | 1-7 | 8-9 | 10-11 | 12
7. Copying — 0 | 1-7 | 8-11 | 12-18 | 19-24
   I  O  +  □  ◇  ⬦
   E  N  D  S  ⚹  ⚹
   I 0 1 2   E 0 1 2
   O 0 1 2   N 0 1 2
   + 0 1 2   D 0 1 2
   □ 0 1 2   S 0 1 2
   ◇ 0 1 2   ⚹ 0 1 2
   ⬦ 0 1 2   ⚹ 0 1 2
8. Writing Name — 0 | – | 1 | 2

**TOTAL** (Max.= 31)

OBSERVATIONS  1 2 3 4 5 6 7 8

## CONCEPTS (green)

| | SCALED SCORE | | | | |
|---|---|---|---|---|---|
| | 0 under 2 yrs | 1 2-3 yrs | 2 3-4 yrs | 3 4-5 yrs | 4 5-8 yrs |

1. Naming Colors — 0 | 1-7 | 8-15 | 16-18
   R O W G BL Y B BR P
2. Identifying Body Parts — 0 | 1-9 | 10-12 | 13-15 | 16-18
   nose  neck  chin  ankle
   hair  stomach  shoulder  hip
   ear  knee  chest  waist
   teeth  thumb  heel
   tongue  elbow  wrist
3. Counting (Rote) — 0-2 | 3-4 | 5-8 | 9-10 | 11
4. Counting (Meaningful) — 0 | 1 | 3 | 5-7 | 9
   1 3 5 7 9
5. Positioning — 0 | 1-2 | 3 | 4 | 5
   on  under  corner  between  middle
6. Identifying Concepts — 0 | 1-14 | 15-20 | 21-26 | 27-28
   biggest  big
   hot
   empty  long
   right  more
   longest  fast
   most  little
   littlest
   cold
   full
   day  short
   shortest  less
   least  slow
   slowest
7. Naming Letters — 0 | – | 1-10 | 11-16
   O B P E R W Y G
8. Sorting Chips — 0 | – | 1 | 1-4 | 5-8
   by color: R  B  Y
   by size:  big  little
   by shape: O  □  △

**TOTAL** (Max.= 31)

OBSERVATIONS  1 2 3 4 5 6 7 8

## LANGUAGE (purple)

| | SCALED SCORE | | | | |
|---|---|---|---|---|---|
| | 0 under 2 yrs | 1 2-3 yrs | 2 3-4 yrs 4-5 yrs | 3 4-5 yrs | 4 5-8 yrs |

1. Articulating — 0 | 1-14 | 15-26 | 27-29
   pin  truck
   bed  rabbit
   cup  dress
   —  chair
   towel  knife
   hand  sandwich
   leg  thumb
   fish  mouth/teeth
2. Giving Personal Data — 0 | 1-3 | 4 | 5 | 6-7
   first name  sex  phone #
   last name  street
   age  city/state
3. Remembering — 0 | 1-3 | 4-5 | 6-7 | 8-9
   clapping  A  B  C
   numbers  A  B  C
   sentences  A  B  C
4. Naming Nouns — 0 | 1-15 | 16 | 17 | 18
   cat  phone  comb
   plane  pencil
   car  clock  ambulance
5. Naming Verbs — 0 | 1-9 | 10-14 | 15-16 | 17-18
   sleep  call  comb
   fly  watch  write
   drive  time  go to hospital
   broken
6. Classifying Foods — 0 | 1-2 | 3-4 | 5-6 | 7-8
   Tally.
7. Problem Solving — 0 | 1 | 2-3 | 4-5 | 6-8
   hungry  0  1  2
   dark room  0  1  2
   rain  0  1  2
   broken  0  1  2
8. Sentence Length — 0 | 1-2 | 3 | 4 | 5-8

**TOTAL** (Max.= 31)

OBSERVATIONS  1 2 3 4 5 6 7 8

**DECISION** _____

Motor score _____ (see page 58 for Cut-off Points by Area Scores)
Concepts score _____
Language score _____ (see page 15 for Cut-off Points by Total Score)
Total score _____
# of Observations _____ (see page 50 for Cut-off Points by Observations)

CHILDCRAFT
EDUCATION CORP.

The screening is accomplished by a team within a setting that simu-lates a typical early childhood environment, such as a preschool or daycare center. This provides ecological validity. However, the child is still screened on a one-to-one basis.

The DDST-R and DIAL-R are *norm-referenced* screening tests. Chil-dren taking such tests are compared with others on whom the test was standardized. Thus, such a test uses a specific population of persons as its interpretive frame of reference.

A *criterion-referenced* screening test, in contrast, measures perfor-mance or mastery of precise skills or content. Scores are interpreted in terms of a prespecified standard of performance. Such a test thus uses a particular content domain as its interpretative frame of reference. Samples of criterion-referenced screening tests for young children are the *Learning Accomplishment Profile* (LAP) (Sanford, 1974), and the *Portage Guide to Early Education* (Bluma et al., 1976). Generally, these tests are most useful when applied to curriculum planning and ongoing evaluation of achievement (pre-test and post-test measures) than as screening tests for identifying special populations (Lichtenstein and Ireton, 1984; Lidz, 1983a). They do not address issues such as how a child learns, how to teach that child, or why there is a problem. However, they do indicate what a child knows and what to teach next. Detailed use of criterion-referenced measures is cov-ered in Chapter 5.

*Screening tests for specific areas.*    In addition to the comprehensive screening tests discussed in the previous section, there are other screening tests that assess only one specific area of development. These areas include health and physical growth, perceptual and cognitive abilities, speech and language development, and social/emotional relations.

*Health and physical information.*   The measurement of growth through the use of height and weight charts is probably the oldest and most universally practiced form of screening (Stangler et al., 1980). Most parents expect and look forward to this event as part of their child's health examination. Another measured parameter of growth during the first two years is the child's head circumference. A commonly used source for evaluating a child's growth is *The National Center for Health Statistics Growth Charts* (Hammill et al., 1976). There are four separate growth charts: two for girls and two for boys. For each sex, one chart covers birth to three years and the other, from two to eighteen years. Using the charts, the physician can screen for failure to thrive at one extreme and obesity on the other.

The *parent interview* is another useful tool for screening for physical problems. A parent questionnaire is useful for screening the child's general health, physical intactness, and health history. The screening interview should check on the child's immunization status. There are seven diseases (diphtheria, tetanus, whooping cough, poliomyelitis, measles, rubella, and mumps) against which all children should be protected.

*Vision screening* can be readily conducted by trained paraprofessionals in the community. This procedure is generally well accepted by the public. Vision tests should screen for amblyopia (lazy eye), refractive errors (nearsightedness and far sightedness), strabismus, and other eye diseases. Several vision screening tests appropriate for preschool children are listed in Table 4.3.

*Auditory screening* often is conducted at the same time as the vision screening for children between three and five years of age. Even with this age group, a skilled technician may assess both areas during the same session. The most commonly used tests are listed in Table 4.4. In addition to pure-tone testing, it is strongly recommended that impedance testing be conducted (Mandell and Johnson, 1984). This is a simple, valid procedure that screens for *otitis media*, a common condition characterized by a fluid-filled and/or infected middle ear.

*Perceptual development.*   Screening tests for perceptual abilities include the *Developmental Test of Visual–Motor Integration* (VMI), the *Motor-Free Visual Perception Test* (MVPT), and the *Tree/Bee Test of Auditory Discrimination*. Many of the screening tests in Appendix B assess some components of perceptual development. The components include basic fundamental skills that emerge without formal training: motor skills (gross and fine motor) and perceptual abilities (visual perception and discrimination, auditory perception and discrimination, body image and visual–motor coordination).

**TABLE 4.3   Screening Tests of Visual Function**

| TEST | AGE RANGE | Amblyopia | Refractive Error | Strabismus | Other Disease |
|------|-----------|-----------|------------------|------------|---------------|
| Vision Tests | | | | | |
| 1. Allen Picture Cards | 2½ years and above | X | X | | X |
| 2. Fixation Test | 2 months and above | X | | | X |
| 3. Illiterate E | 3 years and above | X | X | | X |
| 4. Optokinetic Response | Any age | X | | | X |
| 5. Sjogren Hand Test | 3 years and above | X | X | | X |
| 6. STYCAR | 6 months–7 years | X | X | | X |
| 7. White Vision Chart | 3 years and above | X | X | | X |
| Muscular Balance Tests | | | | | |
| 1. Cover Test | Any age | X | | X | |
| 2. Hirschberg | Any age | | | X | |
| Combination of Vision and Muscle/Machines | | | | | |
| 1. Atlantic City Vision Screener | 3 years and above | X | X | X | X |
| 2. Michigan Screener | 3 years and above | X | X | X | X |
| 3. Screening Insta-line | 3 years and above | X | X | X | X |

Adapted from W. Frankenburg and B. Camp (eds.) *Pediatric Screening Tests*. Springfield, IL: Chas. C. Thomas, 1975, p. 299.

*Cognitive development.*   There are relatively few screening tests that screen only for cognitive development. It is difficult to specify the elements of cognition independent of the other areas of development. One widely used test—*Boehm Test of Basic Concepts*—assesses the child's underlying understanding of space (location, direction, orientation, and dimension), time, and quantity (or number). Many of the screening tests in Appendix B assess some aspect of cognitive development: intelligence, concept formation, memory, thinking processes, sequencing, and classifying.

*Speech and language development.*   There are several speech and language screening tests useful for the young child. Among them are *Expressive One-Word Picture Vocabulary Test, Hannah–Gardner Test of Verbal and Nonverbal Language Functioning, Peabody Picture Vocabulary Test—Revised, Photo Articulation Test,* and the *Preschool Language Assessment Instrument.* The purpose of screening speech and language is to locate and refer for further evaluation children who have any of the following symptoms:

Frequent misunderstanding of speech
Difficulty in expressing needs and wants
Irrelevant responses to speech directed to the child
Decreased sensitivity to sound stimuli
Difficulty in articulating speech sounds

**TABLE 4.4  Auditory Screening**

| NAME OF TEST | TIME | EQUIPMENT REQUIRED | AGE RANGE |
|---|---|---|---|
| 1. Ewing Procedure | 2 minutes or less | Voice and noisemaker | 6–30 months |
| 2. Neonate Screening | 1 minute | Infant Screening Audiometer | 24 hours–1 year |
| 3. Verbal-Auditory Screening of Children (VASC) | 5 minutes | Tape cartridge and Tape Recorder | 3–5 years |
| 4. Preschool Screening Audiometer | 5 minutes | Audiometer and toys | 3–5 years |

Adapted from W. Frankenburg and B. Camp (eds.) *Pediatric Screening Tests.* Springfield, IL: Chas. C. Thomas, 1975, p. 352.

Language screening also can be used to determine the child's dominant language. Public Law 94-142 requires that children be tested in their native language. Thus, the screening should determine the child's language proficiency and communicative competence and the child's dominant language. Children who are fully bilingual are capable of understanding and using two language systems well. Some children, however, mix up the two languages. The assessment should attempt to detect whether this behavior is caused by an underlying language disorder (an inability to understand and communicate ideas in either language) or whether the use of the two languages simultaneously can be characterized as logical, systematic, controlled by the child, and appropriate to the situation and context (Ortiz, 1984).

*Social–emotional development.* Although the social–emotional realm is an important area of consideration, many authorities believe this to be a difficult area to assess with a screening test. Walker (1973), after examining 143 socioemotional measures for preschool and kindergarten children, recommended the use of observational strategies in naturalistic settings. Several observational inventories and checklists have appeared recently, including the *Joseph Preschool and Primary Self-Concept Screening Test, Preschool Behavior Rating Scale,* and the *Revised Child Behavior Checklist.*

**Training Staff**

A reliable developmental appraisal depends upon adequate preparation, training, and supervision of the examiners. Since a tool is only as good as its user, it is important that people responsible for administering screening tests be carefully trained. A nonprofessional person, such as an aide or volunteer, can be trained to administer many of the screening tests. Frankenberg and his associates (1970) suggest a tutorial approach for training one or two nonprofessionals at a time. If the group to be trained consists of ten or more people, then a uniformly prepared format should be used, using written material, films, or videotapes for consistent presentation, role playing, and supervised practice. Because proficiency of test administration tends to decrease when aides think their work is no longer being monitored, it is important to make periodic checks of screening results to assure a high level of screening accuracy. The person in charge of such periodic checks should be a professional who is competent in testing procedures and has received proper training in administering the screening tools used in the program. Materials—such as time lines, written and performance tests, videotapes, and sample forms which help the person in charge to more readily coordinate the entire screening program—are available (Mardell-Czudnowski and Goldenberg, 1984b).

## Planning for Screening

The smooth administration of the screening procedure depends upon careful planning and coordination of many groups, including community leaders, volunteers, school administrators, professionals, paraprofessionals, parents, and the media. Plans should begin at least ten weeks before the screening occurs and include orienting volunteers and alerting the community about the upcoming screening for all preschool children. Children should be registered in advance and assigned appointments for both sensory and developmental screening. Some communities do both types of screening on the same day. The screening plans should include procedures for follow-up contacts with the parents to inform them whether their child has passed the screening, should be rescreened, or needs a diagnostic evaluation.

## Reporting Results

Parents should be adequately prepared and involved in the screening process and be informed in advance about its purposes. During the screening process, the coordinator should establish rapport with parents, make them feel expected and welcome, address them personally, encourage their input, and accept their feelings. The professional should avoid using educational jargon; parents should not feel the professional is talking down to them (Lichtenstein and Ireton, 1984). At the conclusion of the screening procedure, information should be coordinated on multiple functions, such as vision, hearing, and development. At this point, decisions must be made about a need for rescreening of any function and whether a further diagnosis is warranted. Results of the screening should be shared with parents and other caregivers (such as, pediatricians, teachers, and so on) as soon as possible to allay any unfounded concerns and to reassure those parents whose children were identified that further diagnosis is necessary before any conclusive decisions can be made. In some situations, such as with DIAL-R, feedback can be given on the same day.

Screening results to parents should not be overly detailed or definitive. When telling parents the results, professionals should strive to avoid conveying misinformation. Interpretation should be in terms of the child's present functioning rather than through the use of labels.

Parents should not be underestimated in terms of what they know about their own child or how this information can help in the assessment of their child. For instance, parents can be taught to observe and complete developmental checklists, measure and chart their child's growth, and assist in vision and hearing screening.

### Cautions Regarding Screening

Screening activities have many potential benefits but also some real dangers, such as

1. *Screening that leads nowhere.* Screening is only as good as the service that follows. Unfortunately, there are still more screening programs than intervention services.

2. *Screening that leads to inaccurate labeling.* Some techniques are unreliable enough that a certain percentage of children screened and diagnosed will be inaccurately labeled or placed.

3. *Screening that is only for the purpose of labeling.* Too often the only result of screening and diagnosis is providing a label that has negative connotations. It is imperative to train staff to use labels in a positive manner. In contrast, another possible danger is an unwillingness to identify *any* young child for

fear of stigmatizing that child. This behavior only results in denying an exceptional child needed services.

4. *Screening that is an isolated, one-shot event.* Screening should be part of ongoing evaluations and intervention programs.

5. *Screening that only leads to a self-fulfilling prophecy.* Care should be taken so that parents and teachers do not expect less from a child who has been identified as having a problem. It should not alter the child's self-concept and status among peers.

These dangers can be overcome if screening is developed as part of a comprehensive system that includes locating, screening, diagnosing, intervention services, and evaluation. It is important to plan the entire screening program, not just the administration of the tests alone. The flow chart in Figure 4.2 illustrates the screening process in relation to diagnosis, intervention, and evaluation (Zeitlin, 1976).

## THE DIAGNOSTIC PROCESS

The diagnosis, the third phase of the assessment system, is an in-depth evaluation of the child who has been detected through the screening process. During the diagnosis, the child is carefully studied to check on the screening recommendation and to determine if the child does indeed have a problem that warrants special education services.

### Screening and Diagnosis: Comparing Identification Decisions

The two assessment procedures—screening and diagnosis—both provide an answer to the question: "Does the child have a problem?" In some cases, the decisions reached in these two assessment processes are not the same. The following diagram illustrates the implications of the four possible combinations of answers when comparing the recommendations derived from the screening and the diagnosis.

Question: "Does the child have a problem?"
Answers:

|  |  | DIAGNOSIS | |
|---|---|---|---|
|  |  | Yes | No |
| SCREENING | Yes (refer) | High-Risk (accurate referral) | False + (over-referral) |
|  | No (do not refer) | False − (under-referral) | Normal (accurate non-referral) |

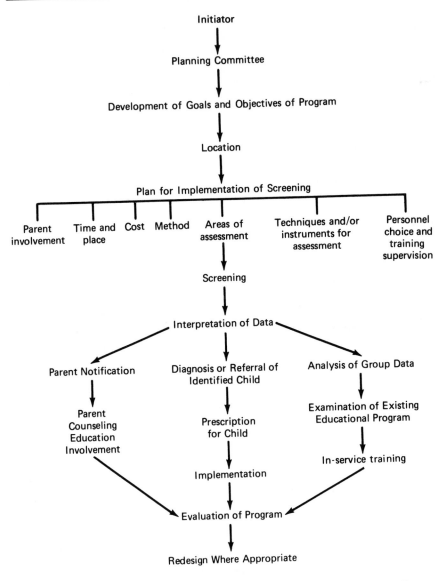

Adapted from S. Zeitlin. *Kindergarten Screening.* Springfield, IL: Chas. C. Thomas, 1976, p. 17.

**FIGURE 4.2** Screening Program

The *high-risk* cell shows children referred by both the screening and the diagnostic process. *False positives* (or over-referrals) are children who are identified in the screening process but found not to require services in the diagnostic process. *False negatives* (or under-referrals) are children who should have been identified but were missed in the screening process. Most children who are screened (88 to 90 percent) will fall into the *normal* cell; that is, the child is not referred by either the screening or the diagnostic process. The number or percentage of under-referrals and over-referrals is determined in part by the selected cutoff points. For example, when screening and diagnosing a population of 50 children, if a low cutoff point is selected on the screening test, the four cells might look like this:

| | |
|---|---|
| 5 | 5 |
| 0 | 40 |

In contrast, with a high cutoff point on the screening test, the four cells might look like this:

| | |
|---|---|
| 5 | 0 |
| 5 | 40 |

The decision about the cutoff point in the screening test determines (1) the number of children selected for diagnosis and (2) the number of children who are missed or "fall through the cracks." Although the diagnosis is costly, missing a child who needs service ultimately can be even more costly. As stated earlier in this chapter, under-referrals are seen as a more serious type of error in decision analysis.

## Areas Investigated in the Diagnosis

The diagnosis investigates, analyzes, and leads to decisions about the following areas:

Severity of the problem
Possible causes of the problem (etiology)
Treatment needed
Most appropriate way to deliver the needed service (placement)

Among the decisions to be made during the diagnosis are (1) what areas are to be investigated; (2) which personnel should be involved in this investigation; and (3) what type of information should be obtained. These are illustrated in Table 4.5. The diagnosis is usually performed by a multi-

Courtesy United Feature Syndicate, Inc.

disciplinary team, its members representing several different specializations. In early childhood special education, this team often is called a transdisciplinary team because the team members are so familiar with the function of each others' specialties that their roles and functions merge.

### Approaches to Diagnosis

There are several different theories or approaches to assessment. Each makes useful contributions to our ability to understand young children with special needs and to diagnose their problems. We suggest using an eclectic approach to diagnosis; that is, combining different theories and approaches to diagnosis. It broadens the assessment information and helps us to see the whole child. Five different approaches to diagnosing are reviewed below.

*Interaction approach.*    This approach considers the various ecological systems in which the child learns and lives. The approach emphasizes looking at both the child and environmental variables and how they affect each other. There is an intricate, interwoven relationship between the child and the surrounding environment. These two variables constantly interact and change each other. It is important to obtain information about the people and the environments that influence the child's learning.

*Developmental approach.*    This approach concentrates on normal development in children in a number of areas. The analysis of the handicapped child's problems are based on knowledge about child growth and development. Figure 4.3 lists some of the major areas of development related to learning. The child's level of development in many of these areas is assessed through norm-referenced tests.

*Information-processing approach.*    This approach concentrates on the manner in which a child receives, interprets, and transmits information. The analysis of testing and teaching tasks can indicate the child's preferred modes of functioning and where strengths and weaknesses in learning occur. This type of assessment has been referred to as dynamic (Feuerstein, 1979; Lidz, 1983b). It is an attempt to reveal the child's problem-solving

**TABLE 4.5  Typical Areas of Investigation in Diagnosis**

| AREA OF INVESTIGATION | PERSONNEL INVOLVED | TYPE OF INFORMATION OBTAINED |
|---|---|---|
| 1. Social History | Social Worker | Information relative to the functioning of the total family unit; note what the child's problem means to the family. |
| 2. Physical Examination | Pediatrician | Child's general health at present; review the child's medical history; note any physical defects that may be present. |
| 3. Neurological Examination | Neurologist | Specific information of any central nervous system impairment if brain damage is suspected; run an EEG to detect possibility of seizures or other malfunctioning. |
| 4. Psychological Examination | Psychologist | Data from the administration of psychometric techniques; use diagnostic tests to measure child's performance against normative standards and projective tests to determine nature of child's emotional responses. |
| 5. Hearing Examination | Audiologist or Public Health Worker | Data from the application of audiometric procedures to determine any type of hearing impairment. |
| 6. Vision Examination | Ophthalmologist or Public Health Worker | Detection of any visual impairment. |
| 7. Speech Examination | Speech Pathologist | Child's ability to understand and/or use words, phrases, concepts. |
| 8. Educational Examination | Special Education/Early Childhood | Diagnostic instruction to determine child's learning style and abilities (general here; more specific within the area of assessment). |

From L. Cross and K. Goin (eds.) *Identifying Handicapped Children*. NY: Walker & Co., 1977, p. 28.

**FIGURE 4.3** Major Areas of Development Related to Learning

**I. Physical**
physical intactness
general health
activity level
vision
hearing
nutrition—eating patterns
neurological structure
endocrine balance

**II. Perceptual Motor**
gross motor—large muscle coordination
fine motor—small muscle coordination
body image—identification of body parts
laterality
directionality
perception of space relations
figure–ground perception
visual motor coordination
auditory discrimination
visual discrimination
perceptual constancy
dominance or sidedness

**III. Cognition**
IQ
thinking processes
concept formation
memory—auditory, visual
sequencing
classifying
creativity

**IV. Speech and Language**
communciation—receptive and expressive language
rhythm
syntax (grammar)
vocabulary

**V. Social Emotional**
self-concept
motivation
adaptive behavior—coping style
social skills—interaction patterns
level of maturity (psychosexual development)
dependence—independence
aspiration level (self-expectation)
nervous tendencies

From S. Zeitlin. *Kindergarten Screening.* Springfield, IL: Chas. C. Thomas, 1976, p. 28.

strategies or styles of response which may account for the child's failures and which may be modifiable once they are identified. The emphasis here is not on *what* the child knows or can do but rather on *how* problems are approached and resolved. The purpose of the information-processing approach is to link assessment directly with intervention.

*Behavioral approach.* This approach to assessment concentrates on observing the child's behavior in a direct and objective manner. This kind of assessment requires us to observe carefully what the child is doing, what conditions trigger certain responses, and how the child's behavior can be changed or modified through changes in the learning environment. In this approach, the child's behavior often is assessed through criterion-referenced tests and frequency measures.

*Neuropsychological approach.* This approach focuses on the relationships between brain functioning and learning. This kind of assessment uses information about the brain from the neurosciences to analyze the manner in which the child processes information and learns.

All these approaches can be used in the diagnosis. Each contributes a different way of looking at the child and directs the assessment in different areas, serving to broaden the total diagnosis.

### Phases of the Diagnosis

The diagnosis consists of the following phases:

1. The case history
2. Interviewing the parent(s)
3. Observing the child
4. Testing
5. Recommending treatment needs and appropriate services

During each of the phases, information about the child is obtained and the phases often are overlapping. Each phase and the way of collecting information is discussed in the balance of this section.

*The case history.* Obtaining information about the child's developmental history is an important activity of the diagnosis. A thorough developmental history includes information about the family; the pregnancy and the delivery; the child's health during the neonatal period; illnesses and pertinent medical events, such as a history of seizures; the ages of developmental milestones; and relevant environmental and social information.

Parents usually are requested to fill out a developmental questionnaire before they come to the parent interview. This helps parents to think about the kinds of information they will have to supply, to check baby books, to probe their memories, and to formulate their own ideas about the nature of their child's problems. The questionnaire also may increase the reliability of the information gathered in the interview.

The parent interview provides an important source of information for the case history, but there also are other sources of information. Depending upon the age of the child and the severity of the problem, the child may have been seen by other professionals who can supply data upon the consent of the parent(s). If the child has been in a preschool program, teachers may be able to offer insights into the child's behavior. The child may have been seen by a pediatrician, dentist, or therapist, who may be able to contribute significant data. Information from such sources should be requested whenever possible.

An outline of the areas that are most often covered on general case history forms is shown in Figure 4.4.

*The parent interview.*   The purpose of the parent interview is to obtain a detailed account of the child's past and current behavior. There is general consensus that parents have the most information about their child. By using an open or unstructured style for the interview, parents tend to reveal useful information such as their feelings, concerns, attitudes, interactions, and expectations. A more structured interview procedure (using predetermined questions) tends to produce more specific information. Rating scales completed by the parents are useful and serve to summarize typical behaviors of the child rather than emphasizing an occasional behavior, such as a single temper tantrum. Two important questions to be asked of parents are "Has your child ever lost a behavior or skill once acquired?" and "Has your child ever failed to make progress?" These questions help identify developmental regressions or plateaus.

Some helpful principles of parent interviewing are

1.  *Be flexible* Let the parent(s) lead the way as long as the conversation is relevant.
2.  *Provide adequate time* Parents cannot feel relaxed when they must give information hurriedly.
3.  *Gather all pertinent information* Sometimes small details serve to complete the picture.
4.  *Accept and interact with the parent(s) as equal(s)* Parents easily recognize when professionals act in a condescending manner.
5.  *Ask open-ended questions* Try to avoid questions that lead to limited responses such as yes or no.
6.  *Minimize distracting behaviors* Unconscious behaviors on the part of the interviewer, such as tapping a pencil on the desk, can be distracting.

Interviewing is an important skill for child-care professionals. It is much more than routine questioning. The interviewer must keep a general outline in mind but be prepared to deviate from that outline when neces-

**FIGURE 4.4**  Areas Often Covered on General Case History Forms

**1. Birth History**
Previous pregnancies
Miscarriages
Mother's health/attitude
Labor
Delivery
Birth weight
Trouble breathing, sucking
Jaundice, cyanosis
Oxygen

**2. Motor Development**
Sat alone
Crawled
Fine and gross motor coordination
Feeding, sucking, chewing
Drooling
Toilet training
Enuresis
Self-help

**3. Language**
Comprehension
Gestures
Echolalia
Perseveration
Onset of words
Current number of words
Onset of sentences
Examples of sentences
Percent understood by parents
Percent understood by other adults
Percent understood by siblings
Percent understood by peers
Child's awareness of problem
Previous assessment
Previous training

**4. Family**
Parents' age, health
Parents' occupation
Parents' education
Parents' income
Marital status
Is child adopted?
Siblings, age, health
Others in home; age, health
History of learning problems in family
Other problems
Language spoken in home

Transportation

**5. Interpersonal Relationships**
General disposition
Playmates and play habits
Parent–child relationships
Other adult relationships
In contact with environment
Discipline
Affectionate
Aggressive
Compulsive
Cries easily
Daydreamer
Fears
Hyperactive
Jealousy
Leader or follower
Perseveration
Sleep habits
Social perception
Tantrums
Psychological assessment(s)
Psychological treatment(s)
Psychiatric assessment(s)
Psychiatric treatment(s)

**6. Medical History**
Convulsions
Fever
Childhood diseases
Cerebral problem(s)
Glandular disturbance
Excessive sweating
Allergies
Drug therapy
Auditory problems
Vision problems
Operation
Accidents
Congenital defects
Name of doctor

**7. Additional Comments**

From L. Cross and K. Goin (eds.) *Identifying Handicapped Children.* NY: Walker & Co., 1977, p. 30.

sary. A meaningful interview requires constant evaluation of what is being said. For more detailed guidance in interviewing techniques, see Benjamin (1981) and Chinn, Winn, and Walters (1978).

*Child observation.*   Systematic observation of the child contributes important information to the diagnosis. Observational information can confirm or refute screening data and thereby reduce the need to administer some diagnostic tests. The validity of the observation depends upon several factors: the observation should not interrupt the child's natural interactions, the procedure should be systematic, the situation should be appropriate, and the report of behavior should be objective and concrete (Umansky, 1983).

Children can be closely observed in many settings: during the testing situation (Bracken, 1983) or at home in their own environment where they may feel more comfortable. They can be observed interacting with parent(s), siblings, or whomever else is typically present in their home environment. The child also may be observed in a diagnostic setting where selected materials are exposed (such as toys, dolls, puppets, paints, and so on) that are designed to elicit a particular response. Or the setting may be relatively unstructured to note the child's behavior under those circumstances. In some cases, the child is placed in a diagnostic classroom to be observed for an extended period of time—two or more weeks. During that time, observations to consider include routine times (cleanup, toileting, snack time, rest time), adult-directed activities, and child-directed activities. The child may be observed alone, with peers, siblings, or with adults. All of these situations are valuable for observing the child and detecting patterns in behavior.

The *anecdotal record* is a widely used observation tool. This is a written objective description of an incident, that is free of the observer's feelings or interpretations. Incidents should be recorded on different days and at different times to obtain a well-rounded picture. The anecdotal record should include a description of the setting in which the event occurred, the stimulus for the event, the child's reaction, and how the event ended.

Other techniques for recording observations of children include logs, diaries, running records, narrative descriptions, checklists, time samples, interactions, and rating scales (Cohen, Stern, and Balaban, 1983; Almy and Genishi, 1979; Boehm and Weinberg, 1977; Stallings, 1977). Systematic observations can be recorded with pencil and paper, audio or videotape, or small portable computers.

A standardized instrument developed as an aid for observation is the HOME (Home Observation for Measurement of the Environment) Inventory (Bradley, Caldwell, and Elardo, 1977; Bradley and Caldwell, 1979). Research with this inventory indicates that it is a more predictive index of cognitive abilities than the child's socioeconomic status.

*Diagnostic testing.* Diagnostic tests provide another measure of the child's current status and performance levels. The test results contribute to the pool of assessment information used in determining if the child has a problem, the nature of that problem, and the kind of treatment needed. Standardized tests provide organized information that is valid, reliable, and clinically useful. Test items sample a child's behavior at specific points in time, and the examiner assumes that the behavior and skills being sampled are representative of a larger repertoire.

*Principles of testing.* The testing of preschool children is especially challenging. In general, the younger the child, the less likely it is that the test results reflect the child's true abilities. Preschoolers typically are not concerned about the quality of their performance; they tend to follow their own impulses, and they are difficult to convince that the test is an important matter (Sattler, 1982; Paget, 1983; Lidz, 1983a; Vane & Motts, 1980). For these reasons, it is particularly important when testing young children to follow sound principles of testing:

Have testing materials arranged systematically; keep unused materials out of sight until needed

Provide consistent limits

Stay attuned to the child's pace

Provide adequate and appropriate praise and reinforcement

Test young children without the presence of others

Parents, teachers, or strangers tend to inhibit the child's spontaneity (Paget, 1983). In certain settings, the examination may be observed through a one-way window.

*Ways to use tests.* The scores obtained on standardized tests offer an objective method for comparing an individual child's performance to that of an average or normed group. The criterion usually used for determining if a subtest score is significantly different is if it (1) varies one and one-half standard deviations from the norm in two or more areas of development or (2) two standard deviations in one area of development. Diagnostic tests should be relevant, credible, timely, and efficient. Reliability correlation coefficients should be reported in the test manual and should be .90 or higher (Salvia and Ysseldyke, 1985). These statistical concepts are discussed in greater detail in psychomeasurement books.

In addition to looking at test scores, it is useful to analyze the tasks that the test requires the child to perform, a technique called *task analysis.* As illustrated in Figure 4.5, each task is analyzed along several dimensions: What processing is required by the child—rote or conceptual? Through which channels is the information coming to the child—visual, auditory, or both? What type of response is expected—motor or verbal? For example,

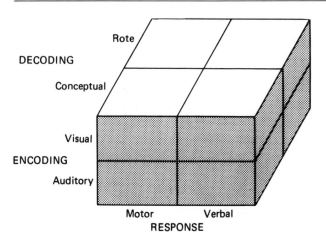

**FIGURE 4.5** Task Analysis of Diagnostic Testing

in the following counting task: "Count for me. You know, 1, 2, . . ." the task is classified as "rote, auditory, verbal." However, in a different counting task: "Give me five blocks. Put them here," the child must demonstrate an understanding of numbers, and the task is classified as "conceptual, auditory, and visual-motor." Thus, a task analysis of test items helps to analyze a child's strengths and weaknesses.

Another use of testing is to assess the interactions among three components: the task, the child, and the environment (Smith, 1980) through *trial interventions*. This method checks out hunches about useful interventions suggested by the testing activities, thereby providing additional assessment information. These trial interventions are teaching lessons used in the clinical setting, home, or classroom. If the interventions are effective, the teacher and/or parent will likely be enthusiastic about continuing the intervention.

Feuerstein (1979) suggests another use of the testing situation. He recommends that the examiner take an active role in the testing process rather than being a neutral, objective observer. The examiner then can use the test items to structure the environment, discover how the child learns best, and facilitate that learning. This is technically a nonstandard use of standardized tests, sometimes referred to as "testing the limits." To avoid invalidating a test score, this procedure, when employed, should follow the standardized procedures. Once the score is obtained, the test can be used for other purposes.

*Examples of diagnostic tests.* Diagnostic tests are available to assess most of the major areas of development mentioned throughout this chapter. Appendix B lists many of the diagnostic tests currently in use.

Following are listed some of the most popular tests. In many cases, tests listed under one category of development also are useful and appropriate in another category. For example, the *McCarthy Scales of Children's Abilities* is listed under Cognitive Tests but it also assesses motor and perceptual skills. A comprehensive battery should be flexible so that as few test instruments as possible are used in assessing a child (Mardell-Czudnowski and Goldenberg, 1983). In some instances, a complete assessment will not include the administration of any tests (Lidz, 1983a). However, preschoolers tend to be inconsistent in their responses to test tasks (Dunst and Rheingrover, 1982; Vane and Motts, 1980). Therefore, evidence based on a single test provides less stable information than evidence from multiple measures derived from several tests (Lidz, 1983a). Most of the following tests are more fully discussed in Appendix B.

*Medical and health tests.*   Testing in this area is usually conducted by a physician. Medical specialists who are likely to examine the child include the pediatrician, neurologist, ophthalmologist, otologist, and endocrinologist. Their testing covers physical intactness, general health, neurological function, activity level, vision, hearing, nutrition (eating patterns), and endocrine balance.

*Perceptual tests.*   These tests cover neurological structure, gross and fine motor coordination, body image, laterality and directionality, perception of space relations, figure–ground perception, visual–motor coordination, auditory discrimination, visual discrimination, perceptual constancy, and lateral dominance. Diagnostic tests of perceptual development include:

Bayley Scales of Infant Development (Motor Scale)
Goldman–Fristoe Woodcock Auditory Skills Test Battery
Southern California Sensory–Integration Tests (Ayres)

*Tests of cognitive development.*   These tests are designed to assess intelligence, thinking processes, concept formation, auditory and visual memory, sequencing, classifying, and creativity. Diagnostic tests in this area of development often are included in comprehensive batteries that also assess other areas of development. The best known and most thoroughly researched tests are

Bayley Scales of Infant Development (Mental Scale)
Columbia Mental Maturity Scale
Infant Psychological Development Scales (IPDS)
Kaufman Assessment Battery for Children (K-ABC)
Leiter International Performance Scale
McCarthy Scales of Children's Abilities (MSCA)

Stanford-Binet Intelligence Scale
Wechsler Preschool and Primary Scale of Intelligence (WPPSI)
Woodcock-Johnson Psychoeducational Battery (WJPEB)

*Speech and language tests.* Speech and language tests assess receptive and expressive language, rhythm, syntax (grammar), vocabulary, and articulation. Diagnostic tests in the speech and language area include:

Carrow Elicited Language Inventory
Developmental Sentence Analysis (DSA)
Illinois Test of Psycholinguistic Abilities (ITPA)
Sequenced Inventory of Communication Development-Revised (SICD-R)

*Social-emotional tests.* These tests are designed to assess self-concept, motivation, adaptive behavior or coping style, social skills, level of maturity, degree of independence, aspiration level, and nervous tendencies. Diagnostic tests in this area of development include:

Adaptive Behavior Scale for Infants and Early Childhood (ABSI)
Goodman Lock Box
Parent and Teacher Temperament Questionnaire
Scales of Independent Behavior (SIB)
Scales of Socio-emotional Development
Vineland Adaptive Behavior Scales

### Recommending Treatment And Services

This phase of the assessment requires *synthesis*—bringing together and interpreting all the assessment information that has been gathered. The purpose of the synthesis is to understand the total child by assembling the diagnostic information into meaningful patterns. The process has been likened to putting the pieces of a puzzle together. The team develops a total picture of the child's abilities and disabilities, strengths and weaknesses. Based on this information, then, placement options are recommended, matching the child's treatment needs with the most appropriate services. In addition, the team decides who will be responsible for various phases of the planned treatment.

All professionals involved in the data-gathering stage should confer as a team, and a case conference team should meet with the parent(s). Written reports of individual findings should be distributed early enough for all to read, think about, and formulate questions before the staff meeting. This saves time at the meeting, enabling everyone to have all the information accessible for discussion. It is important that the report be presented in clear terms, avoiding generalizations, ambiguities, and speculations so parents and professionals from other disciplines understand it

(Sattler, 1982). Information and decisions must be explained to the parents both written and orally in the parents' primary language.

### Cautions Regarding Diagnosis

One must recognize that there are many possible sources of error in the diagnosis. Cross and Goin (1977) have charted the types of possible errors and their sources (Table 4.6).

Testing errors also may result from using a poor test, using a technically adequate test for the wrong purpose, using a technically adequate test with the wrong child (a child whose characteristics differ greatly from the population on which the test was normed), interpreting the test score incorrectly (particularly with children from minority cultures), or from clerical errors (Salvia and Ysseldyke, 1985). One way to protect the child and parents from any or all of these errors is to re-evaluate the findings frequently. Frequent re-evaluation is particularly important for young children. Children in special education programs must be re-evaluated every three years.

## THE EVALUATIVE PROCESS

Evaluating is the process of determining a child's progress and achievement and how well a program is working (Boehm and Sandburg, 1982; Brooks-Gunn and Lewis, 1983). This final stage of assessment is crucial for

**TABLE 4.6   Sources of Error in Developmental Diagnosis**

| SOURCE | POSSIBLE ERRORS |
|---|---|
| 1. History | Failure to take a thorough history; undue reliance on the past without allowing for possibility of change. |
| 2. Interpretation | Incorrect assumption of inability caused by child's failure to cooperate; failure to note the quality of the child's performance; failure to withhold judgment in case of doubt. |
| 3. Observation | Limited setting (i.e., diagnostic center only as opposed to combination of multiple settings); single observations rather than observations of greater duration and frequency; decontextualization of the testing situation. |
| 4. Instrumentation | Lack of multiple measures; administration by unskilled personnel; overemphasis on "objective" data. |
| 5. Placement | Lack of available options; no consideration of existing options. |

From L. Cross and K. Goin (eds.) *Identifying Handicapped Children.* Walker & Co., 1977, p. 33.

providing data concerning the future placement of the child and the success and effectiveness of the program. The evaluating process includes any or all of the following activities:

Establishing entrance and exit criteria
Re-evaluating the child
Evaluating program effectiveness

### Establishing Entrance And Exit Criteria

*Entrance criteria,* standards used for admitting students into a special education program, differ from state to state and often from school district to school district within a state. These differences can cause considerable problems when families move. However, every program needs clearly defined, objective criteria for determining which children to serve.

In addition to entrance criteria, every program must establish *exit criteria*—standards that allow a child to leave the program as soon as it appears likely that he or she will be able to function in a regular classroom setting. Many school districts have established procedures to facilitate this transition; for example, transitional kindergartens that have smaller class size (usually 10–15), an aide, and move at a slower pace, particularly at the beginning of the school year. From there, children may progress to a regular kindergarten or first grade, or a special education setting.

### Re-evaluating The Child

Many school districts spend the spring of each year conducting annual reviews. One aspect of this process, which is required by P.L. 94-142, is to determine the progress of each child in a special program and decide if the child is ready to (1) leave the program, (2) change to another program, or (3) remain in the present program. Since criterion-referenced tests measure mastery of precise skills or content, pretest and post-test scores on such tests help evaluate the child within a program. Such instrument-related assessment is known as *summative evaluation.* It enables the multidisciplinary team to evaluate the specific skills that a particular child has mastered. When these same criterion-referenced tests are used to determine how a child is progressing relative to teaching objectives and which instructional steps need to be taken next, this is known as *formative evaluation.* Both formative and summative evaluation play a role in determining the least restrictive placement of the child. Some districts computerize this aspect of assessment and program management to make sure that all options are considered for every child.

### Evaluating Program Effectiveness

Program evaluation refers to the effectiveness of a program. It uses the collective data of many children rather than data on an individual child.

Aspects to be evaluated include the curriculum being used, the mode of instruction, and the staff. Program evaluation enables the administration and staff to determine whether program changes need to be instituted. Curriculum objectives should be stated in behavioral terms so that program effectiveness can be more easily evaluated, possibly through the use of goal-attainment scaling. This procedure evaluates each program goal on a five-point scale in terms of whether or not the goal was met and to what degree.

---

### CASE EXAMPLE—CHARITY

The following case example of three-year-old Charity illustrates the four segments of assessment: locating, screening, diagnosing, and evaluating.

### 1. Locating

Mrs. Brown first learned of the local school's plan to screen preschool children when her two older children, Jimmy in fifth grade and Anne in third grade, brought home flyers about the preschool screening program. After seeing the poster about the program displayed in the supermarket, Mrs. Brown called the school secretary and made an appointment for her three-year-old daughter, Charity.

### 2. Screening

Mrs. Brown brought Charity, along with her 18-month-old daughter, to school for the screening appointment, where a team was screening preschool children. Mrs. Brown completed the *Parent Information Form* while Charity was being screened. First Charity was screened for vision and hearing problems. Then the team screened Charity in other areas using a preschool screening test (DIAL-R). When the screening was completed, the screening coordinator discussed the results with Mrs. Brown. Charity, at age 3 years 7 months, was functioning within the normal range for vision, hearing, motor and social–emotional development. However, the DIAL-R scores for Concepts and Language of 5 and 8, respectively, were below the cutoff points for a child of Charity's age. Upon review of the parent information form that Mrs. Brown had filled out earlier, the screening coordinator pointed out that Mrs. Brown's own observations concurred with the screening results. Mrs. Brown had indicated that Charity did not begin saying individual words until 22 months and even at 3 years 7 months spoke only in phrases. Mrs. Brown also had checked the back of the parent form indicating that she was concerned about possible speech and language problems. Mrs. Brown made an appointment to return with Charity for a diagnostic session in two weeks. She also took home a more detailed developmental questionnaire to complete with her husband, Reverend Brown, and with the use of baby books or other records.

### 3. Diagnosing

Within the next two weeks, the special education staff analyzed the screening results from the DIAL-R score sheet. Charity was functioning at the two-year-old level on five of the six items routinely administered to children under four years in the Concepts area. On the sixth item—Rote Counting—she was below the two-year-old level. In the Language area, she was functioning at the two-year level on six of the eight items. On one item—Classifying Foods—she was below the two-year level; on the other item—Problem Solving—she was at her age level of three years. The staff decided to involve the following personnel in the diagnostic process: the social worker who would interview the parents and develop a case history; the psychologist who would assess intellectual development and observe Charity; and the speech pathologist who would assess speech and language development.

Charity and her parents attended the diagnostic session. While Charity was warming up to the new situation, her parents chatted with the social worker. They continued their discussion when Charity left with the psychologist. According to her parents, Charity was developing much as her older brother and sister had, with the exception of talking. She used much jargon and pointing, and she was becoming increasingly more agitated when family members did not understand her. Mrs. Brown also said that Jimmy, their fifth-grader, was having a very difficult time learning to read. Reverend Brown said that he also had a reading problem as a child. However, he did not recall that Jimmy had the language problems that Charity was exhibiting.

At the conclusion of the interview, the Browns watched Charity through a one-way window as she worked first with the psychologist and later with the speech pathologist. The psychologist sat with the parents, observing Charity, during the speech and language assessment.

The school psychologist administered the Kaufman-Assessment Battery for Children (K-ABC). All four global scores were within the normal range. However, some subtests that were dependent on a verbal response were depressed, and on one subtest, Charity never understood the task even though she was given the allotted three teaching experiences. When testing the limits for some of the subtests, it became apparent to the psychologist that Charity's problems were primarily in the area of expressive language. Her attention span and comprehension were age-appropriate, she responded well to the limits that were set, and she interacted well with the two testers. In fact, she appeared to be enjoying all the attention she was receiving.

The speech pathologist administered the Sequenced Inventory of Communication Development-Revised (SICD-R). Charity was at age level on all items that measured receptive language (sound and speech discrimination, awareness, and understanding). She had only minor articulation problems, but she was almost two years behind on all expressive language items except those that involved imitation.

One week later, Charity's parents met with the special education staff to discuss the findings. Her parents agreed that Charity had an expressive language problem and were happy to learn that services were available to help her. They enrolled her in the early childhood special education program.

### 4. Evaluating

Charity attended the early childhood special education program four half-days a week for two years. At the end of the first year, when she was 4 years 9 months, she had made eighteen months' progress in speech and language. At the end of the second year, she was functioning almost at age level. She was then mainstreamed into a standard kindergarten classroom with minimal speech support services.

## SUMMARY

Assessment of young handicapped children is a complex procedure that requires much time, preparation, and skill to be successful. The procedure can be divided into four processes: (1) locating, (2) screening, (3) diagnosing, and (4) evaluating.

Locating may include any or all of the following activities: defining the target population, increasing the public's awareness of services, encouraging referrals, and canvassing the community for children in need of services.

Screening may include any or all of the following activities: selecting conditions to be screened, selecting tests, training staff, screening children, and reporting results. There are screening tests for newborn infants, as well as comprehensive screening tests and screening tests for specific areas (health and physical information, perceptual, cognitive, speech and language, and social-emotional). Appendix B lists screening tests in detail for use with preschool children in all areas of development. Cautions regarding screening procedures are listed.

Diagnosing may include any or all of the following activities: obtaining data from all sources, interviewing the parents, testing and observing the child, and determining the treatment needs and most appropriate service(s). There are standardized diagnostic tests for specific areas of physical, perceptual, cognitive, speech and language, and social-emotional development. In addition, Appendix B provides diagnostic tests in detail. Cautions regarding diagnosis are discussed.

Evaluating may include any or all of the following activities: establishing entrance and exit criteria, re-evaluating the child, and evaluating the program.

These four stages of assessment are interrelated and must be coordinated in order to meet the special needs of young children.

## REVIEW QUESTIONS

### Terms to Know

assessment
locating
screening
diagnosing
evaluating
validity
reliability
norm-referenced test

criterion-referenced test
false positive
false negative
etiology
synthesis
formative evaluation
summative evaluation
analysis

1. Define the components of total assessment and the person(s) generally responsible for each component.
2. Why is screening such a crucial component in total assessment?
3. What are the major areas of development related to learning that are generally screened and/or diagnosed? What are the components of each?
4. Describe each of the typical areas of investigation in diagnosis and the personnel involved in each area.
5. List some general guidelines for the testing of young children.
6. Describe procedures for locating preschoolers who require special services.
7. Discuss cautions regarding developmental screening.
8. List factors that lead to a positive and productive parent interview.
9. What areas are generally covered when obtaining a case history?
10. Complete the following chart with names of tests:

**Preschool Tests**

|  | SCREENING | DIAGNOSING |
|---|---|---|
| Physical/Health | | |
| Perceptual | | |
| Cognitive | | |
| Speech–language | | |
| Social–emotional | | |
| Comprehensive | | |

11. Using only a deck of playing cards, describe how to screen a three-year-old's development in the following areas:
    a. gross motor
    b. fine motor
    c. concepts
    d. language
    e. social–emotional

    For each task, determine if it is rote or conceptual; if the input is visual, auditory, and/or haptic; and if the output is motor and/or verbal.

## REFERENCES

ALMY, M. and C. GENISHI (1979) *Ways of Studying Children: An Observation Manual for Early Childhood Teachers* (2nd ed.), NY: Teachers College Press.

APGAR, V. (1953) "Proposal for a New Method of Evaluating the Newborn Infant." *Anesthesia and Analgesia*, 32, 260–67.

BARNES, K. E. (1982) *Preschool Screening: The Measurement and Prediction of Children At-risk.* Springfield, IL: Charles C. Thomas.

BECK, R. (1977) The Need for Adjunctive Services in the Management of Severely and Profoundly Handicapped Individuals: A View from Primary Care. In N. Haring and L. Brown (eds.) *Teaching the Severely Handicapped.* NY: Grune and Stratton.

BENJAMIN, A. (1981) *The Helping Interview.* Boston: Houghton Mifflin.

BERMAN, A. (1977) "LD Resource Materials: The Great Ripoff," *Journal of Learning Disabilities,* 10.

BLUMA, S., M. SHEARER, A. FROHMAN, and J. HILLARD (1976) *Portage Guide to Early Education.* Portage, WI: Cooperative Educational Service No. 12.

BOEHM, A. and B. SANDBURG (1982) "Assessment of the Preschool Child." In C. Reynolds and T. Gutkin (eds.) *The Handbook of School Psychology.* NY: John Wiley.

BOEHM, A. and R. WEINBERG (1977) *The Classroom Observer: A Guide for Developing Observation Skills.* NY: Teachers College Press.

BRACKEN, B. (1983) "Observing the Assessment Behavior of Preschool Children." In K. Paget and B. Bracken (eds.) *Psychoeducational Assessment of Preschool Children.* NY: Grune and Stratton.

BRADLEY, R. and B. CALDWELL (1979) "Home Observation for Measurement of the Environment: A Revision of the Preschool Scale." *American Journal of Mental Deficiency,* 84, 235–44.

BRADLEY, R., B. CALDWELL, and R. ELARDO (1977) "Home Environment, Social Status and Mental Test Performance." *Journal of Educational Psychology,* 69, 697–701.

BRAZELTON, T. B. (1973) *Neonatal Assessment Scale.* Philadelphia: Lippincott.

BROOKS-GUNN, J. and M. LEWIS (1983) "Screening and Diagnosing Handicapped Infants." *Topics in Early Childhood Special Education,* 3, 1, 14–28.

BUROS, O. K. (ed.) (1978) *The Eighth Mental Measurement Yearbook.* Lincoln, NE: University of Nebraska Press.

CHINN, P., J. WINN, and R. WALTERS (1978) *Two-way Talking with Parents of Special Children.* St. Louis: Mosby.

COHEN, D., V. STERN, and N. BALABAN (1983) *Observing and Recording the Behavior of Young Children.* (3rd ed.), NY: Teachers College Press.

CROSS, L., and K. GOIN (eds.) (1977) *Identifying Handicapped Children.* NY: Walker and Company.

DUNST, C. and R. RHEINGROVER (1982) "Discontinuity and Instability in Early Development: Implications for Assessment." In J. Neisworth (ed.) *Assessment in Special Education.* Rockville, MD: Aspen Systems.

FEUERSTEIN, R. (1979) *The Dynamic Assessment of Retarded Performers.* Baltimore: University Park Press.

FRANKENBURG, W. J., and B. CAMP (eds.) (1975) *Pediatric Screening Tests.* Springfield, IL: Chas. C. Thomas.

FRANKENBURG, W. J., A. FANDAL, W. SCIARILLO, and D. BURGESS (1981) *The Denver Developmental Screening Test—Revised Manual.* Denver: Ladoca Publishing.

FRANKENBURG, W., A. GOLDSTEIN, A. CHABOT, B. CAMP, and M. FRITCH (1970) "Training the Indigenous Nonprofessional: The Screening Technician." *Journal of Pediatrics,* 77, 564–70.

GOODWIN, W. L. and L. A. DRISCOLL (1980) *Handbook for Measurement and Evaluation in Early Childhood Education.* San Francisco: Jossey-Bass.

HAMMILL, P., T. DRIZD, C. JOHNSON, R. REED, and A. ROCHE (1976) *National Center for Health Statistics Growth Charts.* Washington, DC: National Center for Health Statistics.

HAYNES, U. (1974) *A Developmental Approach to Casefinding.* Washington, DC: U. S. Department of Health, Education and Welfare. U. S. Public Health Service Publication.

JOHNSON, H. W. (1979). *Preschool Test Descriptions.* Springfield, IL: Chas. C. Thomas.

KNOBLOCH, H., F. STEVEN, and A. MALONE (1980) *Manual of Developmental Diagnosis: The Administration and Interpretation of the Revised Gesell and Amatruda Developmental and Neurological Examination.* Hagerstown, MD: Harper and Row.

LEIGH, J. (1983) "Early Labeling of Children: Concerns and Alternatives." *Topics in Early Childhood Special Education,* 3, 3, 1–6.

LICHTENSTEIN, R. and H. IRETON (1984) *Preschool Screening: Identifying Young Children with Developmental and Educational Problems.* Orlando: Grune and Stratton.

LIDZ, C. (1983a) "Issues in Assessing Preschool Children." In K. Paget and B. Bracken (eds.), *The Psychoeducational Assessment of Preschool Children.* NY: Grune and Stratton.

LIDZ, C. (1983b) "Dynamic Assessment and the Preschool Child." *Journal of Psychoeducational Assessment.* 1, 1, 59–72.

LITTMAN, B. and A. PARMALEE (1978) "Medical Correlates of Infant Development." *Pediatrics.* 61, 470–74.

MANDELL, C. and R. JOHNSON (1984) "Screening for Otitis Media: Issues and Procedural Recommendations." *Journal of the Division of Early Childhood,* 8, 1, 86–93.

MARDELL-CZUDNOWSKI, C. and D. GOLDENBERG (1983) *Developmental Indicators for the Assessment of Learning—Revised Manual* (DIAL-R), Edison, NJ: Childcraft Education Corp.

MARDELL-CZUDNOWSKI, C. and D. GOLDENBERG (1984a) "Revision and Restandardization of a Preschool Screening Test: DIAL Becomes DIAL-R." *Journal of the Division for Early Childhood,* 8, 2, 149–56.

MARDELL-CZUDNOWSKI, C. and D. GOLDENBERG (1984b) *Coordinator Handbook, Training Packet, and Training Videotape.* Edison, NJ: Childcraft Education Corp.

MEISELS, S. (1985) "Prediction, Prevention, and Developmental Screening in the EPSDT Program." In H. Stevenson and A. Siegel (eds.) *Child Development and Social Policy.* Vol. 1 Chicago: University of Chicago Press.

MEISELS, S. and M. WISKE (1983) *Early Screening Inventory* (ESI). NY: Teachers College Press.

MITCHELL, J. (ed.) (1985) *The Ninth Mental Measurement Yearbook.* Lincoln, NE: University of Nebraska Press.

ORTIZ, A. (1984) "Choosing the Language of Instruction for Exceptional Bilingual Children." *Teaching Exceptional Children,* Spring, 208–12.

PAGET, K. (1983) "The Individual Examining Situation: Basic Considerations for Preschool Children." In K. Paget and B. Bracken (eds.) *Psychoeducational Assessment of Preschool Children.* NY: Grune and Stratton.

PRECHTL, H. and A. BEINTEMA (1964) *The Neurological Examination of the Full Term Newborn Infant.* London: Heineman.

SALVIA, J. and J. YSSELDYKE (1985) *Assessment in Special and Remedial Education* (3rd ed.) Boston: Houghton Mifflin.

SANFORD, A. (1974) *Learning Accomplishment Profile.* Winston-Salem, NC: Kaplan School Supply.

SATTLER, J. (1982) *Assessment of Children's Intelligence and Special Abilities.* (2nd ed.) Boston: Allyn and Bacon.

SMITH, C. (1980) "Assessment Alternatives: Non-standardized Procedures." *School Psychology Review.* 7, 46–57.

SOUTHWORTH, L. E., R. L. BURR, and A. E. COX (1981) *Screening and Evaluating the Young Child: A Handbook of Instruments to Use from Infancy to Six Years.* Springfield, IL: Charles C. Thomas.

STALLINGS, J. (1977) *Learning to Look, a Handbook on Classroom Observation and Teaching Models.* Belmont, CA: Wadsworth.

STANGLER, S. R., C. J. HUBER, and D. K. ROUTH (1980) *Screening Growth and Development of Preschool Children: A Guide for Test Selection.* NY: McGraw-Hill.

UMANSKY, W. (1983) "Assessment of Social and Emotional Development." In K. Paget and B. Bracken (eds.) *Psychoeducational Assessment of Preschool Children.* NY: Grune and Stratton.

VANE, J. and R. MOTTS (1980) "Test Response Inconsistency in Young Children." *Journal of School Psychology,* 18, 1, 25–33.

WALKER, D. (1973) *Socioemotional Measures for Preschool and Kindergarten Children.* San Francisco: Jossey-Bass.

ZEHRBACH, R. (1976) *Comprehensive Identification Process* (CIP). Bensenville, IL: Scholastic Testing Services.

ZEITLIN, S. (1976) *Kindergarten Screening.* Springfield. IL: Chas. C Thomas.

# FIVE

# Delivering
# Intervention Services

## INTRODUCTION

The focus of this chapter is the delivery of services for exceptional preschool children. The chapter reviews service options for preschoolers, factors affecting placement, the impact of the law on services, and the team approach to providing services to young children.

Early intervention services for exceptional and at-risk young children and their families offer several types of services, including special education; social services; and emotional, health, medical, or recreational services. The services should be based on the developmental needs of the child and follow the child's IEP (individualized educational program). In early childhood, this is sometimes referred to as the IIP (individual intervention program). The IEP is developed from the assessment of the child and his or her family. If services from more than one agency or discipline are needed, they should be coordinated and integrated.

Studies continue to show that preschool intervention for exceptional youngsters leads to significant improvement in development and learning. As a consequence, services for exceptional preschoolers continue to expand and improve. At present, 42 states have laws that *mandate* services to some portion of the preschool handicapped population (birth through age five). In the states with mandated laws, young handicapped children have the right to receive special education services. Other states have *permissive* legislation. In these states, the schools *may* provide services to this age group. Studies show that states that have laws mandating special education preschool services serve a larger portion of their handicapped preschoolers than states with permissive laws (U.S. Department of Education, 1985).

## ALTERNATIVE PLACEMENTS FOR YOUNG EXCEPTIONAL CHILDREN

An array of service alternatives and placement options is necessary to meet the varied needs of all young exceptional and at-risk children. Arrangements must be flexible to provide for the diverse and changing needs of these children. A number of model programs demonstrating various service options were developed and disseminated through the HCEEP projects (Handicapped Children's Early Education Programs) (Bailey and Wolery, 1984: Illinois Board of Education, 1980; Karnes and Zehrbach, 1977). The options for exceptional preschoolers can be classified into three groups: home-based, center-based, and the combination home- and center-based services.

## Home-Based Services

In the home-based type of service, a professional child-care provider goes to the child's home, typically one to three times per week. The major responsibility of the child-care provider is to train the parent(s) in the home to work with the child. First, within the home setting, an assessment of the child's present skills is made. Then the professional determines which skills the child has already mastered and which the youngster should be helped to acquire. Next, the professional works with the parent to plan the needed training activities. Finally, the professional demonstrates to the parent how to help the child acquire the skills and teaches the parent how to monitor the child's progress.

Thus, in home-based programs parents become the child's primary teacher. This type of program demands much of the parent in terms of time, dedication, and motivation. In some cases, the professional will solicit the assistance of older siblings, grandparents, and even neighbors to help the parents perform these tasks.

In certain situations, home-based programs are the most appropriate type of service. It is a particularly viable option with very young children (infants and toddlers), in rural communities when the child lives in an isolated area, and also in cases where transportation problems would prevent the child from getting to a center-based program. Home-based programs have the advantages of (1) teaching the child in a natural setting and (2) fully involving parents in their child's learning (Illinois State Board of Education, 1980; Bailey and Wolery, 1984). Figure 5.1 is an example of a record form that can be used to obtain information during home visits.

## Centered-Based Services

In the center-based program, the parent or school-arranged special transportation brings the child to a central facility. The services at the facility can be comprehensive, with staff members representing expertise in many of the related disciplines and services—including early childhood teachers, speech and language pathologists, medical personnel, psychologists, adaptive physical education teachers, physical therapists, occupational therapists, and social workers. The center also may provide parent training and offer organized parent support group meetings. Parents are encouraged to carry through the training at home.

Children usually attend from two to five days per week, and the school day is three to five hours long. A comprehensive curriculum is developed according to the needs and developmental stages of the child. Center-based programs have facilities, equipment, instructional materials, and toys that parents would not have in the home. In addition, children can

**FIGURE 5.1** Parent Education Home Visit Record

PARENT EDUCATION HOME VISIT RECORD

Date: _____
Time _____ to _____

Student _____
Teacher _____ Class _____
Persons present: _____
Items for discussion:

Parent feedback:

Specific objectives established and agreed upon by parent and teacher:

Teacher recommendations:

Suggested time for next conference: _____

develop social skills by playing with the other children. Center-based services are particularly useful for 3- to 6-years-olds.

Transportation may be a problem in some cases because of the difficulty of getting the child to the center. Some parents cannot transport their child to the center for services on a regular basis. Further, buses are expensive and the trip may be very long for the child. Center-based programs often are found in urban areas, although there are center-based services in rural areas as well. Special transportation is considered a "related service" for special education programs.

## Combination Home- and Center-Based Services

This is a flexible program that combines services to young children in the home and in a center. For example, the child may come to the center several times a week and also a professional may visit the child in the home every other week. The kinds of services provided in the home and center will depend upon many factors: the child and parents' needs, the age of the child, and the nature of the handicap. The major advantage of the combination service is its flexibility. It can be designed to meet each child's unique needs.

## Consultation Services

In this type of service, parents periodically bring their child to a center where the child is seen by a team of professionals, perhaps once a week. The professional who sees the child also may train the parents on how to work with the child at home. This type of service often is used for handicapped infants. As with the home-based program, the parent assumes the responsibility for much of the intervention and teaching of the child.

## Transition

Transition involves the child's placement from one type of organized program and placement to another. Going into a new placement can be a traumatic experience and should be carefully planned, coordinated, and monitored.

*Transition after the birth-to-three program.* Transition from a birth-to-three program to a three- to six-year-old early childhood special education program often is frightening for both parent and child. The toddler will be moving from a smaller program with a one-to-one relationship with a caseworker to a larger program with more children and more expectations. Careful planning and coordination is needed to help the toddler and parent make this transition smoothly.

*Transition after the preschool years.* Decisions about placement must be made at the completion of the early childhood special education program for three- to six-year-olds. Some children will be integrated (or mainstreamed) into a standard class, a process that requires sensitivity, cooperative planning, and sufficient communication (Turnbull, Winton, Blacher, and Salkind, 1982). Other children will be placed in other kinds of settings at the completion of their preschool program, such as self-contained special education classes or special schools. By the time transition decisions are made, however, teachers and other related personnel will have had the opportunity to observe the child over a long period of time to assess the child's placement needs. Among the placement options at the completion of the early childhood programs are the following:

1. *A standard kindergarten or first grade classroom* In some cases a child makes such rapid progress in the special education program that he or she is no longer eligible for special education services. The parent may elect to continue early childhood programming in a nonhandicapped environment. Placement can be in the kindergarten if the child is of eligible age and readiness.
2. *A transitional class* In this setting, careful observation and special education intervention would continue for a period of time.
3. *A resource room* In this option, the child would be both in a standard classroom for part of the day and in a small special education setting for a portion of the day.
4. *A self-contained special education class* This class could be located either in the local school or in the larger special education district, which would permit a more intensive special education curriculum.
5. *A residential facility* This setting is used for certain severe cases or where the home is unable to provide the needed care.

Whatever placement is recommended, it is important to take steps to assure a smooth transition to the continuing placement. Receiving teachers (be they kindergarten, first grade, or special education teachers) should have a chance to observe the child, talk with the parents, attend the annual review, and be familiar with the child's individualized education program (IEP). The early childhood special education teacher should spend some time on-site with the receiving teacher at the beginning of the new placement and acquaint the receiving teacher with the child's special needs. In most cases, the child will be moving from a small instructional group to a larger, less structured environment.

To ensure a successful transition from preschool to the new setting, Fowler (1982) suggests the following steps be considered:

1. Identify differences between the special education preschool and the new placement that may adversely affect a child's adjustment.
2. Prepare the child for transition from the preschool class by teaching behavior routines and skills that the child will need in the new setting.
3. Consider alternative arrangements in the new setting to help the child acquire the needed behaviors and skills that the child did not learn in the preschool.

4. Establish and maintain communication with the teachers in the new setting before, during, and after the child's transition.

## FACTORS TO CONSIDER IN PLACING CHILDREN FOR INTERVENTION SERVICES

Appropriate placement depends upon a number of factors: the age of the child, the type of handicapping condition, the severity of the handicap, the type of community (urban or rural), and whether classes are categorical or crosscategorical.

### Age of the Child

An important consideration is the child's age. The birth-to-three age group, consisting of infants and toddlers, needs home-based or consultation services. Infants require an intensive one-to-one intervention service over an extended period of the day. Parents often take on this responsibility because they spend more time with the infant. Toddlers may benefit from a combination center- and home-based program. For preschoolers in the 3- to 6-year-old range, the center-based program often is the most appropriate placement. In this setting, they are likely to benefit from a social situation and are able to work in a group. These youngsters also are capable of riding a bus to and from school.

### Type of Problem

Another important concern is the nature of the child's handicap. A handicap such as deafness requires very unique intervention and usually must take place with teachers of the hearing impaired. Other handicaps, such as learning disabilities, require more developmental and cross-categorical types of intervention services.

### Severity of the Problem

Another important factor is the level of severity. The severity of a handicap often is classfied into four levels: mild, moderate, severe, or profound. Children with mild or moderate handicaps need very different types of services from those with severe or profound handicaps. Mild–moderate problems usually can be dealt with in groups in center-based programs. Children with severe–profound handicaps often need more individual services and require more services from related professionals.

### Type of Community

Sociological factors of the community also must be considered. In rural areas, there are special problems of transportation and the isolation of the parents. Children with a particular type of handicap may be scattered over many hundreds of miles. In some communities, weather affects the ability to provide services when roads are closed because of rain/snow or extreme cold. Urban areas are more likely to provide center-based programs. However, transportation may be difficult for urban parents as well.

### Categorical or Cross-Categorical Placement

Another issue in placement is whether the child should be served in a categorical placement (with children with the same handicapping condition) or in a cross-categorical setting (a grouping of children who have several types of handicaps). With young children, this problem is particularly pressing because educators are reluctant to stigmatize the preschooler by labeling the child. Further, it is difficult to differentiate the specific category of the problem with the young child. For instance, many symptoms are similar for learning disabilities, emotional disturbance, and mental retardation. Therefore, early childhood educators prefer to delay the differential diagnosis, if possible, and not decide upon the category of handicap until the child is observed over a period of time. Thus, the child is placed in a cross-categorical setting, where children with several types of handicaps, as well as nonhandicapped and gifted children, are placed together for instruction. This setting permits further observation and evaluation to take place. Such cross-categorical settings may simply be designated as *developmental classes* or *early childhood services*.

Even though the child receives instruction in a cross-categorical setting, it is necessary under P.L. 94-142 in most states to classify the child's primary exceptionality during the evaluation process. This required information becomes child-count data for the State Education Agency and for the U.S. Department of Education. Many children receive the categorical statement of *Language Impaired* as their primary handicap.

### Nature of the Kindergarten Program

One of the primary functions of early childhood special education should be to prepare children for standard academic experiences if appropriate. For many children, this means that the placement goal is the school's regular kindergarten class. The placement of exceptional children in a standard classroom with nonhandicapped children is often referred to as *mainstreaming*. Mainstreaming has legal as well as educational implications, and it is therefore discussed later in this chapter in the section concerning the law.

In considering the standard kindergarten as a possible placement for a child, however, it is important to study the nature of that school's kindergarten curriculum. There is much variability among kindergarten programs, depending upon the local educational philosophy and administrative objectives for the kindergarten curriculum. In the past, traditional kindergarten programs were organized to focus on social interactions and group compatibility for large group instruction. At the present time, there is increasing pressure for kindergartens to change their focus to a more academic, structured, and teacher-directed learning environment (Walter and Vincent, 1982). The skills needed by the child to succeed in the academic-type kindergarten include: (1) attending skills; (2) independent work completion skills; (3) appropriate peer interaction skills; and (4) compliance to rules. In addition, some states are developing legislation to expand the traditional half-day kindergarten to a full day. Some educators predict that this expansion in time will increase the academic content of the kindergarten program. Changes in the kindergarten curriculum to a more academic focus will create major adjustments for exceptional children and their families.

### Services for Infants and Toddlers

Although the provision of services for young exceptional children ages three to five is indeed complex, it is even more so for the infant and toddler group, birth to three years of age. Handicapped infants are likely to have obvious and rather severe problems requiring medical and other related services. Also, the needs of their confused, distraught, often guilt-ridden parents and families are very great. To add to the complexity, no single agency has the total responsibility for provision of services to this group of children.

Although there is a general lack of services for handicapped infants and toddlers, experiences with pilot programs are beginning to be reported (McCollum and Stayton, 1985). Many of these programs are home-based, serving infants and their parents in the home.

As mentioned earlier, Public Law 94-142 does not include the birth-to-three age group. However, the Developmental Disabilities Act does include this group, since it covers children from birth through age 21. In addition, a number of states now have laws requiring service for this age group of handicapped children. After reviewing funded HCEEP services for the birth-to-three population, Karnes, Linnemeyer, and Shwedel (1981) reached the following conclusions:

1. *Intervention in infancy is sound practice.* The earlier the intervention, the better are the chances of reducing the adverse effects of the handicapping condition. In some cases, the handicap can even be eliminated.

2. *"Bonding" is more difficult to accomplish with a handicapped infant.* Bonding is the necessary process of infant development in which a strong affective relationship is established between the baby and the caregiver (usually the mother). With a handicapped infant, it is particularly difficult to establish this essential relationship, and parents often need direct assistance.

3. *A multidisciplinary team that represents several disciplines and agencies is important.* One profession or one agency cannot provide all the knowledge, skill, and expertise needed.

4. *Parents become the baby's first teacher.* Parents of handicapped infants require parent training to help them in this difficult task. As key members of any team concerning their child, they must be involved in all aspects of the program.

## THE LAW AND SERVICES FOR YOUNG EXCEPTIONAL CHILDREN

Federal and state laws influence many aspects of the life and schooling of young exceptional children. The rights of all handicapped individuals, including young children, are protected through this legislation. The rules and regulations affect assessment, teaching practices, and the delivery of intervention services.

### Public Law 94-142

The legislation that has had the greatest influence on educational services for handicapped children in our schools is the federal law known as Public Law 94-142, The Education for All Handicapped Children Act. Passed by Congress in 1975, the law became effective in 1977. Under this landmark legislation, all handicapped children and youth aged three through twenty-one have the right to a free, appropriate public education. Further, each state must have a plan that complies with the federal law. As a result, this law has affected children and schools in every part of the United States.

Under P.L. 94-142, handicapped children are defined as those who because of their impairments need special education or related services. The handicapping categories and characteristics of these handicaps are discussed in Chapter 2.

Although the age range specified in P.L. 94-142 is three through twenty-one, there are exceptions in the law in regard to the three- to six-year-old populations. If an individual state *does not require* special education for handicapped three- to six-year-olds in their state law, the federal law cannot supersede the state legislation.

Public Law 98-199, passed by Congress in 1983, underscores the federal role in special education by extending and affirming many of the features of P.L. 94-142. This act provides an expansion of early childhood special education programs: (1) it grants permission to use federal funds under the preschool incentive grant to children below the age of three and (2) it establishes grants to states for developing and implementing comprehensive plans to provide early childhood education for handicapped children from birth through age five.

Section 504 of the Vocational Rehabilitation Act of 1973 often is discussed along with P.L. 94-142. Section 504 is a civil rights law, mandating equal program *accessibility* for handicapped individuals. It is this law that requires public buildings, including schools, to accommodate handicapped individuals. For example, ramps are to be provided for people who use wheelchairs.

Several important features of P.L. 94-142 that affect children, their parents, and teachers are discussed in the following sections: Eligibility for Special Education Services, the Individualized Education Program (IEP), the Least Restrictive Environment, and Procedural Safeguards.

## Special Education Eligibility: Entry and Exit Criteria

Before a child receives services, the evaluation team must determine whether the child is eligible for special education services. Participation in early childhood special education requires eligibility in one of the special education categories. The handicapping conditions specified in P.L. 94-142 are mentally retarded, hard of hearing, deaf, speech and language impaired, learning disabilities, visually handicapped, seriously emotionally disturbed, orthopedically impaired, other health impaired, deaf–blind, and multihandicapped. The child may also be identified as gifted or talented.

Unlike school-age students, eligibility for young children cannot be established through academic performance. Eligibility criteria for young children are based on developmental delays. One Special Education Services Cooperative established eligibility based on developmental delays in four areas of development: (1) communication skills; (2) cognitive processing; (3) preacademic productivity; and (4) interpersonal relationships and personal adjustment. This organization established the following eligibility and exit criteria:

Mild delays: three- to five-month delays in any one developmental area.
Moderate delays: six- to nine-month delays in any one developmental area.
Severe delays: ten- to twelve-month developmental delays in two developmental areas.

The same criteria serve as exit criteria to determine when a child will leave the early childhood special education program and make a transition to the standard educational program or another special education program.

## The Individualized Education Program (IEP)

One of the major provisions of P.L. 94-142 is the requirement that an _individualized education program_ (IEP) be formulated for each child identified as handicapped. The IEP serves two functions:

1. _The IEP is a written plan for a particular child._ As a written statement developed by the case conference team, the IEP prescribes specific educational goals and objectives, as well as the child's placement.

2. *The IEP is a management tool for the entire assessment and teaching/intervention process.* Serving a much broader purpose than the written document itself, the IEP is the core of the entire process of assessment and teaching. As such, it assures that the education individually designed for the child is appropriate and that the special education services actually are delivered and monitored.

The major phases of the IEP process are shown in Figure 5.2.

*1. Referral.* The child who is suspected of having special needs can be referred through a number of sources. Often children are identified for referral through a screening procedure given by the community (see Chapter 4). Children also can be referred through other agencies, by hospitals and physicians, or by the parents or other family members.

*2. Multidisciplinary evaluation.* At this stage of the IEP process, specialists representing various disciplines and related professions obtain necessary information by assessing the child's performance and observing the child's behavior. For example, for one child the multidisciplinary team might include a psychologist, a vision specialist, a hearing specialist, a speech and language pathologist, a physical therapist, and an early childhood educator. The multidisciplinary team determines the child's eligibility for special education services.

**FIGURE 5.2**

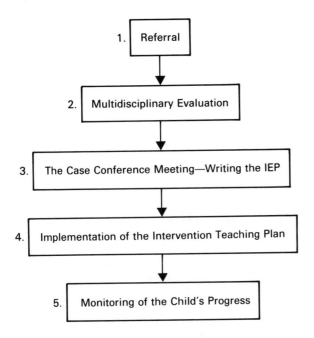

Several parts of the law regulate the multidisciplinary evaluation: (1) testing must be administered by trained personnel; (2) the tests must be appropriate, validated for the purpose used, and be free of cultural or racial bias; (3) evaluation materials must be administered in the student's primary language; and (4) the evaluation team must represent several disciplines and include at least one teacher or other specialist in the area of the suspected handicap.

*3. The case conference meeting—writing the IEP.*    After the multidisciplinary information is gathered, the parents are contacted to arrange the case conference meeting. It is at this meeting that the IEP may be written.

*Participants at the IEP meeting.* Participants must include the following:

1. A representative of the public educational agency (the school district)
2. The child's teacher (if the child is not yet in school, an early childhood special education teacher)
3. One or both parents
4. The child when appropriate (this usually applies to adolescent-age students)
5. Other individuals, at the discretion of the parents or school

*Content of the IEP.* The individualized education program for each child must include:

1. A statement of the child's present levels of performance.
2. A statement of annual goals, including short-term instructional objectives.
3. A statement of the specific special education and related services in which the child will be able to participate in the regular educational programs.
4. The projected dates for the initiation of services and the anticipated duration of the services.
5. Appropriate objective criteria, evaluation procedures and schedules for determining, on at least an annual basis, whether the short-term instructional objectives are being met.

Thus, among the many critical decisions that are made in the case conference meeting are the child's eligibility for special education services, the annual goals, the specific objectives of the intervention services, the educational placement, when services are to begin, and how the child's progress will be evaluated. (Examples of an IEP annual goal and short-term objectives are shown in Figures 5.3, 5.4(A), 5.4(B), and 5.4(C).)

*4. Implementation of the intervention/teaching plan.*    This is an important portion of the IEP process. Now the child is placed into the agreed upon setting and receives instruction designed to help him or her reach the IEP goals and objectives.

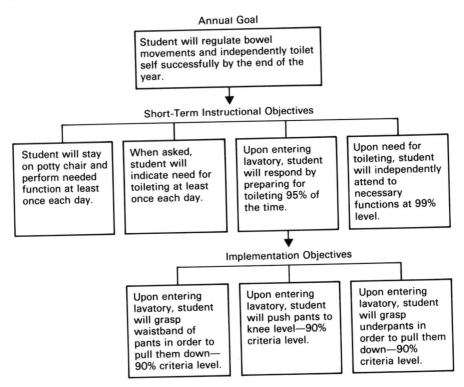

From *Illinois Primer on Individualized Education Programs*. (1981) Illinois State Board of Education. Springfield, Il: Dept. of Specialized Education Services, p. 35.

**FIGURE 5.3** Example of Annual Goal and Short-Term Objectives

*5. Monitoring of the child's progress.* This stage of the IEP process calls for review (at least annually) and re-evaluation of the plan in terms of the child's progress. Plans must be included in the IEP to show how this evaluation will be accomplished, who will conduct it, and what assessment instruments and criteria will be used.

### Procedural Safeguards

Several laws affecting assessment procedures and placement are known as *procedural safeguards*. They are designed to protect the rights of handicapped children. The most important of these safeguards are summarized here:

1. Parents must consent in writing to having their child evaluated and to the plans and placement set forth in the written IEP.
2. The assessment must be conducted in the child's native language and the findings reported to the parents in the parents' native language.

Instructional Area: Self-help Skills

Present Educational Levels: Rosalie can place her shoes on the correct feet, cross her shoelaces, and pull them tight. However, she needs physical prompts to complete making the bow.

Rosalie is toilet trained and can feed herself.

Annual Goal: Rosalie will independently tie her shoe.

| Short-Term Objective (Terminal Behavior) | Optional: Instructional Methods/Media Materials | Evaluation of Instructional Objectives | | Duration of Objectives (Optional) | |
|---|---|---|---|---|---|
| | | Evaluation Procedures to be Used (Conditions) | Criteria of Successful Performance | Date Started | Date Completed |
| 1. With the use of physical and/or verbal prompts, Rosalie will tie a single-loop knot. | | 1-3. Frequency of performance on objective. | 1. 90% independence/10 consecutive trials. | | |
| 2. Rosalie will independently tie a single-loop knot. | | | 2-3. 90% accuracy/10 consecutive trials. | | |
| 3. Rosalie will independently tie a double-loop knot. | | | | | |

**FIGURE 5.4(A) Example of Annual Goal and Short-Term Objectives**

Instructional Area: Psychomotor Skills

Present Educational Levels:

Gross Motor: Rosalie can sit unaided and can stand, with support, for approximately twenty minutes. She is ambulatory when given total physical assistance. Rosalie can use a wheelchair independently.

Annual Goal: Rosalie will increase mobility in the classroom, using a walker or rolator.

| Short-Term Objective (Terminal Behavior) | Optional Instructional Methods/Media /Materials | Evaluation of Instructional Objectives | | Duration of Objectives (Optional) | |
|---|---|---|---|---|---|
| | | Evaluation Procedures to be Used (Conditions) | Criteria of Successful Performance | Date Started | Date Completed |
| 1. While standing at a handrail, Rosalie will alternate sliding her feet forward and backward. | Handrail | 1. Physical therapist and teacher documentation of performance. | 1. 90% independence/5 consecutive days. | | |
| 2. While standing at a handrail, Rosalie will alternately raise and lower each foot approximately three inches from the floor. | | 2. Physical therapist and teacher documentation of performance. | 2. 90% independence/5 consecutive days, given verbal prompts. | | |

From *Illinois Primer on Individualized Education Programs*, p. 36.

**FIGURE 5-4(B) Example of Annual Goal and Short-Term Objectives**

Instructional Area: Academic Achievement

Present Educational Levels:

Communication Skills: Rosalie attends to verbal stimuli. She identifies pictures of nouns, verbs, and 16 out of 25 adjectives. She is able to follow a two-step command. Rosalie names approximately 35 objects. She can initiate adjective-noun phrases when responding to "What is this?" Spontaneous speech consists of one- and two-word phrases. Intelligibility, volume, and rate are within normal limits.

Annual Goal: Rosalie will improve communication skills.

| Short-Term Objective (Terminal Behavior) | Optional Instructional Methods/Media /Materials | Evaluation of Instructional Objectives | | Duration of Objectives (Optional) | |
|---|---|---|---|---|---|
| | | Evaluation Procedures to be Used (Conditions) | Criteria of Successful Performance | Date Started | Date Completed |
| 1. Rosalie will increase her production of 3 (4) word phrases in a one-to-one setting. | Emerging Language Program | 1. Performance on task. | 1. 90% accuracy/ 5 consecutive sessions. | | |
| 2. Rosalie will increase her production of 3 (4) word phrases in spontaneous speech. | Small group activities | 2. Performance on task. | 2. 90% accuracy/ 2 consecutive weeks. | | |

Source: Illinois Primer on Individualized Education Programs, p. 37.

FIGURE 5.4(C) Example of Annual Goal and Short-Term Objectives

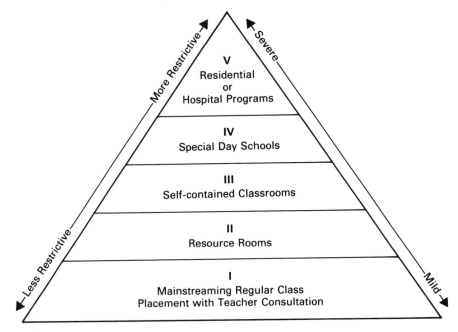

**FIGURE 5.5**  A Model of the Continuum of Educational Program Alternatives in Relation to Restrictiveness and Severity

3. Tests and procedures used for the evaluation and placement must be free of racial or cultural bias.
4. The parents have the right to see all information collected and used in the decision making.
5. Parents and children have the right to an impartial due process hearing if they disagree with the IEP decisions.
6. The confidentiality of all reports and records of the child is protected under the law.

### Continuum of Alternative Placements

P.L. 94-142 requires that schools provide an array of educational placements to meet the varied needs of handicapped children. Among the types of options are regular classes, resource room classes, self-contained special classes, special schools, and other types or combinations of placements that may be needed. In selecting the placement for delivering services for a particular child, the case conference team should consider factors such as severity of the handicap, the need for related services, the child's ability to fit into the routine of the selected setting, and the child's social and performance skills. Often the team recommends a delivery system that combines elements of several types of placements. Following is a listing of possible placements, ranked from the least restrictive to the most restrictive:

Regular classroom with no basic change in teaching procedures
Regular class with indirect services within the regular class
Regular class with direct services and instruction within the regular class
Regular class with resource room services
Self-contained special classroom with part-time instruction within the regular class
Self-contained special class, full-time on a regular school campus
Self-contained special class in a private day school facility
Public residential school facility
Private residential school facility
Hospital program
Home-bound instruction

*Least restrictive environment.* The writers of P.L. 94-142 recognized that successful handicapped adults have learned to function comfortably in the larger society of the nonhandicapped world. The intent of the law, therefore, is to help prepare handicapped children for that integration through experiences in school with nonhandicapped peers. The feature of P.L. 94-142 designed to assure this integrated experience is known as the *least restrictive environment.* This means that handicapped children are to be educated with nonhandicapped children to the extent appropriate. Placement decisions must reflect consideration of the least restrictive environment for each child. The more placement includes nonhandicapped children, the less restrictive that environment is considered to be.

The term *restrictive* as used in this context has to do with placement with nonhandicapped children. Being with nonhandicapped children is considered less restrictive. Being with only handicapped children is considered to be more restrictive.

Figure 5.5 illustrates several of the most common placement options in relation to the restrictiveness of the environment and to the severity of the handicap. This type of model was first suggested by Deno (1970). Each level of the model, beginning with Level I and progressing through Level V represents an increasingly restrictive placement in terms of diminishing contact with nonhandicapped children.

*Mainstreaming.* The term *mainstreaming* is commonly used to describe the transition and integration of handicapped children into a standard classroom. Mainstreaming is not synonymous with the concept of the "least restrictive environment." The intent of the law is to provide educational experiences for handicapped children in a setting with nonhandicapped children *as appropriate.* It is not the intent of the law to place all handicapped children into standard classes. For some children, the least restrictive placement is not a standard class but another placement from the Continuum of Alternative Placements. In a study on the effects of integration, Odom, Deklyen, and Jenkins (1985) found that the placement of nonhandicapped with handicapped preschoolers did not interfere with the normal development of the nonhandicapped child.

The intent of mainstreaming could be lost by failing to provide sufficient special education classes and personnel. There is danger that a poorly initiated mainstreaming movement can mean a backlash from teachers, parents, and the lay public. Several points should be kept in mind (Zigler and Muenchow, 1979):

1. Appropriate training for teachers and other personnel who work with handicapped children is needed. In the case of preschool children, this includes volunteers, teachers, and related personnel.
2. Without adequate support personnel to assist regular class teachers with the handicapped, mainstreaming is doomed to failure. This means that preschool teachers, daycare teachers, Head Start teachers, and so on need supportive help from special educators for handicapped children in their charge.
3. Mainstreaming should not be viewed as a way to save money. Properly conducted, a mainstream program will cost as much as the self-contained special education classes.
4. Mainstreaming and its evaluation does not take place in a social vacuum. The point here is that for some children, "normalization" placement in a nonhandicapped setting is the wrong type of placement.

Some possible approaches to be considered for providing a mainstreaming setting for three- to five-year-old handicapped children are suggested by the Illinois State Board of Education (1979):

1. Have the special education program for three- to five-year-olds located within the regular elementary building and allow them to partake in certain kindergarten activities during designated periods of the day or week. Coordinate activities between early childhood and preschool bilingual classes located in the same building by scheduling group activities together, such as field trips, music, art, snacks, physical education, language lessons, and the like.
2. Have special education programs for the special preschool children located in separate facilities but coordinated with local kindergartens in the public school by programming for the special preschool children to be with the kindergarten class for specified periods during the week.
3. Integrate more severely and profoundly handicapped preschoolers with less severely involved children. In essence, this endorses the concept of meeting least restrictive environment requirements through coordination internally with special education programs. For the more severely handicapped children, this setting may constitute a least restrictive alternative.
4. Utilize schools that have been abandoned because of declining enrollment as a setting for early childhood special education programs and institute additional programs within the building, such as Head Start, a kindergarten class, youth groups, and other child developmental programs.

5. Open early childhood special education programs in junior and community colleges or high schools where there are established child development programs for the students and coordinate programs and activities between the two groups.

6. Coordinate early childhood special education programs (either school facilities or separate facilities) with existing community resources for preschoolers. Dually enroll exceptional preschoolers with local Head Start programs for specified days or weeks.

## THE TEAM APPROACH TO COMPREHENSIVE SERVICES

The kinds of problems affecting young handicapped children include physical, language, social, emotional, family, health, and cognitive factors. To provide comprehensive service for children with several problems, a team of professionals who can contribute expertise in a number of areas is needed. In addition to the teacher of the handicapped preschool child, other specialists provide assessment or therapy. Team members could include physicians, nurses, psychologists, social workers, physical therapists, occupational therapists, speech clinicians, audiologists, recreation workers, nutritionists, volunteers, parents, and others. The teacher, although not an expert in any of these specialties, should understand enough of each specialty to communicate intelligently and integrate the findings of each specialist in working with the child.

All of the specialists concerned with a particular child are considered the *child development team*. The teams can be *multidisciplinary, interdisciplinary*, or *transdisciplinary*. On the *multidisciplinary* team, the specialists work side by side, each performing the assigned responsibility.

On the *interdisciplinary* team, the specialists have developed common perceptions and they share responsibilities. Getting a group of specialists to function as an interdisciplinary team is a difficult and challenging goal. Each specialist comes onto the team with a different set of skills and a different perspective of the child. These differences can constitute the strength of the team or they can be a potential for role conflict. For example, if a feeding problem confronts a child, the nutritionist, nurse, physical therapist, speech pathologist, dentist, and physician could each provide helpful information. They could also disagree about the cause of the problem or the appropriate method of treatment. The way to help the child is to get the team to work together as an interdisciplinary unit (Holm, 1978).

The term *transdisciplinary team* is sometimes used to integrate the members of the team. Specialists are willing to cross the borders of their disciplines and assimilate knowledge from other areas. At times they can substitute for each other in a particular activity. In short, they work together as a cohesive unit. What is emphasized is the integration of therapy services and the avoidance of duplication of services by individual specialists. Often a multidisciplinary team approach results in the removal of a young child for separate therapy sessions with each designated specialist. The transdisciplinary approach, however, attempts to jointly plan goals and objectives that will integrate therapies, rather than splinter them.

It is at the staffing (or case conference) that the various specialists are asked to pool their findings. Holm (1978) has some specific suggestions for a team leader to hold a successful team staffing:

1. Be sure that all participants know each other and are aware of each person's professional affiliation.
2. Provide basic information in written form.
3. Have an outline or organized plan for the discussion.
4. Encourage all staff members to participate. They should both listen and talk.
5. Stimulate responses and exchange among members.
6. Summarize the discussion and state the decisions that are made at the appropriate point of the meeting.

## SUMMARY

There are several service delivery options for the young exceptional child. In *home-based* services, the child-care professional visits the home on a regular basis and teaches the parent(s) how to teach the child. Much of the responsibility falls upon the parent. In *center-based* services, the child comes to a fully equipped center and receives services from professionals in many disciplines. The *combination home- and center-based* program combines elements of both of these programs. Through *consulting* services, the parent is trained at a center but takes on much of the responsibility for teaching. The focus of *transition* programs is the well organized transfer of the child from one placement to another during or after the preschool years.

There are a number of important factors to consider in making decisions about service delivery and placement. These include the child's age, the type of handicapping condition, the severity of the problem, the type of community (urban or rural), and categorical or cross-categorical placement. The birth-to-three population constitutes a special group of handicapped children and requires very

special kinds of services.

Public Law 94-142 is extremely important federal legislation for the handicapped preschooler. It assures free appropriate public education for every handicapped child. Whether three- to six-year-olds are included in this legislation depends upon each state's law. The individualized education program (IEP) is the process through which decisions about placement and services are made. Procedural safeguards protect the rights of the handicapped child and include protection in evaluation, due process, and confidentiality. The continuum of alternative placements is the array of services that the school district must provide to meet individual needs. *Mainstreaming* is placing handicapped children with non-handicapped children in regular classes. For some handicapped children, the mainstreamed setting is not the most appropriate placement.

A team approach to comprehensive services is needed to integrate the services of all the specialists working with the child. The team can be multidisciplinary, interdisciplinary, or transdisciplinary.

## REVIEW QUESTIONS

### Terms to Know

least restrictive environment
continuum of alternative placements
categorical
noncategorical
mainstreaming

Public Law 94-142
IEP
procedural safeguards
home-based services
transdisciplinary team

1. Name four placement options for the preschool exceptional child.
2. Define the *least restrictive environment*. Give an example of a least restrictive and most restrictive environment.
3. What is meant by *continuum of alternative placements?*
4. Give some advantages and disadvantages of *mainstreaming*.
5. Why is P.L. 94-142 so important?
6. What happens at an IEP meeting?
7. Find out what your state laws are concerning young exceptional preschool children.

## REFERENCES

BAILEY, D. and D. WOLERY (1985) *Teaching Infants and Preschoolers with Handicaps.* Columbus: Charles E. Merrill.

DENO, E. (1970) "Special Education as Developmental Capital." *Exceptional Children,* 37, 229–37.

FOWLER, S. (1982) *Transition from Preschool to Kindergarten for Children with Special Needs.* ERIC, ED 231 102. Lawrence, KS: Kansas University, 39 pp.

HOLM, V. (1978) "Interdisciplinary Child Development Team." In K. Allen, V. Holm, and R. Schiefelbusch (eds.) *Early Intervention: A Team Approach.* Baltimore: University Park Press, pp. 99–122.

ILLINOIS STATE BOARD OF EDUCATION (1979) *Early Childhood Education for the Handicapped: Recommended Procedures and Practices.* Springfield, IL: Department of Specialized Services.

ILLINOIS STATE BOARD OF EDUCATION (1980) *Executive Summary: Early Childhood Education for the Handicapped: Special Study.* Springfield, IL: Department of Specialized Educational Services.

ILLINOIS STATE BOARD OF EDUCATION (1981) *The Illinois Primer on Individualized Education Programs.* Springfield, IL: Department of Specialized Educational Services and Illinois Regional Resource Center.

KARNES, M., S. LINNEMEYER and A. SCHWEDEL (1981) "A Survey of Federally Funded Model Programs for Handicapped Infants: Implications for Research and Practice." *Journal for the Division of Early Childhood,* 5, 25–39.

KARNES, M. and R. ZEHRBACH (1977) "Alternative Models for Delivery Services to Young Handicapped Children." In J. Jordan, A. Hayden, M. Karnes, and M. Woods (eds.) *Early Childhood Education for Exceptional Children.* Reston, VA: Council for Exceptional Children.

McCOLLUM, J. and V. STAYTON (1985) "Infant/Parent Interactions: Studies and Intervention Guidelines Based on the SIAI Model." *Journal of the Division of Early Childhood,* 9 (Spring) 125–35.

ODOM, S., M. DEKLYEN and J. JENKINS (1985) "Integrating Handicapped and Nonhandicapped Preschoolers: Development Impact on Nonhandicapped Children." *Exceptional Children*, 51, 41–48.

P.L. 95-602 (1978) *Rehabilitative Comprehensive Services and Developmental Disabilities Amendments of 1978.*

TURNBULL, A., P. WINTON, J. BALCHER and N. SALKIND (1982) "Mainstreaming in the Kindergarten Classroom: Perspectives of Parents of Handicapped and Nonhandicapped Children." *Journal of the Division for Early Childhood*, 6 (December), 3–13.

U.S. DEPARTMENT OF EDUCATION (1985) *To Assure the Free Appropriate Public Education of All Handicapped Children*, Seventh Annual Report to Congress on the Implementation of the Education of the All Handicapped Children Act. Washington, DC: Government Printing Office.

WALTER, G. and L. VINCENT (1982) "The Handicapped Child in the Regular Classroom." *Journal of the Division for Early Childhood*, 6, 84–95.

ZIGLER, E. and S. MUENSCHOW (1979) "Mainstreaming: The Proof Is in the Implementation." *American Psychologist*, 34, 993–94.

# SIX

# The Curriculum: Principles and Practices

## INTRODUCTION

The second part of this book deals with the teaching of young handicapped and at-risk children. Chapter 6 presents an overview of the curriculum and useful principles and practices for teaching. Each subsequent chapter discusses intervention strategies for a different curriculum area: motor and perceptual skills (Chapter 7); communication skills and language (Chapter 8); cognitive skills (Chapter 9); and social and affective skills (Chapter 10).

This chapter overviews the goals, content, and design of the curriculum for early childhood special education programs. A *curriculum* is the planned arrangement of experiences designed to bring about desired changes in the child's behavior.

In effective programs, the curriculum is thoughtfully planned to assure that children have adequate and appropriate opportunities and experiences to learn and to grow. For young children with special needs, a comprehensive curriculum offers youngsters experiences in a broad range of activities. Specifically, the curriculum should include activities with physical movement, language experiences, cognitive expansion, social events, and creative expression.

The curriculum for young children with special needs combines elements from the curriculum models of both early childhood education and special education. Some key elements of the curricula from these two fields and the combined early childhood special education programs are discussed in the following sections.

## EARLY CHILDHOOD CURRICULUM MODELS

In early childhood education programs, the curriculum is designed for preschool children who fall within the normal range of development. Over the years, there have been many changes in the philosophy of early childhood education, and each change triggered programmatic changes in the early childhood curriculum. Among the various philosophies that have influenced the teaching practices in early education are the ideas of the MacMillan sisters, who recognized the importance of early education and started the first nursery schools in London; the theories of Freud linking the critical relationships of emotions and behavior to learning; the concepts of John Dewey, who stressed the importance of firsthand experiences to learning; the recommendations of Montessori to use structured environmentally planned learning materials; and ideas of Piaget concerning the sequence of cognitive development.

Preschool curriculum models can be classified into four categories: (1) the *enrichment* curriculum, which is designed to encourage natural learning through incidental expansion of learning experiences; (2) the *directed teaching* curriculum, which is a carefully designed and structured teacher-directed program; (3) the *cognitive emphasis* curriculum, which is designed to promote thinking skills in the young child; and (4) the *caretaking,* or custodial situation, which is a program for the working parent and may be a placement in a daycare center, or with a neighbor or a good friend. In addition, there is a *combination* curriculum, which combines elements from all four approaches. Each of these curriculum models is briefly described.

### Enrichment Curriculum

The enrichment philosophy frequently shapes the curriculum of the standard nursery school format. Based on the "whole child" theory of early childhood education, the enrichment curriculum emphasizes a comprehensive view of the child's education and is concerned with all aspects of child growth—physical, emotional, linguistic, social, and cognitive. A goal of the enrichment curriculum is to offer the opportunity for the child to have many experiences for a variety of purposes.

Underlying the enrichment curriculum are the theories of developmental psychology which reflect a maturational view of child development. This view stresses that there is a natural growth sequence for the young child. The role of the teacher is to enhance the natural growth processes by providing learning opportunities within an environment that is enriching, encouraging, and nurturing. The premise is that under favorable, open circumstances, the child's own inner drive and need to learn will naturally stimulate learning activities and behaviors. Thus, skills and abilities will emerge and naturally develop. This approach is *child oriented* since it is concerned with the individuality of the child. It also is called *present oriented* because the prime concern is the child's immediate needs—not the child's long-range and future needs in society.

In the enrichment curriculum classroom, one will typically find special activities areas; for example, an area for play with large blocks, a place for dress-ups and playhouse materials, a quiet play section, and a creative arts area. Enrichment programs typically have periods of the day assigned for outdoor play and for indoor play. Language activities are encouraged through storytelling and conversations. Field trips to the outer world are designed to broaden children's experience levels; they may visit places such as museums, the post office, stores, and parks. Although the teacher arranges a generalized but flexible time schedule for the day, activities are child-selected. The teacher capitalizes on opportunities for incidental and informal learning. A priority goal for the enrichment class is to encourage child exploration.

### Directed Teaching Curriculum

The directed teaching curriculum concentrates on the direct teaching of specific skills selected by the teacher. Based upon the principles of behavioral psychology, this curriculum approach emphasizes direct intervention to bring about selected learning skills in young children. The role of the teacher is to carefully plan and structure learning experiences to build specific pre-academic and academic skills. Materials and activities are carefully designed to develop these selected skills.

In the directed teaching curriculum the teacher first determines the kinds of preacademic behaviors that are needed to perform in academic areas such as reading and arithmetic. These behaviors are then directly taught to the child as early as possible. The teaching of academic skills of reading and arithmetic during the preschool years is emphasized also.

The directed teaching approach is sometimes described as a "compensatory model" of curriculum. The underlying premise is that middle-class children receive a hidden curriculum in their home environment. By providing this "hidden curriculum" to children who missed such experiences, disadvantaged children are compensated and have a better chance of learning. For example, middle-class children are more likely to learn the skills of recognizing letters of the alphabet in their home. The impetus behind the development of *Sesame Street* was to bring the hidden curriculum to disadvantaged children through television.

In summary, the directed teaching curriculum is *goal oriented* because it is concerned with the child's adaptation into society. It also is *future oriented* because it advocates teaching specific skills as early as possible— skills the educator believes the child will need at some future time.

### Cognitive Emphasis Curriculum

The cognitive emphasis curriculum is based on the ideas and theories of cognitive psychology, with many of the concepts and curriculum programs stemming from the work of Jean Piaget (1971). Of major concern is the way children develop cognitive or thinking abilities—memory, discrimination, problem-solving ability, concept formation, verbal learning, and comprehension. One of Piaget's important insights about children is that they do not think like adults, but they go through distinct stages of development that are characterized by particular types of thinking (see Chapter 9). In the cognitive emphasis curriculum, attention is given to the child's underlying thinking processes and the cognitive learning that develops through direct experiences and action. Unlike the direct teaching curriculum, this approach is not concerned with training specific academic areas, such as reading and arithmetic, but in building thinking skills.

In one widely reported early childhood project, the Perry Preschool Project (Schweinhart and Weikart, 1980), for example, the stated purpose of the teaching activities is to develop the child's cognitive skills. The Montessori-type curriculum (Montessori, 1964) might also be viewed in this context because the child's learning environment and materials are structured to enhance cognitive growth.

### Custodial Care Curriculum

In today's world, many parents who work outside of the home need to arrange for custodial care for their child. These services may be obtained through a daycare facility or a private home. In these settings, children are supervised for the portion of the day that the parent needs to be away. In some cases, it is for the entire day; while in others, child care services are needed for only part of the day. The child may arrive as early as six in the morning and stay as late as six in the evening. Curriculum planning for children in this type of setting depends upon many factors, including the level of knowledge and training of the supervisory and child-care staff, the age of the child, and the number of children within the facility. Most often custodial care is fairly loosely structured, with much of the day taken up in napping, feeding, and toileting schedules.

### Combination Curriculum

In general practice, most programs for young children combine elements of several curriculum models. They provide some open experiences that are child-selected, offer some directed teaching of specific skills, encourage the development of cognitive skills, and may even extend day services to meet the needs of the working parent(s). In recent years, combination programs have grown out of the research findings in early childhood, the needs and demands of parents, and the competitive nature of early childhood private programs.

## THE SPECIAL EDUCATION CURRICULUM

The special education curriculum consists of the special services for handicapped children ages three through 21 that are not available in the standard education program. Curriculum changes from standard education are made in the content of the lessons, the types of skills taught, and the learning environment. Because it must meet the needs of many different kinds of handicapped children, the special education curriculum is necessarily varied. Certain handicaps require unique adaptations and techniques; for example, in teaching deaf, blind, or physically handicapped children. Certain concepts are key to the special education curriculum.

The special education curriculum must be individualized to take into account the *individual differences* of each child. (This concept is discussed later in this section.)

The child's curriculum plan should evolve from a careful examination of the tasks to be learned; that is, *task analysis.* (This concept is discussed later in this section.)

The special education curriculum should be *flexible,* permitting teachers to take advantage of selective teaching techniques, materials, and methods to meet and solve the varied instructional demands of handicapped children.

Special services of *related specialists* (such as speech and language pathologists, adaptive physical education teachers, or social workers) often are incorporated into the child's curriculum plan to provide the needed support and assistance. (See Chapter 5.)

Children identified as handicapped should have a written *individualized education program* (IEP) to guide the planning of the child's curriculum. (See Chapter 5.)

The child's curriculum plan should incorporate the philosophy of the *least restrictive environment.* That is, plans should include activities with nonhandicapped children to the greatest extent possible. Often this philosophy is referred to as *mainstreaming,* and its implementation may lead to placing the child for some period of time in a nonhandicapped classroom (Walter and Vincent, 1982). (See Chapter 5.)

### Meeting Individual Differences

The major purpose of the special education curriculum is to meet the needs of atypical children by taking into account their individual differences. Two types of individual differences should be considered (Kirk and Gallagher, 1986): (1) *Interindividual* differences are the ways in which handicapped children differ from nonhandicapped children and (2) *intraindividual* differences are uneven abilities in various areas of functioning within a single child. Both inter- and intraindividual differences are important considerations in curriculum planning for the exceptional preschool child.

**Interindividual differences.**   When the performance of one child is compared with that of a group of children of the same age, this is referred to as *interindividual differences*. Special education programs developed because the skills and abilities of exceptional children differed so markedly from those of the other children in the standard classroom that special kinds of services were needed.

Many of the tests used in psychology and education are norm-referenced tests, which are designed to measure interindividual differences. These tests evaluate children by measuring their ability to perform a skill; and they show that at specific ages, some children have acquired more of a certain skill while others have acquired less of the same skill. Norm-referenced tests—particularly those for young children—report a child's performance in several ways, including age scores, percentile ranks, or standard scores. (See Appendix B.)

With young children, the interindividual comparison often is reported as an age score. The age score indicates how children in the norm population (the sample used to develop the test) scored, based on their chronological age. For example, if the test score indicates the child's language score as 4–6, this means that the child's score on the language test is comparable to the language performance of the average child of four years and six months.

Many of the tests for young children are designed developmentally and are called *scales*. That is, they are constructed so the child first is given very simple tasks, and then as the evaluation progresses, the items gradually become more difficult. It is expected that the child's performance will improve proportionately on the scale as the child progresses in chronological age.

In summary, interindividual differences refer to how the child differs from others of the same age. Interindividual differences are measured through norm-referenced tests, which are useful for classifying children, determining the category of handicap, and helping place a child with a group of children with similar skills. Norm-referenced tests, however, do not tell the teacher what specific curriculum program the child needs. This information is more effectively gathered through intraindividual tests.

**Intraindividual differences.**   The term *intraindividual differences* refers to a comparison of the various abilities within an individual child. The exceptional child may display strengths in some abilities but weaknesses in other abilities. For example, the child may do well in motor skills but display limitations in language skills. Or the child may learn easily through visual stimuli but do poorly in auditory tasks. Also, one child may find arithmetic easy but reading very difficult.

Evaluation instruments that measure a child's intraindividual abilities analyze variations within the child. Rather than comparing the child's abilities to normed group data, these tests describe the child's individual abilities in comparison to him- or herself. The abilities examined with intraindividual tests can include skills in gross motor, fine motor, memory, auditory perception, visual perception, receptive language, expressive language, social, cognitive, and academic skills. (See Appendix B.)

Determining a child's strengths and weaknesses in each of these ability areas can help in designing the individualized curriculum. The teacher seeks answers to questions such as: What are the child's discrepancies in development? What can the child do well, and what tasks are difficult for this child? Such information can be used to organize an instructional program for an individual child, taking into account the child's strengths and weaknesses, without regard to how he or she compares with other children.

### Task Analysis

*Task analysis* is the process of examining how an individual child learns and then applying this information to the skills that the child is expected to acquire. The purpose of task analysis is to gather information that can help the teacher make curriculum decisions that will be beneficial for the child. There are two dimensions to *task analysis* as it is used in special education. One dimension analyzes the *child* in terms of abilities and disabilities—what the child can and cannot do. The other dimension of task analysis analyzes the *task* itself—the nature of the skills or content the child is expected to learn.

*Analysis of the child.* In using task analysis to study the child, the teacher examines how well the child understands and performs the task. An important question from this perspective is how does the child receive, store, and retrieve information? Which avenue of learning does the child seem to prefer: visual, auditory, or tactile? Does the child avoid certain pathways of learning? Is intrusion necessary? In visual learning, the child receives information by using the visual system; visual information is scanned and processed through the eyes and then the central nervous system. In auditory learning, the child uses the auditory system to receive information; auditory information is received through the ears and processed through the central nervous system. Learning through the tactile system involves the activities of touch and movement. It is also important to determine the amount of assistance to be provided by the teacher.

Another issue in task analysis is whether the child is being asked to perform a task of reception or expression. When the task requires the child to take in information, this is considered *reception*. (Watching *Sesame Street* is an example of receptive learning.) When the child is required to give out information or to perform an act, this is considered *expression*. (Following a direction or making an oral reply are examples of expressive learning.) The child may be able to perform receptive tasks but not expressive tasks.

To illustrate the dimension of task analysis of the child, the activity of answering a telephone call can be examined: The sensory systems involved are auditory (hearing the ring); visual (seeing the phone and recognizing it as something to talk into); tactile and kinesthetic (touching the phone and picking up the receiver). The use of all the senses makes the task intersensory. Hearing the sound can be analyzed as receptive, while the response of picking up the phone and talking are expressive acts.

Further, the child's ability to handle a task can be analyzed in terms of the child's specific type of handicap. For example, the child with a visual handicap may not see the phone clearly; the child with an auditory handicap may not hear the ring; the child with a motor handicap may not be able to physically handle the phone easily; the child with a language disorder may have difficulty talking; and the child with a cognitive deficit may be unable to associate the sound of the ring with the phone.

Thus, an analysis of the child's abilities and disabilities, along with strengths and weaknesses in learning systems, provides important information for teachers in planning the curriculum for the individual child.

*Analysis of the task.* In using task analysis to study the task itself, the teacher concentrates on organizing the skills the child is expected to learn. First, the task to be learned is broken up into the components or steps. Once the elements of the task are identified, they are set into an ordered sequence of difficulty. Finally, the curriculum is designed to teach each successive step of the task. This is essentially a behavioral approach to curriculum construction; it emphasizes setting established expected behavioral outcomes and it requires accurate measurement of the child's performance.

To illustrate how analysis of a learning activity reduces the performance into sequential steps, the self-help activity of brushing teeth is used. The activity can be ordered into the following sequential steps:

1. Walk or move to the sink, turn on the water, and reach for the toothbrush and toothpaste container.
2. Unscrew the cap of the toothpaste/push the pump lever.
3. Place the cap on the sink surface.
4. Pick up the brush and get it wet.
5. Put the paste on the toothbrush.

6. Put the tube of toothpaste down on the sink.
7. Brush teeth.
8. Put the brush down.
9. Rinse mouth out with water.
10. Turn the water off.
11. Put the brush away.
12. Replace the cap on the toothpaste.

*Integrating the two approaches to task analysis.*   In planning the curriculum for a handicapped child, both dimensions of task analysis are needed. First, it is necessary to conduct an analysis of a child's strengths and weaknesses and the child's current performance levels. After setting curriculum goals and skills to be learned, task analysis is used to organize those skills in terms of component parts and the sequential steps for learning. Finally, information from both types of task analysis must be coordinated. These steps are summarized:

1. *Task analysis of the child.* Specify how the individual child functions: the things the child can and cannot do, learning preferences and strengths and weaknesses in learning systems, the child's performance levels, and the amount of adult assist needed.
2. *Task analysis of the curriculum.* Examine the tasks the child is expected to learn. Break the task into the components needed to perform the task.
3. *Relate the curriculum task to the child.* Coordinate the information gathered from both the analysis of the child and the analysis of the curriculum skills. This process leads to the development of a curriculum that is beneficial for an individual child.

## THE EARLY CHILDHOOD SPECIAL EDUCATION CURRICULUM: A MERGING OF TWO DISCIPLINES

The curriculum for young children who are at-risk or handicapped includes elements from both early childhood education and special education. Early childhood education contributes the philosophy of the "whole child" and the importance of considering all aspects of child growth in planning the curriculum. Special education contributes the concepts of individual differences and the process of task analysis in planning the curriculum. Thus, the early childhood special education curriculum must meet the special needs of the child's handicap, but it also must provide a balanced program that considers all aspects of the child's growth and welfare (Anastasiow, 1981).

### Family Involvement

A critical element in the early childhood special education curriculum is the consideration of the total family system. The family system consists of

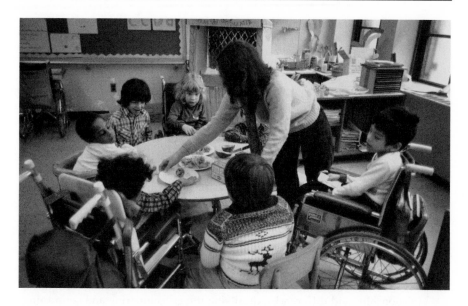

the child's network of interpersonal relationships and can include mother, father, grandparents, sisters, brothers, and others who have a relationship with the child. The child's learning within the school environment is closely linked to events and relationships within the family system.

For example, handicapped and at-risk children and their family system face unusual kinds of stress on many occasions, which can interfere with the child's learning. The curriculum should include plans for helping the child as well as the parents and the entire family system develop strategies to cope with these stressful situations (Zeitlin, 1981). (See Chapter 3 for a further discussion of the role of the family.)

### Elements of the Curriculum

A comprehensive curriculum should offer at-risk and handicapped preschoolers the needed stimulation and practice in many skill areas. These activities help the child develop skills for current living and also lay the foundation for later academic learning (Hayden and Smith, 1978; Kaczmaret and Dell, 1981). Intervention and teaching activities for each of these curriculum areas are presented in the related chapters in the balance of this book.

*Self-help skills and self-concept*—These skills enable children to take care of themselves and include activities such as dressing, eating, and personal hygiene. Learning self-help skills promotes the development of a positive self-concept and feelings of independence. (See Chapters 7 and 10).

*Gross motor activities*—Activities for gross motor skills involve the large muscles used to move the arms, legs, torso, hands, and feet. They include walking, crawling, climbing, jumping, throwing, and rolling activities. (See Chapter 7.)

*Fine motor activities*—These skills involve the small muscles used to move the fingers, wrists, eye–hand coordination, and coordination of the two hands. They include puzzles, finger games, cutting and pasting, painting, buttoning, and lacing. (See Chapter 7.)

*Communication activities*—The ability to use language to communicate one's thoughts is key to learning. Receptive language describes the ability to understand the language of others and includes the activities of listening and responding to instructions and hearing stories. Expressive language describes the ability to initiate communications and involves the activities of talking, conversation and explaining. (See Chapter 8.)

*Visual activities*—These are activities that develop visual discrimination, visual memory, and visual–motor integration. They include recognizing differences and similarities in pictures and shapes, and coordinating vision with body movement, such as eye–hand coordination. (See Chapter 7.)

*Auditory activities*—These are activities that help the child practice auditory identification of sounds, auditory discrimination of sounds, and auditory memory. Activities include word games, rhyming games, and word memory games. (See Chapter 8.)

*Cognitive activities*—Cognitive activities help the child practice thinking skills. They include reasoning, storing and remembering information, recognizing relationships and differences, classifying things, comparing and contrasting, and problem solving. Many play activities help children develop cognitive skills. (See Chapter 9.)

*Social activities*—An important element of the curriculum is the development of social skills. This includes learning to interact and get along with others by forming age appropriate relationships with other children and adults. (See Chapter 10.)

### Scheduling Components of the Curriculum

A sample class schedule for an early childhood special education one half-day class is shown in Table 6.1. The half day may be scheduled during the morning session or the afternoon session.

### PRINCIPLES FOR EARLY CHILDHOOD SPECIAL EDUCATION PROGRAMMING

There are several key principles for curriculum planning in early childhood special education. As indicated in Figure 6.1, each of these principles must be considered in relation to the others.

1. *Plan for teaching the "whole" child.* The curriculum should be balanced with emphasis on the child's general growth and development, including physical, social, emotional, cognitive, and language aspects of child development.

2. *Meet the child's special needs.* The curriculum should take into account the child's individual needs, limitations, and the goals and objectives developed for the child's IEP (Individualized Education Program). Have realistic expectations. The child's handicap may impact on what can be accomplished and limit performance.

**TABLE 6.1  Early Childhood Special Education**

CLASS SCHEDULE

| A.M. Time | P.M. Time | Activity* |
|---|---|---|
| 8:45–9:00 | 12:30–12:45 | Calendar: days of week, weather |
| 8:45–9:00 | 12:30–12:45 | Show and Tell |
| 9:00–9:30 | 12:45–1:15 | Movement activity—Wednesday and Friday |
| 9:00–9:30 | 12:45–1:15 | Gym—Tuesday and Thursday |
| 9:30–10:15 | 1:15–2:00 | Individual work; includes free choice of activity, a fine-motor project, cognitive activities, and socialization activities as cited on IEPs. |
| 10:15–10:20 | 2:00–2:05 | Cleanup |
| 10:20–10:40 | 2:05–2:25 | Snack: set table, wash hands, brush teeth. |
| 10:40–10:45 | 2:25–2:30 | Reading: children choose a book and "read" to themselves, to each other, or with an adult. |
| 10:45–11:05 | 2:30–2:50 | Group: activities vary daily to include review of cognitive concepts, music, fingerplays, individual projects, discussion of pertinent events, and group decisions, as cited on IEPs. |
| 11:05–11:15 | 2:50–3:00 | Dismissal: put on coats, distribute notes. |

*Therapist works one-to-one or in groups, both in the classroom and in private/individual therapy settings.

3.  *Sequence the units of information.* Curriculum planning requires careful ordering of instructional units into teachable steps. This may mean breaking a skill the child is to learn into subskills or steps. Make sure the child learns each step of the lesson before proceeding to the next step. Modifications may be necessary along the way.

4.  *Pace the teaching for the child's needs.* Plan the day so that the activities are varied. Alternate between active and quiet activities, between organized projects and free play. Do not go so quickly that the child is overburdened; on the other hand, do not go so slowly that the child is not challenged. Use a variety of instructional approaches to take advantage of new materials, methods, and settings.

5.  *Reward the child's efforts.* The curriculum should include plans for positively encouraging and reinforcing the child's efforts, even when only partial success is achieved. Many kinds of recognition and rewards for efforts can be used, ranging from verbal praise to concrete rewards.

6.  *Work with the family.* Establish a good working relationship with the child's parents and family. The curriculum should include both home and school learning. Schools and parents must establish a trusting relationship to encourage the transfer of learning between home and school.

## DESIGNING A COMPREHENSIVE CURRICULUM

The early childhood special education teacher tries to take advantage of all learning opportunities. Although the teaching is usually accomplished in a school setting, a child's learning is not limited to schoolrooms or school

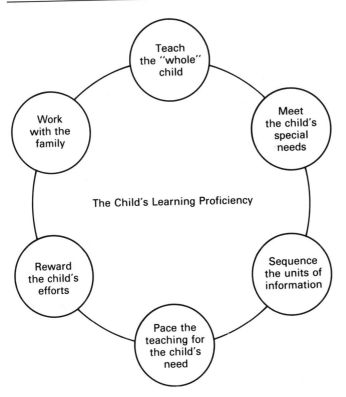

**FIGURE 6.1**   Principles for Teaching Young Children with Special Needs

buildings. Instruction can take place in many other places, such as parks, school buses, field trips, the public library, the corner pet shop, or in the home.

In designing the curriculum, the teacher must decide on the *content* (the subject matter and skills the child is to learn) and the *methods* (the techniques and materials that will most effectively teach that content). Once the content and methods are selected, effective teaching requires that the information, materials, and methods for a lesson be assembled and offered to the learner in a planned and organized manner.

Four major considerations of curriculum design are (1) the *purposes* that are to be accomplished through the curriculum plan: (2) the *educational experiences* to achieve those purposes: (3) the effective *organization* of the learning experiences; and (4) the *evaluation,* to determine whether the goals and objectives have been reached. Each is discussed in the following section.

### Setting Purposes for the Curriculum

The foundation for a curriculum is set by selecting the major purpose or purposes of the program. The selection of purposes depends to some extent upon the educational orientation of the curriculum developer. Two different philosophical orientations can affect the setting of purposes: (1) the subject-matter orientation and (2) child-centered orientation.

*Subject-matter orientation.* Teachers with this perspective are inclined to be more concerned with teaching the content or subject matter of the lesson. The curriculum is organized to adjust the order, speed, and complexity with which the subject material is presented. Often called a *basic skills approach* to curriculum development, this view sets goals of competence in the fundamental skills of basic subjects that each child is expected to acquire.

*Child-centered orientation.* Teachers with this perspective are inclined to be more concerned with the process of child growth and development—with the child's unique needs, learning patterns, and motivation. Materials and methods are selected that will meet the child's individual needs and will be motivating and stimulating to the child. Often called a *child-centered approach* to curriculum development, the view focuses on the child rather than the content.

*Combining both orientations.* In actual practice, curriculum planning for the young exceptional child requires both perspectives. The curriculum plan should provide for the learning of specific predetermined skills and knowledge, but it also should provide for the child's growth and development through participation in a variety of stimulating experiences. Therefore, in setting purposes it is important to (1) identify the content of skills to be learned; (2) understand the child's needs in terms of learning styles, rate of learning, handicapping conditions, abilities and disabilities; and also (3) identify gaps between the present level of skills and some standard level of expected performance in a content area.

Once general purposes and goals have been selected, these goals must be subdivided into specific objectives. By stating each specific or short-term objective along with the expected changes in performance that are anticipated, it is easier to plan the teaching and to monitor change. Each objective should include the conditions for learning and the material to be used (Mager, 1962). Thus, short-term objectives provide the steps for reaching the general purpose or overall goal.

### Selecting Experiences to Meet Purposes

The teacher also must select a series of learning experiences to help the child reach the goal. Learning experiences are most effective when activities are dynamic and the child is an active participant. The setting should be organized in a way that invites the child to learn. Ample time and opportunities to practice the skills should be included in the curriculum plan.

---

### CASE EXAMPLE—NAOMI: GOALS AND OBJECTIVES

Four-year-old Naomi is a child with a problem in language. The general goal (or purpose) and short-term objectives for Naomi are

**Goal**

To increase the quantity of expressive oral language.

**Short-term Objectives**

1.  Naming objects through imitation
2.  Spontaneous naming of random objects
3.  Naming colors through imitation (given a set of specific colors)
4.  Spontaneous naming of colors without cues
5.  Constructing two-word phrases through imitation
6.  Spontaneous construction of phrases using a vocabulary pool from previous lessons
7.  Using self-initiated small phrases in reply to simple questions.

The level of acceptable performance for each objective should be set. For example, it could be set as the number of times that correct terms are used (that is, 80 percent of the time or 8 out of 10 times). Also, it would be appropriate to specify the environmental conditions in which the behavior should be demonstrated. For example, given a visual presentation (pictures of the primary colors of red, blue, yellow, and green) the child will name the colors through imitation (modeling) with 100 percent accuracy during a 30-minute therapy session.

---

Many kinds of experiences and a wide range of methods can be used to meet specific objectives. Often one learning experience can be used to meet more than a single objective. For preschool children, the activity itself becomes the support for other closely aligned goals. Running, jumping, crawling, and poking are fun activities for a young child and help satisfy the child's need to move. The pleasure gained from the sheer physical sensation of movement is linked to the activity itself.

Sometimes many children participate in the same activity, yet each child has an individual perception of that experience. One preschooler may be very interested in the information being presented and give undivided attention. Another child may find the activities interesting at the start, but become distracted by some small toy or unfamiliar sound. Even though the same learning activity has been selected for the two children, the experience is quite different for each of them. It is more difficult to arrange learning situations when the child is easily distracted or thinks the particular activity is not interesting. In such situations, the teacher must be particularly creative modifying the planned activity and broadening the content to limit distractions while kindling the child's interest. The teacher should consider each child's needs and when organizing learning experiences for that child.

### Organizing Learning Experiences

*Units, topics, and lessons.* There are three levels of curriculum organization: (1) *a lesson,* (2) *a topic,* and (3) *a unit.* The *lesson* is the smallest element and includes all of the plans for a single day's instruction. (For example, a lesson could be on elephants.) The *topic* is broader in scope and involves plans for several lessons. (For example, the topic may be on animals in the zoo.) The *unit* is the largest element of the curriculum structure. The information for the unit is more extensive, is constructed around a major interest or purpose, and is worked upon for a longer period of time. (For example, the unit may be on the zoo.)

Unit: The zoo
Topic: Animals of the zoo
Lessons: Elephants

The *lesson plan* is a written guide to help organize, assemble, and plan the day's instruction step by step. The lesson plan includes several phases: (1) the objective of the lesson; (2) the materials that will be used; (3) the procedures for the lessons; and (4) the method for evaluating what has been learned. As an illustration, in the early childhood curriculum, some time is usually spent on the *unit* of the calendar. The purpose of the calendar unit is to help the children understand time relationships and the succession of days of the week, month, and dates for each of the days of the month. As part of the daily activities, the *lesson* on calendars may involve correctly placing a single number on a chart of that specific month and week. It may involve counting the days of the week or days of the month to find the correct date. The *topic* may be the succession of the months within a year. It may be necessary to have many lessons to complete the calendar for a specific month.

*Principles of Curriculum Organization.* The organization of effective learning experiences depends upon three principles: (1) continuity, (2) sequence, and (3) integration.

*Continuity* is the recurring use of concepts among and within other parts of the lesson. For example, if recognizing color is selected as an objective, then this concept will be presented again and again in various parts of other units. Continuity is a thread by which major concepts are supported or reinforced with continued emphasis. Continuity often is thought of as a spiraling process, a method by which repetition occurs at regular intervals but at successively higher levels of complexity (Bruner et al., 1967).

*Sequence* is the successive steps of the curriculum. Each unit is built upon a previous experience but expands upon the skill in a broader application. Pieces of information may be presented in succession, but with each added layer of knowledge there is greater depth or complexity to the content.

*Integration* is the way in which all of the curriculum elements relate to each other. Experiences should be organized so that there is unity among the program elements. The skills selected for instruction should be usable in other areas. *Generalization* is the systematic occurrence of appropriate behavior within new situations. The curriculum should help the child generalize what has been learned. The program should coordinate learning experiences rather than teach isolated skills (Kaczmaret and Dell, 1981). For example, teaching the fine motor skill of the pincer grasp (using the thumb and index finger to pick up small objects) can be accomplished during many activities: during snack, cleanup, and/or an art project. In turn, this acquired skill assists the child in holding a tool for writing or cutting.

### Evaluating Learning Outcomes

The final aspect of curriculum design is the plan to evaluate the outcome or the result of the instruction. Did the child reach the goal and learn as expected?

The reason for teaching is to bring about change in the behavior of the child. To evaluate the curriculum one must ask what the consequences of the lessons are in terms of the child's behavior. If the child is unchanged or unaffected by the lesson, then the purposes of the curriculum have not been reached. It is important to continuously appraise a child's performance and to obtain measures more than once. Usually, it is advisable to have a measure of performance prior to the instruction and another measure after that instruction is completed. In this way the teacher can see if there was change over a specific period of time.

There are several ways to monitor a child's progress. The teacher can evaluate behavior by simply observing the child's reactions. The teacher can also collect work samples that demonstrate the performance of the child, a technique called *sampling*. The evaluation method, however, should provide some tangible evidence of skill mastery.

An example of content goals and behavioral evidence of its accomplishment for a kindergarten is shown in Table 6.2.

The child should be given many opportunities over time to demonstrate that the skill has been mastered. For example, if the objective of the lesson is to increase the child's ability to express ideas orally, the evaluation must provide opportunities for the child to demonstrate oral expressive behavior. Bailey, Harms, and Clifford (1983) suggest five ways that changes in behavior can be measured readily in young children: (1) *engage-*

*ment* (meaningful involvement in an activity); (2) *independence* (completing an activity without direct teacher supervision); (3) *aggression* (physical or verbal behavior initiated to cause hurt to another person or object); (4) *social interaction* (interactions with other children); and (5) *happiness* (behavior indicating joy and pleasure).

## SUMMARY

A *curriculum* is a planned arrangement of experiences that are designed to bring about changes in a child's behavior.

The curriculum for early childhood special education combines elements from two fields: (1) early childhood education and (2) special education.

There are several curriculum models for early childhood education. The *enrichment curriculum* emphasizes teaching the "whole" child and encouraging opportunities for exploration and child-oriented learning. The *directed teaching curriculum* emphasizes the direct teaching of teacher-selected skills. The *cognitive emphasis curriculum* is designed to enhance thinking skills. The *custodial care curriculum* meets the needs of working parent (s) and emphasizes care-taking aspects, such as is found in daycare centers. The *combination curriculum* combines elements from the four previous curriculum types.

The curriculum for special education is designed to meet the needs of exceptional children. Key concepts in special education programs are (1) meeting individual differences and (2) task analysis. Two concepts of individual differences are *interindividual differences* (how the child compares to others of similar age) and *intraindividual differences* (how abilities within an individual child compare with each other). Two approaches to task analysis are analysis of the *child* and analysis of the *task*.

The early childhood special education curriculum must involve the family system—the network of relationships that impact the child. Principles to be considered in teaching include (1) the "whole" child, (2) special needs; (3) sequencing; (4) pacing; (5) reinforcing efforts; and (6) working with the family.

The structure of the curriculum consists of three levels: a lesson, a topic, and a unit.

Four major considerations of curriculum design are; (1) purposes of the curriculum; (2) the educational experiences; (3) organization; and (4) evaluation.

## REVIEW QUESTIONS

### Terms to Know

curriculum
task analysis
interindividual differences
intraindividual differences

"whole" child
lesson plan
short-term objectives
enrichment curriculum

1. Using the calendar for a year, give an example of a coordinated lesson, topic, and unit for early childhood special education for each month of the school year.

**TABLE 6.2  Content Goals and Behavioral Evidence of Accomplishment**

| CONTENT GOALS | BEHAVIORAL EVIDENCE | KINDERGARTEN GRADE LEVEL |
|---|---|---|
| | Each indicator is one of many that can assess a student's performance. Others may be used if they are more appropriate for the learner. | |
| The student should: | The student can: | |
| 1. Identify basic colors. | 1a. Identify color of crayons.<br>b. Name the colors as they are shown.<br>c. Color an object a specific color as directed.<br>d. Match one color to its mate using teacher-made materials. | |
| 2. Recognize likenesses and differences in color, shape, position, and size of objects. | 2a. Group attribute blocks.<br>b. Choose the object that is different in a group.<br>c. Distinguish differences in pictures, letters, or numbers.<br>d. Sort pictures into categories. | |
| 3. Identify everyday familiar sounds. | 3a. Listen to sounds and identify them.<br>b. Identify animal sounds in songs (i.e., "Old MacDonald").<br>c. Recognize voices of classmates. | |
| 4. Know left and right. | 4a. Draw a line from left to right.<br>b. Follow a sentence with hand moving from left to right.<br>c. Know difference of left hand and right hand.<br>d. Look at pictures from left to right. | |
| 5. Recognize rhyming words. | 5a. Recognize words that rhyme when listening to a story or nursery rhyme.<br>b. Answer yes or no when asked if two words rhyme.<br>c. Recall orally one word that rhymes with another. | |

**TABLE 6.2  Content Goals and Behavioral Evidence of Accomplishment (cont.)**

| CONTENT GOALS | BEHAVIORAL EVIDENCE | KINDERGARTEN GRADE LEVEL |
|---|---|---|
| 6. Understand directional words. | 6a. Place an object in a given direction.<br>b. Point to positions on a picture. | |
| 7. Follow oral directions. | 7a. Perform three commands in sequence.<br>b. Participate in "Simon Says."<br>c. Act out directions on movement records. | |
| 8. Be able to coordinate eye and hand movement. | 8a. Lace picture cards.<br>b. Cut on a line.<br>c. Draw around an object. | |
| 9. Know the upper- and lower-case letters of the alphabet. | 9a. Recall orally the flash card letters selected at random.<br>b. Match the upper and lower case of each letter.<br>c. Write alphabet letters when dictated. | |
| 10. Hear the beginning sounds of consonants. | 10a. Name the letter when teacher makes the beginning consonant sound.<br>b. Respond with a word when given a consonant. | |
| 11. Sequence pictures. | 11. Arrange three pictures in proper order. | |
| 12. Retell a story in order. | 12. Listen to a story and retell it. | |
| 13. Show interest in books and stories. | 13a. Pay attention during storytime.<br>b. Pretend to read to other children.<br>c. Look at books during quiet time.<br>d. Relate story details to pictures. | |

2. What elements are included in constructing a comprehensive curriculum?

3. Three components to be considered in organizing learning experiences are *continuity, sequence,* and *integration.* How does each contribute to the organization of learning experiences?

4. Give your analysis of the sequence of the steps of learning toileting skills.

5. Four early childhood curriculum models are discussed in this chapter. Which model appeals to you and why?

6. Curriculum practices in early childhood special education combine ideas from both early childhood and special education. What are some of the contributions of each field to early childhood special education?

7. Do a task analysis of making a peanut butter and jelly sandwich:
   a. from an analysis of the child perspective.
   b. from an analysis of the task perspective.
   c. from an analysis of the child perspective for a child with a paralysis of one arm.

8. Assume you are the chairperson of a foundation that will fund educational research in early childhood special education curricula. What topics would you suggest for further study?

## REFERENCES

ANASTASIOW, N. (1981) "Early Childhood Education for the Handicapped in the 1980's: Recommendations." *Exceptional Children,* 47, 276–82.

BAILEY, D., T. HARMS, and R. CLIFFORD (1983) "Matching Changes in Preschool Environments to Desired Changes in Child Behavior." *Journal of the Division for Early Childhood,* 7, 61–68.

BRUNER, J. et al. (1967) *Studies in Cognitive Growth.* NY: John Wiley.

HAYDEN, A. and R. SMITH (1978) *Mainstreaming Preschoolers: Children with Learning Disabilities.* U.S. Department of Health and Human Services. Washington, DC: Government Printing Office.

KACZMARET, L. and A. DELL (1981) "Designing Instructional Activities for Young Handicapped Children." *Journal of the Division for Early Childhood,* 2, 74–83.

KIRK, S. and J. GALLAGHER (1986) *Educating Exceptional Children.* Boston: Houghton Mifflin.

MAGER, R. (1962) *Preparing Instructional Objectives.* Palo Alto, CA: Fearon.

MONTESSORI, M. (1964) *The Montessori Method.* NY: Bently.

PIAGET, J. (1971) *Biology and Knowledge.* Chicago: University of Chicago Press.

SCHWEINHART, L. and D. WEIKART (1980) *Young Children Grow Up: The Effects of the Perry Preschool Project Through Age Fifteen.* Ypsilanti, MI: High Scope Press.

WALTER, G. and L. VINCENT (1982) "The Handicapped Child in the Regular Classroom." *Journal of the Division for Early Childhood,* 6, 84–95.

ZEITLIN, S. (1981) "Coping, Stress, and Learning." *Journal of the Division for Early Childhood,* 2, 102–8.

# SEVEN

# Teaching Motor and Perceptual Skills

## INTRODUCTION

The subject of this chapter—motor and perceptual skills—reflects the first learnings of young children. The chapter (1) analyzes the integration of the sensory, motor, and perceptual systems; (2) reviews the normal sequence of motor and perceptual development; (3) reviews theories concerning atypical motor and perceptual development; (4) analyzes the characteristics of motor impairments; and (5) suggests instructional strategies for teaching motor and perceptual skills.

Children come into the world as active, curious creatures, eager to learn. In order to learn and benefit from the world about them, children need fundamental motor capabilities. The infant's early movements and reflex reactions provide the foundation for all subsequent learning. For infants, learning begins with their own body movements. For young children, motor activities and perceptual experiences set the stage for more complex motor, perceptual, and cognitive learning. As children learn through sensory and motor experiences, they develop motor and perceptual skills that promote intellectual and cognitive growth (McClenaghan and Gallahue, 1978; Corbin, 1973; Espenschade and Eckert 1980).

Young children who lack normal motor experiences or who have delays in motor development are deprived of the foundation of the early

learning process. These children need careful assessment of their motor abilities and disabilities and the provision of planned motor intervention and instruction (Folio & Fewell, 1983; Schurr, 1975; Caldwell and Stedman, 1977).

## SENSORY, MOTOR, AND PERCEPTUAL SYSTEMS

The learning of motor and perceptual behavior is complex, involving several different systems. Through the *sensory system,* the child receives sensory stimuli from the environment. Through the *motor system,* the child engages in physical bodily movement. Through the *perceptual system,* the child recognizes and interprets sensory information. Children become increasingly adept at directing their body in motor activity and intergrating the sensory, motor, and perceptual systems through a progressive development of these systems.

There are different theories of motor behavior and how these systems are integrated during the learning process. Each theory of motor behavior describes interconnecting threads between levels of sensation, perception, and motor learning. For example, Bower (1977) describes the process as intersensory differentiation. Piaget (1969) explains it through the dual process of assimilation and accommodation.

Bruner (1973) explains movement with precision as the means by which the child demonstrates an understanding and interpretation through intention, feedback, and patterns of action mediation. Cratty (1975, 1979) classifies early perceptual patterns as latticed behaviors and attributes which are intertwined in psychomotor and cognitive domains of behavior.

### The Sensory System

The sensory system is composed of the five sense organs: the eyes, ears, nose, mouth, and skin. The child receives the stimuli or sensations from the environment through sight, sound, smell, taste, and touch. For example, infants might see the movement of a mobile above their bed, hear the noise of a rattle, or feel the touch of their mother on their face. These sensations are pieces of information that are funneled through the nervous system pathways to the brain, where they are stored for later use. The child learns to integrate the various components of the sensory system and to link them with motor acts.

### The Motor System

There are several levels of motor system functions. They range from innate reflex motor behavior of the newborn infant to complex motor acts.

---

## CASE EXAMPLE—GREGG: MOTOR DIFFICULTIES

Gregg, age 4 years and 5 months, was attending the local park district preschool program. During the regular conference session scheduled for all new children in the program, the preschool teacher shared some concerns about Gregg with his parents. Although Gregg's social adjustment to preschool playmates seemed adequate, he was having some serious problems during group activities. He refused to participate in any of the instructional lessons requiring motor skills. Gregg's motor coordination was very awkward; he seemed to have problems with his balance; and he fell frequently during running games. He even fell off his chair while working and he could not catch or throw a ball. When Gregg was unable to perform the motor activities that the other children in the class were engaged in, he often became discouraged and angry. Paper and crayon projects also were difficult for him, and he performed so poorly that he deliberately avoided this type of activity. He was unable to cut with scissors or direct a crayon to do what he wanted. Gregg could only complete paper and crayon lessons when the teacher gave him special help during every step of the activity.

Gregg's parents said they were not surprised that motor activities in preschool were difficult and frustrating for him. They noted similar problems at home. They said that he has also become a management problem at home, becoming moody and defiant when given the simplest task. Gregg's parents said that when he was younger they had expressed their concerns about Gregg's delays in motor development to the pediatrician. Gregg was delayed in sitting, crawling, and walking. He did not crawl until 11 months and walked at 18 months. Currently, his walking gait still seems to be awkward. He has difficulty holding utensils and eating by himself. He still needs much help to dress himself. At times, he cannot manage his trousers quickly enough to use the toilet.

Gregg's parents and the preschool teacher requested that the local public school system do an assessment to evaluate Gregg's needs. The evaluation team found that Gregg does indeed have significant gross and fine motor delays. The team recommended that Gregg be placed in the early childhood special education program and that he receive adaptive physical education intervention, as well as an OT (occupational therapy) screening. He will be closely observed and reevaluated after a period of three months to determine further needs.

---

*Innate reflex motor behaviors.* These are automatic actions that enable infants to practice motor patterns over which they eventually will have voluntary control. The first actions of newborn infants are mostly reflex in origin—innate involuntary movements and needed supports for basic survival. Through consistent practice, these lower level functions become automatic. Through repeated experience and some selective choice, they can lead to higher level motor functions (Gardner, 1975). Innate reflex behaviors diminish in occurrence as the child develops greater voluntary control of the motor response system.

The reflexive motor behaviors of the newborn infant include *rooting, sucking, swallowing, startle (Moro) reflex,* the *Babinski reflex,* and *stepping.* Evaluation of the infant's innate reflex motor behaviors are often components of neonatal assessment scales (Brazelton, 1969; Prechl and Beintema, 1964).

Rooting, sucking, and swallowing are necessary for the location of food. *Rooting* is the turning of the head and mouth in search of the breast nipple. A soft touch to the awake infant's cheek will set this reflex into motion. *Sucking* allows the ingestion of liquids for nourishment. It can be initiated through a soft touch on the mouth or cheek. The lips purse and make inundating motions. *Swallowing* follows sucking but is in operation even during sleep. There is a need to keep the throat and nasal passages clear for breathing, so swallowing also helps to remove any mucus or fluid drainage of the sinuses.

The *Moro reflex* is a startle response, a sharp jolted action that follows a sudden change in sensation for the young infant. An example of a stimulus that can trigger the startle reflex is a sudden loud noise. In response to the noise, the infant's head falls back, the arms are thrust out to the sides of the body, and the legs stretch and extend. The infant cries and brings both arms together. The startle reflex diminishes in frequency and intensity as the infant's nervous system matures, until the residual response becomes a minor body flinch.

Another early reflex that diminishes through normal development is the *Babinski reflex.* This reflex is initiated by stroking the sole of the infant's foot. The infant responds by spreading or fanning his or her toes. This reflex normally disappears four to six months after birth.

*Stepping reflexes* are seen when the newborn is supported in an upright position and the feet are placed on a hard surface. The infant will make walking steps, alternating feet; but these reflexes also disappear a few weeks after birth.

As the child develops greater voluntary control of the motor response system, these innate reflexes normally diminish and eventually disappear.

**Muscle tone and control.**   *Muscle tone* refers to the potential a muscle has for action. Muscle capacity and control increase to provide support for an upright position and balance to assist in walking. As the child develops muscle control, many motor skills become refined. By age six, the child can perform many motor acts. However, it is important to note that there is a wide variance of motor skill and performance at early ages.

Normal motor behavior reflects a continuous progression of improved muscle control and capacity. Internal bodily processes are stabilizing. Breathing, digestion, and elimination become automatic processes. As external reactions of the infant are integrated, there is an increase of voluntary motor efficiency.

*Flexor tone* and *flexion* are essential muscle characteristics of the normal full-term infant. The arms and legs are somewhat fixed in a bent position and are rarely seen fully extended. This means that the arms and legs usually are positioned close to the body and are not easily straightened.

*Muscle activity.* An individual muscle is limited in its performance. A muscle can perform only two actions: it can contract and it can relax. When it contracts, the muscle becomes shorter. When it relaxes, the muscle lengthens. *Muscle activity* is dependent upon the position of the bones of the body (posture) and the attached muscle. The energy for this muscle activity is transmitted through nerves. Electrical impulses emanate from the brain and are transmitted through the spinal cord and outer nerve endings to the muscles. All muscle action is controlled by the specialized centers of the brain.

*Motor acts.* A *motor act* is a skill involving movement. It is a physically expressed movement of the human body and its parts. *Motor performance* involves large muscle action: muscles and bones moving together in a purposeful manner.

Once the brain receives the sensory information and identifies the content, proper action is dispatched. The response information is carried back through the nervous system pathway. The child performs an observable motor act. Examples of motor acts of infants occur when the infant follows or reaches for a mobile, turns the head toward a rattle, or responds with a facial expression to the mother's touch (Gardner, 1975; Robb, 1972).

Movement must become automatic to be effective. For movement to be normal, there must be a normal range of motion in each individual joint (Shepherd, 1980).

### The Perceptual System

*Perception* is the interpretive function of the brain. It is the translation or release of sensory impressions into some representational level that is stored and recalled. Interpretation is dependent upon previous experience and information. In reality, the functions of motor activity and perception are so closely related that it is difficult to separate one from another (Carterette and Friedman, 1973). The term *perceptual–motor* reflects this close interrelationship.

## SEQUENTIAL DEVELOPMENT OF MOTOR AND PERCEPTUAL BEHAVIORS

Research and observation show that there is a normal developmental sequence for motor and perceptual learning. Motor performance and the quality of movement begin at a simple stage and gradually become more complex as the child learns to integrate and combine simple motor movements into complex motor patterns (Bruner, 1973). Even children who have delays in acquiring movement patterns progress through this developmental motor sequence as they mature.

### Maturation and Readiness

The concept of *maturation* refers to physical and behavioral developments that occur through an innate growth process. The process of maturation affects all areas of development in children, including the sequential learning of motor skills. Thus, both learning and maturation are integral components of general development.

Another important concept in all areas of learning and development is the notion of *readiness*. Certain kinds of learning and behavioral changes cannot occur until the child has obtained the needed maturational level or is ready for that particular learning. Motor readiness depends upon many factors: heredity, past learnings, environmental experiences, and physical capabilities. For example, readiness for walking depends upon hereditary traits; past experiences with standing, balance, and cruising around furniture; and the child's stage of physical development.

### Principles of Sensorimotor Development

There are five major principles of sensorimotor progression (Conner, Williamson and Siepp, 1978; McGraw, 1969).

1. *Sequential development* Foundations of movement occur in a definite pattern and are integrated to combine and form new motor acts. The rate may vary but the sequence is usually fixed.

2. *Overlapping sequences* Babies are in a constant state of change. One skill may be in the process of being mastered along with the introduction of succeedingly difficult tasks.

3. *Dissociation* Sensorimotor maturity is demonstrated by independent body movement patterns. Gradually, the infant moves from a total responding organism to one that can separate body parts and select independent movement. The infant progresses from using the whole arm action to swipe at an object to the limited grasp of the object with only the fist or fingers.

4. *Cephalocaudal development* Development proceeds from the head to the feet. Motor control and coordination are achieved in the upper parts of the body and then progress down to the lower extremities. Head and trunk control precede leg control.

5. *Proximal–distal development* Development also progresses from the center of the body to the periphery or extremities. There is greater control of the shoulder and arm actions before there is individualized finger dexterity.

Table 7.1 shows sensorimotor development from birth to age four. This development illustrates the hierarchy of motor skills and the gradual increase of motor control.

**TABLE 7.1   Sensorimotor Development**

| MONTHS | TRUNK AND LIMB CONTROL | HAND AND FINGER CONTROL |
|---|---|---|
| 0–4 | Head turning-control<br>Head lifting on forearms | Flexion of arms and legs<br>Partial extension<br>Hand to mouth, finger sucking<br>Unilateral arm, leg movement |
| 4–6 | Supports body weight with arms<br>While on stomach supports weight<br>by stretching arms and legs out<br>from support<br>Dissociation of head, limbs | Reaches for visual objects<br>Brings hands together<br>Bring objects to mouth<br>Feet to mouth<br>Bilateral arm, leg movement |
| 6–8 | Prone pivot<br>Trunk extension<br>Backward push<br>Trunk control<br>Supported upright sitting | Radial hand grasp<br>Shakes objects<br>Bangs objects |
| 8–12 | Trunk rotation<br>Segmented body movement<br>Chest off floor (support on hands, knees)<br>Propels body forward<br>Belly crawling, creeping<br>Unsupported upright sitting<br>Body rocking, bouncing (flexion and extension)<br>Pull to stand<br>Cruising | Thumb, index finger grasp<br>Voluntary grasp, release<br>Purposeful squeeze<br>Inferior pincer grasp<br>Individualized finger agility |
| 12–18 | Creeping<br>Forward walking, supported<br>Forward walking, unsupported | Plantar flexion<br>Hip extension, toes extension<br>Superior princer grasp |
| 18–24 | Independent erect standing<br>Changes positions from sit to stand<br>Changes positions from prone to supine<br>Fast walking<br>Wobbly gait<br>Walks upstairs, assisted<br>Walks downstairs, assisted<br>Kicks ball forward | Independent use of thumb<br>Releases object at target<br>Pours objects from container<br>Uses whole arm movements in painting<br>Throws ball overhand, two hands |
| 24–36 | Pedals trike<br>Reciprocal walk, alternate arm swing<br>Ascend and descend stairs (nonalternate feet)<br>Running<br>Jump, holding on | Dresses self<br>Attempts buttoning<br>Zippers<br>Buckles<br>Strings beads<br>Uses scissors, pencils |

**TABLE 7.1 (Cont.)**

| MONTHS | TRUNK AND LIMB CONTROL | HAND AND FINGER CONTROL |
|--------|------------------------|-------------------------|
|        | Step-jump<br>Hop<br>Walks on tiptoe | |
| 36–48  | Fast run<br>Skillful jump, continuous-forward<br>Skillful hopping<br>Can walk a balance beam<br>Can climb on playground<br>  equipment<br>Can imitate one body part<br>  movement | |

### Piaget's Stages of Child Development

The research and writings of the Swiss psychologist Jean Piaget (1969) emphasize the nature of the developmental sequence that occurs as the child matures. Piaget observed that as children mature, their mode of thinking and their cognitive abilities change. The progressive development begins with the basic reflex activities of the newborn and leads to complex acquired behaviors of abstract thinking. Several sequential stages of child development are identified: (1) the sensorimotor stage (ages birth to two); (2) the preoperation stage (ages two to seven); (3) the concrete operational stage (ages seven to eleven); and (4) the formal operations stage (age eleven or older) (Piaget, 1952). Of course, these ages are only suggestive; the actual ages for the occurrence of each stage is different for each child. The important finding of Piaget's work is that these stages develop sequentially; each stage depends upon a foundation of learning of the previous stage. Of major concern in this chapter is the sensorimotor stage. Other stages of Piaget's stages of development are discussed under cognitive skills (see Chapter 9).

Piaget's sensorimotor stage of development covers the first two years of life, the period from birth until the emergence of language. The sensorimotor stage is the most fundamental stage of development; that is, all higher learning depends upon the learning that occurs during the sensorimotor stage. During this period of time, the child changes from a self-satisfying reflex-bound creature to a child who can adapt and is capable of rather complex environmental interactions. Simple motor habits are formed and voluntary control comes into operation.

Other aspects of Piaget's theory of learning, including the development of cognitive structures through the processes of assimilation and accommodation, are discussed in Chapter 9.

## ATYPICAL MOTOR DEVELOPMENT: THEORETICAL PERSPECTIVES

Basic principles about motor learning as they affect exceptional children are

1. *Human learning begins with motor learning.* As human beings move, they learn. An understanding of the dynamics of learning necessarily involves an understanding of movement and motor development.
2. *There is a natural sequence of developmental motor stages.* Each stage must be successfully acquired by the child before the next stage is added.
3. *Academic and cognitive learning is based on successful motor learning experiences.* A child's academic and cognitive problems may be due to insufficient motor experiences and gaps in motor learning.
4. *Planned motor intervention can provide children with missing motor experiences.* Building motor skills prepares the child for academic and cognitive learning.

In the field of special education, there are a number of theories about how motor and perceptual development differ in exceptional children and the effects of motor dysfunction on other areas of learning. Three theories of the effects of inadequate motor development on handicapped children are reviewed in this section, each representing the views of a different discipline. (1) The theories of Kephart are based on concepts from learning and motor theory. (2) The theories of Ayres are based on concepts of sensory integration. (3) The theories of Cratty are based on the concepts of adaptive physical education.

### Kephart: Learning and Motor Theory

Newell Kephart (1971) strove to understand handicapped children by adapting basic concepts of learning and motor theory. His ideas have been a major force in understanding the role of motor and perceptual development in motor and perceptual disorders. A number of concepts laid the foundation for Kephart's ideas.

Perceptual–motor development is very important in children's overall learning, helping them develop a solid and reliable concept of the world about them. Children who do not have normal perceptual–motor experiences cannot develop a stable and reliable perceptual–motor notion of the world. They encounter problems when confronted with symbolic materials and thinking tasks. These children are disorganized motorically, perceptually, and cognitively.

In the process of motor learning, the child must learn much more than a sequence of motor skills. Motor development consists of the learning of motor patterns and a sequential refinement of basic motor generalizations. In Kephart's view, the child must learn four basic motor generalizations: (1) balance and posture (learning about keeping one's balance); (2)

locomotion (learning about moving toward an object); (3) contact–manipulation (learning about grasping for objects); and (4) receipt and propulsion (learning about catching and throwing objects) (Chaney and Kephart, 1968).

The orderly development of motor skills depends upon the child's ability to match perceptual information with motor information. The child must learn to match the motoric world (that is physically experienced) with the perceptual world. For example, when a child sees a block (perceptual information), the child must match it with the physical experiences of holding, throwing, and biting the block (motor information). Inaccuracies of the perceptual–motor match are seen as causes of many learning problems. Children who lack perceptual–motor experiences and skills do not have the basic foundation for cognitive learning.

According to Kephart, the child with developmental problems needs intensive remediation of perceptual–motor skills. Perceptual–motor experiences give the child a more secure and trustworthy sense of the qualities of the physical universe, which in turn provides the foundation for later academic learning.

### Ayres: Sensory–Motor Integration

Jean Ayres (1975, 1978, 1981) presents a theory of motor learning from the perspective of occupational therapy. Recognizing the complex principles of brain physiology and function, the job of occupational therapists is to prescribe specific motor therapy and exercises to modify the brain function of patients with various kinds of debilitating motor problems. Ayres has applied this knowledge and experience to children with developmental problems. Her theory is that these children have deficits in sensorimotor integration. Special motor activities are therefore designed to improve the child's sensory–motor integration, and it is thought that this improvement will lead to improvement in many other areas of the child's development.

*Sensory–motor integration* is a neurophysiological process through which sensory information is organized and interpreted. Learning is described as a highly complex function of the central nervous system, which takes in, sorts out, and connects information from the environment. The child receives environmental information through the sensory system; the brain integrates this information with stored data that was acquired through past experiences; and a complex feedback system integrates data from several sensory avenues. Since the child's brain has the quality of plasticity, or adaptability, the assumption is that the brain system can be organized through movement activities.

Thus, sensory integration theory suggests that brain function in handicapped children can be modified through therapy designed to stimulate sensory integration within the brain and thereby normalize behavior.

The visual and auditory sensory systems receive much educational emphasis because of their obvious classroom applications. Sensory integration involves stimulating three other sensory systems: the vestibular system, the tactile system, and the proprioceptive system. The *vestibular* system enables one to detect motion; the *tactile* system involves the sense of touch and stimulation of skin surfaces; the *proprioceptive* system involves the stimulation from within the body itself (the digestive system, nerves, joints, ligaments, and bone receptors). Occupational therapists offer methods of therapy that include activities to stimulate these three systems. *Tactile* stimulation occurs through touching and rubbing skin surfaces; *vestibular* stimulation occurs through activities such as swinging, spinning, and being rolled on a large ball; and *proprioceptive* stimulation occurs through scooter board activities (Hinojosa, 1982).

*Tactile defensiveness* describes the behaviors of children with impairments in the tactile and vestibular systems. These children tend to withdraw from tactile sensations. They dislike having their hair combed, hugging or touching, playing with fuzzy textures, or rolling up their shirt-

sleeves. In some cases, these children will manipulate objects only with the tips of their fingers, avoiding the palms of their hands, or they will walk on their toes, rather than on the whole soles of their feet. These children may have difficulty relating to other children because they will interpret typical jostling play as aggressive or attacking and will respond accordingly. Some children may touch or explore the environment and seek out tactile stimuli but they must be the ones to initiate and control the stimuli. If touched by someone else, the child may react negatively. Often children displaying many of these serious behaviors are defined as autistic or autistic-like youngsters.

The indiscriminate use of sensory integration for all handicapped children is controversial and lacks conclusive research support (Sellick and Over, 1980). Some authorities suggest that decreases in vestibular stimulation may be a component of disturbed interaction patterns between new mothers and their handicapped infants (Thomas, Becker, and Freese, 1978). However, Sandler and Coren (1981) found that vestibular stimulation—rocking and spinning—was useful with premature infants.

### Cratty: Adaptive Physical Education

Cratty (1975, 1979) approaches the problem of motor and perceptual development from the perspective of the field of standard and adaptive physical education. Cratty emphasizes the importance of game activities to help the child with developmental delays improve generalized movement, to develop a feeling of achievement and total well-being, and to garner social peer acceptance. The standard physical education activities are modified to meet the special needs of children with motor problems. Adaptive physical education helps the child improve fundamental movement skills, develop stronger and more agile physical abilities, and improve motor performance. As a result, the child's stability, agility, flexibility, and strength increase along with general motor efficiency.

One problem with standard physical education classes is that children are directed toward activity mastery; for example, grades are given for the quality of the basic motor skill rather than the process-oriented development of motor patterns. Another problem for preschoolers is that they are not usually in attendance in public schools so that they do not have the opportunity to participate in the standard physical education classes until they reach kindergarten or primary grades.

Kalakian and Eichstaedt (1982) support the need for adaptive physical education. They suggest that physical education services follow a revision of the cascade model of least restrictive special services. (See Figure 5.5, Chapter 5.) Progress is to be evaluated by participation and development rather than through event mastery. Figure 7.1 shows a cascade of adaptive physical education services for children with motor needs.

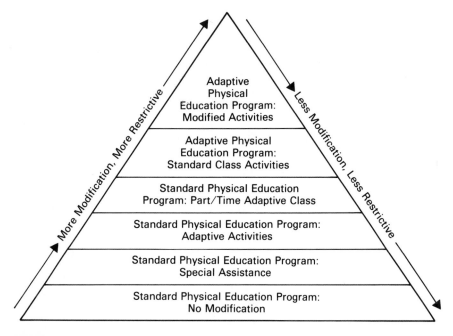

**FIGURE 7.1**

## CHARACTERISTICS OF MOTOR IMPAIRMENTS

There is a normal wide range of motor skill development in young children. The stages of development are not completed by all children of a given age at equal intervals. Often a child who has a considerable lag will make large and uneven growth spurts in motor achievement. Uneven rates of growth may indicate only a different developmental pattern. However, when differences in movement and motor capabilities affect the child's educational progress, parents and teachers need to consider options for assistance and remediation. Dysfunctions in motor proficiency and motor skill performance reflect the child's handicap and the severity of the handicapping condition.

### Atypical Motor Stages

The child whose motor milestones are different from the established norm may show one of the following patterns:

*Stage skipping:* A child may skip one or several of the regular stages and achieve a mature motor pattern at an earlier age than expected.

*Stage deviation:* A child may fail to make significant progress and remain at an immature stage indefinitely.

*Partial stages:* A child may acquire partial skills and not fit into a particular stage.

*Stage lag:* A child may linger at an early stage of skill development for a while, then quickly pass through several stages to a mature pattern.

## Motor Dysfunctions

Atypical motor development can take many forms. A motor system must be intact and free from physical limitations in order for normal progression to occur. Motor abnormalities can include muscle weaknesses, joint formation problems, or malformation. The term *motor delay,* or *lag,* suggests that the behavior will be acquired but on an altered time frame. If the motor behavior does not occur or if the output is significantly different from the normal range, then the delay becomes a deficit or deviation (Henderson, Morris, and Frith, 1981). Delays in muscle development can be classified through the components of *muscle tone, muscle control,* and *muscle strength.*

**Deficits in muscle tone.** Tone deficits are muscle-tension related, and the stretching capacity of muscles is of great importance. A tense child will have increased tone; a sleeping child will have decreased tone. An exaggeration to either extreme on a regular basis creates a condition called *hypotonicity* or *hypertonicity.*

When muscles are limp and do not demonstrate resistance to a stretch, the loss of tone is described as *hypotonicity.* The child experiencing this problem probably will have little effectual movement and a lack of postural stability. Just supporting the body in an upright fashion may be taxing for such a child. Balance and reaction-time problems are often noted with Down's syndrome children, as compared to other mentally handicapped children (Henderson et al, 1981). In many cases, hypotonia and decreased pelvic stability contribute to these deficits (Connolly, Morgan, and Russell, 1984; Melyn and White, 1973).

*Hypertonicity* is a condition of tight muscles, in which the muscles are constantly excited and stretched. In order to accomplish movement, an overexertion of force is necessary.

Two types of hypertonicity are *spasticity* and *rigidity.* Muscles that are *spastic* require force to overcome the resistance to stretch but there will be some movement. Sometimes the resistance is overcome but the resulting movement is erratic. On the other hand, *rigid* muscles resist any movement.

**Deficits in muscle control.** Rapid, jerky, involuntary movements of the arms and legs are called *tremors.* Involuntary muscle vibrations impair the child's balance and coordination. These movement disturbances may be seen as poorly controlled sets of subskills.

*Deficits in muscle strength.* There may be significant differences in muscle strength within the child's body. For example, greater or lesser muscle strength may be found on the right or left side of the body. Also, muscle impairments may affect one side of the body more than the other. A muscle weakness is called *paresis;* a total inability to move is called *plegia.*

Progressive muscle weakness such as muscular dystrophy usually is evident within the first three years of life. The disease progresses until the child is unable to move. Usually diagnosed clinically by the age of three, muscular dystrophy is documented with a history of walking difficulties and frequent falls as well as poor balance.

### Brain Injury

The causes of dysfunctions in motor development are often connected with damage or lack of control in one or more of the centers of the brain (Johnston and Macgrab, 1976). Observable differences in motor integration can warn of early deficit patterns and offer the possibility for early intervention and potential improvement in motor performance.

Cerebral palsy is a motor dysfunction caused by brain injury. Because of damage to their central nervous system, children with cerebral palsy have abnormal patterns of movement and abnormal states of motor tone. As these children mature, their abnormal motor patterns are reinforced through feedback to their sensory systems. Interference with the central nervous system also results in lower level motor functions at inappropriate chronological ages. When the cortical area of the brain is damaged, there may be a release of primitive reflexes normally seen in younger, less developed children (Shepherd, 1980).

## INTERVENTION STRATEGIES FOR CHILDREN WITH MOTOR DYSFUNCTIONS

Methods of intervening and helping the child with motor and physical disorders come from many sources: physicians, occupational and physical therapists, early childhood specialists, and adaptive motor specialists. In this section, intervention strategies are organized under the following topics: adaptive supports, sensory stimulation, and motor development activities.

### Adaptive Supports

The severity of the motor deficit can cause significant physical adjustments for the young child. The age of the child at the onset of the condition and the limitation of movement will greatly affect motivation and progress (Jennings, Conners, Stegman, Sankaranarayan, and Mendelsohn,

1985; Commey and Fitzhardinge, 1979; Kitchen, Ryan, and Rickards, 1980). The child with extensive limb restriction will need specialized supports to compensate for motor deficits. Muscular weaknesses may require the addition of special chairs, tables, braces, or wheelchairs.

The child with more severe physical or orthopedic problems may use braces or artificial limbs (often called orthotic or prosthetic appliances). Although a first encounter with the many straps, belts, fasteners, and joints may be intimidating, it is quite important for the early childhood teacher to be knowledgeable about them so that bruises, abrasions, restricting range of motion, and possible loss of circulation do not result from poor or incorrect fit (Fredrick and Fletcher, 1985). Often, young nonverbal children cannot communicate well enough to express levels of discomfort.

Only the child's physician, orthotist, prosthetist, or physical therapist can provide the necessary technical or medical assistance to monitor adjustment to these appliances. However, the early childhood teacher should ask the specialist to explain the device, including (1) the purpose for the device and times when it is necessary to wear it; (2) signs of poor fit, condition, or

incorrect adjustment; (3) specific activity limitations, alterations, or adaptations for the child; (4) the amount of physical assistance the teacher should provide; and (5) how the appliance fastens, adjusts, and is removed.

It is important for teachers to stress the positive results of wearing the device. If other class members reject a child with such a device, it is critical that the teacher and child discuss the device and explain its purpose and how it works to other children. Also, it is necessary to reassure children in the class that the condition is not contagious. Young children have great difficulty separating causes of physical problems and the direct effect upon each of them. It may be frightening for some children to look at these devices and not project their own involvement with them. Once the device is explained and each child understands the purpose of the assist, the teacher should incorporate the special needs of the child into daily activities.

Teaching materials may be altered, also, as an adaptive support. For example, fine motor movements can be aided with the use of foam, wood, plastic, specially designed scissors, and taped additions to pencils or crayons. Stabilizing and reducing the slippery surface helps the child with grasping problems. Using foam and placing a writing tool through the foam gives the child a larger mass to hold. Also, specialized pencil grip holds are available for strapping the pencil to the hand if grasp is difficult.

Technology has served to improve adaptive devices for handicapped people. Electronic devices are responsive to even minimal movements. Also, computers give more access to children with physical and motor limitations. It is now possible for a child to learn to use a computer equipped with special modifications to fit the special needs of that child. Computer adaptations are further discussed in Chapter 9.

### Sensory Stimulation

Sensory stimulation activities are designed to increase the child's sensory input. General sensory stimulation can be accomplished through many developmental activities. Rolling on textured surfaces, such as grass and sculptured carpeting, increases stimulation for the child. Playing with water, dough, and sand provides texture-stimulating activities. Rubbing the body with powder and lotion is cutaneous stimulation. Bouncing on inflatable equipment, playing with musical toys, and negotiating an obstacle course are good physically stimulating experiences.

Spastic muscle tone may require controlled sleeping situations, such as the use of an inflated air mattress, bolsters, or rolled towels to reduce the effects of limited muscle response to a resting state (Korner, Kraemer, and Haffner, 1975). In some cases, sustained pressure on particular joints and muscles will increase muscle response. A light embrace, meant as a sign of approval, may actually be an unpleasant experience for some children—while a spanking may turn out to be reinforcing.

Tactile stimulation can be provided in a variety of ways. A few examples are rubbing the child's hands, feet, or trunk with a blanket or towel; lying in a hammock that wraps around the body; writing on a carpet square with chalk, then erasing it with the arms, elbows, or feet; reaching for toys in a carpeted barrel; lying or rolling on a carpeted surface; rolling up in a blanket, then unrolling; walking barefoot in sand, grass, or leaves; playing with water; playing with play dough or clay; painting with finger paints, pudding, or shaving cream; engaging in puppet games; and digging for objects buried in sand. Further assistance from a physical therapist, occupational therapist, or adaptive physical education teacher may be necessary to plan and implement sensory stimulation activities.

Tables 7.2 and 7.3 present a sequence of gross and fine motor behaviors along with methods of stimulation.

**TABLE 7.2   Sequence of Gross Motor Behavior and Methods of Stimulation**

| MOTOR BEHAVIOR | METHOD OF STIMULATING MOTOR BEHAVIOR |
|---|---|
| **Head and Neck Control**<br>Turns head to side<br>Raises head from prone position<br>Supports head in an upright position | Stimulate the infant to raise head with the use of a moving light or noisy toy. |
| **Sitting with Support**<br>Sits in a lap with minimal support<br>Independently sits with prop (pillow)<br>Independently sits in objects with reduction of support | Gradually reduce the need for support and increase the length of time for nonsupport.<br>Increasing reduction of support gives the infant new situations to adjust to. |
| **Rolling Over**<br>Rolls over from back to stomach | Place infant on back and guide roll to left or right. |
| **Raising Body**<br>Supports the upper body on forearm | Stimulate the infant by placing on stomach and using a noisy toy or colorful object to draw attention. |
| **Sitting Without Support**<br>Sits in chair independently<br>Sits on the floor independently | Gradually increase the length of time for nonsupported sitting and alternate a variety of places for sitting: floor, chair, highchair, swing, and jumperseat. |
| **Precrawling**<br>Initiates forward movement—prone | Use a toy or food as an incentive and draw the infant's attention toward it. |
| **Pull to a Sitting Position**<br>Pulls to a sitting position—prone<br>Requires less adult support in task | The adult is an assist and support for the child.<br>The adult will support the child in attempts to accomplish the task. |

**TABLE 7.2 (Cont.)**

| MOTOR BEHAVIOR | METHOD OF STIMULATING MOTOR BEHAVIOR |
|---|---|
| **Creeping**<br>Locomotes forward on hands and knees | Offer objects to infant to increase distance accomplished. |
| **Pull to Standing Position**<br>Pulls to standing position with support<br>Pulls to stand with less physical support<br>Uses objects as assist for pull to stand | Offer infant the use of adult support to pull to stand from a sitting position and reduce amount of support. Also make objects available for use as supports. |
| **Sidestepping with Support**<br>Sidesteps around objects while standing | Encourage moving to left and right in moving around objects. |
| **Standing with Support**<br>Stands with minimal adult assistance<br>Stands using objects for adult support<br>Stands without any support | Begin with physical support, and then the adult will gradually reduce support. First, hold with two hands and reduce to one hand and then to fingers. |
| **Walking**<br>Walks with back support<br>Walks with front support<br>Walks with object support<br>Walks with support from side<br>Walks without support<br>Practices walking skills | Begin with front and back support of infant and gradually reduce physical support. Practice the skill with regularity. |
| **Stairwalking**<br>Creeps upstairs<br>Creeps downstairs<br>Walks upstairs with support<br>Walks downstairs with support<br>Walks upstairs without support<br>Walks downstairs without support<br>Practices stairwalking skills<br>Uses alternate feet in stairwalking<br>Walks stairs in a continuous alternation of feet | Provide safe opportunity for child to attempt to accomplish the skill. Small set of stairs is a good start. Provide supervision for the practice of this skill. The adult should be physically near the child while this skill is being practiced until such time as it is mastered. |
| **Running**<br>Alternates feet<br>Alternates feet and has both in air<br>Increases tempo of running and length of time in midair | Establish an area that is free of objects and will allow the child an opportunity to practice the task. Playgrounds, parks, walks, and hallways are good areas. Be sure that shoes are not slippery or new. |
| **Throwing**<br>Uses the whole arm prior to the release of the object<br>Releases object with backward or forward thrust with no body rotation | Offer small objects that can be easily grasped, such as beanbags or soft toys. When using balls, use a small ball that the child can hold easily if you plan to |

**TABLE 7.2 (Cont.)**

| MOTOR BEHAVIOR | METHOD OF STIMULATING MOTOR BEHAVIOR |
|---|---|
| Releases object with rotation of trunk and step off one foot<br>Releases object with step, pivot, and timed throw | throw for accuracy. If you are going to throw for distance, use a large ball—inflated but soft. Provide a target for the throw and alternate accuracy and distance priorities. Begin with a large ball and decrease size of ball to accommodate the child's hand and grasp. |
| **Catching**<br>Rolls a ball to another person<br>Receives a ball (small object), body cradling for the catch<br>Receives an object with arms clasped to grasp<br>Receives an object with arm preparation | Begin with rolling activities and increase to toss at a short distance. Throw to the child at the middle of body height so as to make the catch possible. Observe the child's stance to catch and alert the child to prepare arms for the catch. Plan activities that use catching skills for practice. |
| **Striking**<br>Strikes a stationary resting object<br>Strikes a rolling or airborne object<br>Strikes a moving object while you move<br>Strikes a moving object and catches it | Provide opportunities to expose the child to situations that will allow practice of this behavior. Begin with large objects (balls) and decrease size as well as increase distance. Vary the speed of the moving object. |
| **Leaping**<br>Leaps forward<br>Increases height of leap<br>Increases distance of leap<br>Leaps continuously | Provide an opportunity to move freely. Give the child a model to follow or a set of actions to copy. |
| **Jumping**<br>Jumps from step, holding onto support<br>Jumps from one foot to the other foot<br>Jumps up from two feet<br>Jumps down from two feet<br>Runs and jumps forward from one foot to other<br>Jumps forward from two feet<br>Jumps down from one foot to two feet<br>Runs and jumps forward from one foot to two feet<br>Jumps over object from two feet<br>Jumps from two feet in a continuous manner<br>Jumps backwards<br>Jumps backwards in a continuous manner | Provide situations that will induce the child to use the skill. Offer models for the child to copy. Set a special time for practice of the skill. Offer physical support to initiate the action. Place objects down in an obstacle path for the child to jump over. Show the child that you are pleased with any effort. Encourage practice. Play games that use the skill. Accept all performances with approval. |

TABLE 7.2 (Cont.)

| MOTOR BEHAVIOR | METHOD OF STIMULATING MOTOR BEHAVIOR |
|---|---|
| **Hopping**<br>Hops on one foot<br>Hops on the other foot<br>Hops continuously on either foot<br>Hops alternating feet | Give physical support for balance. Remove the support as the child can manage alone. Encourage practice and show the child that you are pleased with any effort. Young children begin this task by holding onto the foot that is not used and then progressing to independently lifting the one foot off the ground during the hop. Play games that use the motor skill. |
| **Skipping**<br>Moves forward using a step and hop<br>Steps and hops using step on one foot and hop on other (gallop)<br>Steps and hops using step on one foot and hop on the same foot (skip) | Provide a model for the child to copy. Separate the parts of the skip into a step and a hop. Integrate the two steps into a smooth pattern. It may require extended practice. Encourage the child to practice and show that you are pleased with any effort. It may help for the child to say "step-hop-step-hop" while doing the task. |

TABLE 7.3 Sequence of Fine Motor Behavior and Methods of Stimulation

| MOTOR BEHAVIOR | METHOD OF STIMULATING MOTOR BEHAVIOR |
|---|---|
| **Hand Grasp**<br>Transfers two blocks in one hand | Provide objects of adequate size and shape for practice. |
| Retains two blocks in one hand<br>Turns doorknob<br>Demonstrates palmar grasp<br>Demonstrates dagger grasp | Offer toys that encourage turns; i.e., nest eggs, barrels, plastic jars/lids Stimulate picking up or handling behavior through play activities. |
| Demonstrates scissor grasp<br>Demonstrates pincer grasp | Offer objects that are safe and easy to handle; i.e., raisins and a plastic container. Put clothespins on and off a rope. |
| Unwraps small piece of candy | Offer candy, suckers, sugar-free candy. |
| **Threading**<br>Threads large beads onto a lace with one hand<br>Threads large beads with two hands<br>Theads small beads<br>Threads beads following a simple pattern | Establish a large chest of buttons, spools, beads for practice. Make a simple pattern and ask the child to duplicate it. Give a more complex pattern or ask children to make their own. Use plastic lacing material that is firm to the grasp and easy to hold. |

**TABLE 7.3 (Cont.)**

| MOTOR BEHAVIOR | METHOD OF STIMULATING MOTOR BEHAVIOR |
|---|---|
| Threads string into 1–3 holes<br>Threads string into 5–6 holes<br>Threads string into shoe/pattern<br>Threads string into lacing card | Offer handmade threading cards, shoes of differing sizes and number of eyelets. Mark threading cards for **stop** and **start** with red and green colors. |
| **Form Boards**<br>Places shapes in shape box<br>Stacks rings on ring tree (assisted)<br>Stacks rings on ring tree (unassisted)<br>Stacks five rings on ring tree in correct order<br>Stacks ten rings on ring tree in correct order<br>Places one shape in singular formboard<br>Places three shapes in formboard<br>Places shapes of decreasing size in formboard<br>Places numerals in appropriate formboard<br>Places cylinders in formboard | Arrange activity area with formboards, ring trees, and standard shapes or forms. |
| **Puzzles**<br>Assembles 2–4 piece unconnected puzzle (object formboard)<br>Assembles a 3–5 piece puzzle<br>Assembles a 6–10 piece puzzle<br>Assembles an 11–15 piece puzzle<br>Assembles a 16–20 piece puzzle | Establish puzzle area with puzzles of varying difficulty. Begin with puzzles that have knobs for grip. |
| **Pencil and Paper Activities**<br>Spontaneously scribbles when given crayon or pencil and paper<br>Colors within confines of paper<br>Demonstrates push–pull motion<br>Imitates circular motion<br>Colors within some directed margin<br>Draws a vertical line from imitation<br>Draws a horizontal line from imitation<br>Traces and imitates a V<br>Traces and imitates a circle O | Materials should be large and easy to grip. Paper should be blank. Large lined paper may be used for letter/name printing. Primary pencils or wider crayons will help. Templates may be used to assist in copying of shapes. Use bold strokes for model. Limit number of items for copying. |
| **Cutting/Pasting**<br>Cuts with 4-hole training scissors with aid of adult<br>Picks up cotton ball with scissors<br>Cuts with 2-hole scissors (assisted)<br>Cuts with 2-hole scissors (unassisted)<br>Cuts 3–5 slits in paper<br>Cuts bold lines<br>Cuts paper in half<br>Cuts square with bold lines<br>Cuts curved lines | Offer cutting tasks in small amounts. Select cutting tool to meet level of skill. Metal cutting guides may assist a child with poor grip or low muscle strength. |

**TABLE 7.3 (Cont.)**

| MOTOR BEHAVIOR | METHOD OF STIMULATING MOTOR BEHAVIOR |
| --- | --- |
| Cuts piece of string | |
| Pastes paper randomly | Select an area where pasting and clay |
| Pastes paper by design | handling are acceptable. |
| **Clay Handling** | |
| Manipulates clay by rolling it in a ball (circular) | Offer small quantities of dough/paste or clay for the child to use. Model |
| Manipulates clay by rolling it in a sausage roll (back and forth) | appropriate pasting and clay handling techniques for the child to follow. |
| Manipulates clay by pushing it with fingers | Placement of sheet or newspaper under |
| Manipulates clay to form meaningful objects | paste and clay area facilitates cleanup procedures. |

### Motor Development Activities

The early childhood special education classroom provides an environment that encourages motor development in a structured setting. The child's IEP (individualized education program—see Chapter 5) specifies information that will be helpful in designing the motor activities. For the child with motor problems, the IEP will document the child's current levels of motor performance and areas of motor delay, specify motor goals and objectives, and designate the amount of service/specialists needed to provide for those goals and objectives.

In addition to the classroom teacher, motor instruction may be given through related service specialists—such as occupational therapists, physical therapists, or adaptive physical education teachers. These professionals, in turn, may make recommendations for additional services.

The following are examples of motor development activities.

1. *Preschool games* Many preschool games and toys—such as pounding pegs with a hammer, hammer and nail games, and dropping forms into slots—can be useful to practice fine motor control.
2. *Clipping clothespins* Clothespins can be clipped onto a line or a box. Children can be timed in this activity by counting the number of clothespins clipped in a specified time.
3. *Water control* Carrying and pouring water from pitchers into measured buckets to specified levels can be encouraged. Use smaller amounts and finer measurements to make the task more difficult. Use of colored water makes the activity more interesting.
4. *Lacing* A cardboard punched with holes or a pegboard is suitable for this activity. A design or picture is made on the board, and the child weaves or sews with a heavy shoelace, yarn, or similar cord through the holes to follow the pattern.

5. *Tracing* Trace lines, pictures, designs, letters, or numbers on tracing paper, plastic, or stencils. Use directional arrows, color cues, and numbers to help the child trace the figures.

6. *Cutting with scissors* Have the child cut with scissors, choosing activities appropriate to needs. Be sure to have left-handed scissors available. There are also "guiding scissors" which allow the teacher to hold the scissors simultaneously with the child. Easiest to cut are straight short lines marked near the edges of the paper, which make a fringe. Then cut along straight lines across the paper. Some children might need a cardboard attached to the paper to help guide the scissors. Cut out marked geometric shapes—such as squares, rectangles, and triangles. Draw a different color line to indicate change of direction in cutting. Cut out curving lines and circles. Cut out pictures. Cut out patterns made with dots and faint lines.

7. *Paper folding* Simple paper-folding activities are useful for the development of eye–hand coordination, following directions, and fine motor control.

8. *Stencils or templates* Have the child draw outlines of patterns of geometric shapes. Templates can be made from cardboard, wood, plastic, old X-ray films, or containers for packaged meat. Two styles can be made: a solid shape or frames with the shape cut out.

9. *Paper and pencil activities* Simple coloring books, readiness books, and dot-to-dot books frequently provide good paper-and-pencil activities for fine motor and eye–hand development.

10. *Copying designs* Children look at a geometric design and copy it onto a piece of paper.

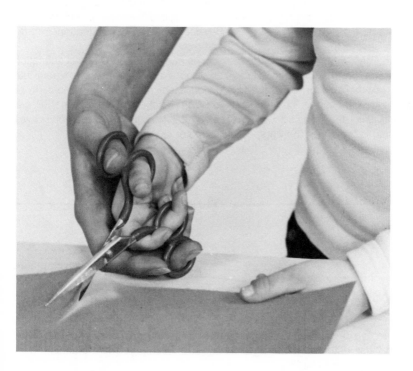

## SUMMARY

One of the first things the infant experiences and learns is body movement. Young children who lack motor experiences or have delays or impairments in motor development are deprived of the foundation in the learning process.

Motor learning is complex, involving the integration of three systems: the sensory, motor, and perceptual systems. The child receives information through the sensory system (visual, auditory, tactile, kinesthetic, proprioceptive). The motor system consists of several levels of movement. The perceptual system interprets the sensory information. These systems must be integrated in motor and perceptual behavior.

There is a normal sequence of motor and perceptual development. Piaget's stages of child development emphasize this developmental sequence. The first stage, sensorimotor learning, provides the foundation for later cognitive and academic learning.

There are several theoretical perspectives of atypical motor development, each stemming from a different discipline. Kephart's theory adapts motor and learning theory to better understand handicapped children. Ayres's theory of motor learning is based on the perspective of occupational therapy. Cratty's theories advocate the benefits of adaptive physical education.

There is a normal wide range of motor skill development in young children. When motor dysfunctions interfere with learning, special interventions are needed. Children may have many deficits in motor behavior. These can be due to deficits in muscle tone, muscle control, muscle strength, or central nervous system damage.

The child with extensive limb restriction will need specialized supports to compensate for motor deficits—such as wheelchairs, braces, artificial limbs, and writing or eating devices. It is important that early childhood teachers be familiar with them and their use.

Sensory stimulation activities are designed to increase the child's sensory input. Some children need carefully planned intervention through tactile and proprioceptive channels. Direction from a physical therapist or occupational therapist may be necessary.

The early childhood special education classroom provides an environment that encourages motor development in a structured setting. The child's IEP will document specific goals and objectives for motor skill improvement.

## REVIEW QUESTIONS

**Terms to Know**

sensation
rooting
sensorimotor integration
perceptual systems
motor act

adaptive physical education
principles of motor development
hypertonicity
reflexes
adaptive supports

1. List the five principles of sensorimotor progression and describe each. How would these differ in an average three-year-old compared to a trainable mentally handicapped child?

2. What is cephalocaudal and proximal distal development? Give an example of each at ages one and three years.
3. Atypical motor development can be identified in different ways. When is a difference considered deviant?
4. If a child requires physical or occupational therapy, what does it involve?
5. List three characteristics of a child with a disorder in the tactile system.
6. Plan a motor-based instructional activity for a four-year-old with a balance problem.
7. List three reflex behaviors.
8. Explain Piaget's stage theory.
9. What is a muscle tremor? Under what conditions is it seen?
10. Competent fine motor skills are necessary in preparation for standard classroom success. Work out a developmental sequence for the skill of cutting a curve with a scissors and two techiques to assist a child in acquiring competence in this task.

## REFERENCES

AYRES, A.J. (1975) "Sensorimotor Foundations of Academic Ability." In W.M. Cruickshank and D.P. Hallahan (eds) *Perceptual and Learning Disabilities.* (Vol. 2) Syracuse, NY: Syracuse University Press.

AYRES, A.J. (1978) "Learning Disabilities and the Vestibular System." *Journal of Learning Disabilities,* 11, 18–29.

AYRES, A.J. (1981) *Sensory Integration and the Child.* Los Angeles: Western Psychological Services.

BOWER, T.G. (1977) *A Primer of Infant Development.* San Francisco: W.H. Freeman.

BRAZELTON, T.B. (1969) *Infants and Mothers.* Dell Publishing Co.

BRUNER, J. (1973) "Organization of Early Skilled Action." *Child Development,* 44, 1–11.

CALDWELL, B.M. AND D.J. STEDMAN (eds.) (1977) *Infant Education: A Guide for Helping Handicapped Children in the First Three Years.:* Walker and Co.

CARTERETTE, E.C. and M.P. FRIEDMAN (1973) *Handbook of Perception.* NY: Academic Press.

CHANEY, C.M. and N.C. KEPHART (1968) *Motoric Aids to Perceptual Training.* Columbus: Chas. E. Merrill.

COMMEY, J.O. and P.M. FITZHARDINGE (1979) "Handicap in the Preterm Small for Gestational Age Infant." *Journal of Pediatrics,* 94, 779–86.

CONNOLLY, B.H., S. MORGAN, and F.H. RUSSELL (1984) "Evaluation of Children with Down's Syndrome Who Participated in an Early Intervention Program." *Physical Therapy,* 64, 10, 1515–19.

CONNOR, F.P., G.G. WILLIAMSON, and J.M. SIEPP (1978) *Program Guide for Infants and Toddlers with Neuromotor and Other Developmental Disabilities.* NY: Teachers College Press.

CORBIN, C.B. (1973) *A Textbook of Motor Development.* Dubuque, IA: W.C. Brown.

CRATTY, B.J. (1975) *Remedial Motor Activity for Children.* Philadelphia: Lea and Febiger.

CRATTY, B.J. (1979) *Perceptual and Motor Development in Infants and Children.* Englewood Cliffs, NJ: Prentice-Hall.

ESPENSCHADE, A.S. and H.M. ECKERT (1980) *Motor Development.* Columbus: Charles E. Merrill.

FOLIO, M. and R. FEWELL (1983). *Peabody Developmental Motor Scales.* Allen, TX: DLM Teaching Resources.

FREDRICK, J. and D. FLETCHER (1985) Facilitating Children's Adjustment to Orthotic and Prosthetic Appliances." *Teaching Exceptional Children,* Spring, 17 (3), 228–30.

GARDNER, E. (1975) *Fundamentals of Neurology.* Philadelphia: Saunders.

HENDERSON, S.E., J. MORRIS, and U. FRITH (1981) "The Motor Deficit in Down's Syndrome Children: A Problem of Timing." *Journal of Child Psychology/Psychiatry,* 22, 233–44.

HINOJOSA, J., et al., (1982) "Occupational Therapy for Sensory Integrative Dysfunction." *The American Journal of Occupational Therapy,* 36 (12) 831–34.

JENNINGS, K.D., R.,E. CONNERS, C.E. STEGMAN, P. SANKARANARAYAN, and S. MENDELSOHN (1985) "Mastery Motivation in Young Preschoolers: Effect of a Physical Handicap and Implications for Educational Programming." *Journal of the Division for Early Childhood,* 9 (2), 162–69.

JOHNSTON, R.B., and P.R. MACGRAB (EDS.) (1976) *Developmental Disorders: Assessment, Treatment, Education.* Baltimore, MD: University Park Press.

KEPHART, N.C. (1971) *The Slow Learner in the Classroom.* Columbus: Charles E. Merrill.

KALAKIAN, L. and C.B. EICHSTAEDT (1982) *Developmental/Adapted Physical Education—Making Ability Count.* Minneapolis: Burgess.

KITCHEN, W.H., M.M. RYAN, and A. RICKARDS (1980) "A Longitudinal Study of Very Low Birthweight Infants: An Overview of Performance of 8 Years of Age." *Developmental Medicine and Child Neurology,* 22, 172–88.

KORNER, A.F., H.C. KRAEMER, and E. HAFFNER (1975) "Effects of Waterbed Flotation on Premature Infants: A Pilot Study." *Pediatrics,* 56, 361.

McCLENAGHAN, B.A. and D.L. GALLAHUE (1978) *Fundamental Movement: A Developmental and Remedial Approach.* Philadelphia: W.B. Saunders.

McGRAW, M. (1969) *The Neuromuscular Maturation of the Human Infant.* NY: Hafner.

MELYN, M.A. and O.T. WHITE (1973) "Mental and Developmental Milestones of Non-institutionalized Down's Syndrome Children." *Pediatrics,* 52, 542–45.

PIAGET, J. (1952) *The Origins of Intelligence in Children.* trans., M. Cook. NY: International University Press.

PIAGET, J. (1969) *The Mechanisms of Perception.* trans., G.N. Seagram. NY: Basic Books.

PRECHTL, H. and D. BEINTEMA (1964) *The Neurological Examination of the Full Term Newborn Infant.* London: Heineman.

ROBB, M.D. (1972) *The Dynamics of Motor Skill Acquisition.* Englewood Cliffs, NJ: Prentice-Hall.

SANDLER, A. and A. COREN (1981) "Vestibular Stimulation in Early Childhood: A Review." *Journal of the Division for Early Childhood,* 3, 48–55.

SCHURR, E. (1975) *Movement Experiences for Children.* Englewood Cliffs, NJ: Prentice-Hall.

SELLICK, K.J., and R. OVER (1980) "Effects of Vestibular Stimulation on Motor Development of Cerebral Palsied Children." *Developmental Medicine and Child Neurology,* 22, 476–83.

SHEPHERD, R.B. (1980) *Physiotherapy in Paediatrics.* Oxford: Alden Press.

THOMAS, E.G., P.T. BECKER, and M.P. FREESE (1978) "Individual Patterns of Mother–Infant Interaction." In G.P. Sackett (ed.) *Observing Behavior.* Baltimore: University Park Press.

# EIGHT

# Teaching Communication Skills and Language

## INTRODUCTION

This chapter discusses problems that young children have in communication—including language, speech, and nonverbal modes of exchanging ideas and messages. The chapter overviews communication skills, traces the process of acquiring communication skills in young children, explores conditions that interfere with normal language development, examines disorders of speech and language, and offers suggested strategies and materials for enhancing the development of communication skills.

The ability to communicate and to use and understand language serves many functions in people's lives. It enables them to learn about the past, dream about the future, comprehend abstract ideas, and socialize with others. Although other animals (for example, bees, birds, dolphins, chimpanzees) have developed methods of communication, only humans possess the species-specific characteristics of language and speech. Thus, speech and language are unique human behaviors, separating people from other living creatures.

## OVERVIEW OF COMMUNICATION SKILLS

Acquiring the ability to communicate is a vital area of development for young children. To be able to share ideas and messages with others, young

## CASE EXAMPLE—JOEY: SPEECH AND LANGUAGE DISORDERS

Joey, age four years five months, was referred to the Early Childhood Special Education program because of severe delays in language development. Upon entry to the program, Joey exhibited an expressive vocabulary of only eight words during a one-week period. While a score of 117 on the Leiter suggested his intellectual functioning was well within normal limits, Joey exhibited poor concept development, with no receptive or expressive identification of any concepts. Motor planning also was poor, and imitation of movement and postures was difficult for him. However, Joey's excellent social skills allowed him to compensate for his other deficiencies in many classroom routines.

Traditional early childhood special education approaches to remediation were implemented, involving a variety of modalities and methods to emphasize basic concepts and expressive language. Both group and individual experiences were provided in the classroom, as well as occupational therapy and speech/language therapy. However, after five months in the early childhood program, virtually no progress had been made and none of the short-term objectives had been achieved.

A team meeting was held with all direct service personnel to discuss programming alternatives. A review of Joey's lack of progress led team members to suggest that Joey was not associating any verbal symbols with objects or actions. In order to determine if Joey was capable of making this association, an informal assessment technique was used. The classroom teacher had Joey blow a bubble with a bubble pipe while she said the word "bubble" to him. Joey was able to make and maintain the association using that word on successive days. The association was possible when visual, motor, kinesthetic, and auditory cues were used simultaneously.

A language remediation plan was then developed, using this type of approach. The team selected six locations and persons within the school that were considered essential to Joey's program. Using instant photographs of Joey taken at a particular location (for example, his desk in the classroom) a verbal statement describing a location or person was made using a NOUN + VISUAL cue. Joey then was given a verbal direction to move to the location in the picture ("Go desk"), and he was expected to respond with appropriate movements.

After this association was made, it was necessary to provide language expansion activities to facilitate generalization. Joey was shown photographs of himself completing an action and given the cue NOUN + VERB + VISUAL or NOUN + VERB + HAPTIC. Finally, Joey was able to label pictures of NOUN + VERB without a verbal or visual stimulus. At this point, his language started to emerge more rapidly.

Within three months, it was possible to evaluate Joey's progress. Results showed his language as having: nouns (20 percent); verbs (4 percent); 2-word combinations (52 percent); 3 or more word combinations (14 percent); sentences (2 percent); and other utterances (8 percent). Joey began to play with peers and use short phrases. At this point, the team anticipates that Joey's spontaneous language will continue to grow with continued language stimulation. The next objective is to help Joey develop and use sentences of greater length and complexity.

children must learn to use the two primary skills of verbal communication—speech and language—as well as nonverbal modes, such as gestures.

### Differences Between Speech and Language

It is important to distinguish between the two primary communication skills of speech and language. *Language* is a structured system of signs, sounds, and symbols that have commonly understood meanings. *Speech,* on the other hand, is the tool for conveying this system orally—the activation of language. Some of the key differences between speech and language are summarized:

| Language | Speech |
|---|---|
| The knowledge in one's head. | The realization of that knowledge in verbal behavior. |
| All the words in a person's mental dictionary and the rules for combining those words into an infinite number of novel sentences. | The actual utterances spoken to others in specific situations. |
| Language exists even in moments of silence. | Speech exists only in moments of actual speaking or listening. |
| | Speech is the activation of language and thought. |

Thus, language and speech abilities enable one to communicate with others and with oneself, and to think. Such a strong interdependent relationship exists between language and thought that it is difficult to distinguish between them. In fact, Whorf (1956) suggested that the language one uses determines how one thinks.

### Components of Language Development

Language development is often classified into three components: (1) inner language; (2) receptive language; and (3) expressive language. *Inner language* reflects evidence of thinking. Vygotsky (1962) refers to this process as "inner speech"; Piaget (1962) calls this stage "preoperational thought." At this level the child integrates and organizes the sensory and perceptual experiences that he or she is continuously encountering. Some examples of the child's thoughts at the inner language level of development are associating the spoon with food, relating the telephone with the sound of its ringing, associating a toy car with the activity of pushing it along the floor, or organizing dolls and doll furniture in a meaningful way. Inner language establishes the foundation for the development of higher level communication skills.

*Receptive language* refers to the ability to listen, to receive the language of others, or to comprehend what others are saying. Receptive language generally is thought to develop simultaneously or in conjunction with inner language, supplying the child with the necessary words with which to think, associate, and assimilate impinging experiences. Receptive language appears intact when the child attends to noises and voices or shows awareness of sound (for example, turns the head to localize sound) and shows understanding by responding appropriately to a request. When a child responds to an oral command ("show me your shoe") or word by going to an object (shoe) or performing an activity (pat-a-cake), the child possesses receptive language skills. The average child begins to exhibit these characteristics between the age of six to ten months.

*Expressive language* is the process of producing meaningful linguistic sounds. Expressive language (other than mimicking) develops only after receptive language. The child must have some comprehension of a specific grammatical form or construction before it can be produced in a meaningful manner; that is, input precedes output. However, the time gap between these developmental stages may be quite short. The average child begins to say words meaningfully between the ages of ten to eighteen months.

Before using expressive language, the child goes through several pre-language stages. The stages and ages of normal language development include:

1.  *Cooing, crying:* response to internal stimulation (birth to four months)
2.  *Babbling:* repetition of sounds for their own sake—a manifestation of identification with humans (three to six months)
3.  *Jargon:* babbling with intonation and stress (six to eight months)
4.  *Approximation or echolalia:* saying words without meaning (six to twelve months)
5.  *Holophrasing:* use of one word for large thoughts (nine to fourteen months)
6.  *Telegraphic speech:* combination of single words but omitting words that carry little information (eighteen to twenty-four months).

It appears that the very intention to communicate verbally or otherwise requires a specific level of sensorimotor development (Leonard, 1978). (See Chapter 9 for Piagetian stages.) This usually occurs during the second half of the second year when the child gains the adult's attention by showing and pointing to objects and obtaining objects by enlisting adults as vehicles to those objects.

Yet another way of looking at all of the aspects of language is through an interactional model (Bloom and Lahey, 1978). In this framework, the *content* (the *what* of the language) interacts with the *form* (the *how* of language) and the *use* (the *why, when,* and *where* of language).

A rule to keep in mind regarding normal language development is that new forms first express old functions, and new functions are first expressed by old forms (Slobin, 1973). The child will use a new linguistic form (for example, a word of expression or syntax) for a function (concept) with which he or she is already familiar but has been expressing in a more primitive way. For example, the child begins to use the words "big" and "many" instead of "more" to express more complex meanings. On the other hand, when the child uses a new function (has acquired a particular meaning or concept), it will be communicated with the form already mastered. For example, a two-year old uses the word *"milk"* to express the concept of the color *white*. In this case, the child has the concept but not the word to express it.

## COMMUNICATION SKILLS IN THE EARLY YEARS

### Language Milestones

The acquisition of language begins long before children speak their first word—at birth or possibly even in utero. Interactions and adaptations to the environment take the form of reflexes, such as grasping, sucking, and eye movements. According to Bruner (1976), the baby is sociocentric from the beginning because it is stressful to be in a nonsocial, noncommunicative situation. Within a few months, a baby's cry shows signs of communicative patterns; for example, a cry followed by a pause to listen for reactions before another cry. By two months, the infant can produce a cry that demands or one that awaits a response from the caregiver. In a few more months, the baby begins to communicate nonverbally; for example, by extending the arms to be picked up. Thus, early language development appears to consist of learning how to map or translate language into ideas or concepts that already have been acquired on a nonlinguistic basis (Bowerman, 1978). The time and order in which various linguistic forms emerge are determined by the child's cognitive development. This cognitive development interacts with the language the child hears in the environment.

At the same time that cognitive development affects language, language input may play a critical role in helping even the young child master concepts that cannot be discovered through direct perception alone (Blank, 1974). In addition, language enables the child to categorize objects and events. This language framework for categorization may trigger off certain semantic concepts, showing the interdependence of cognition and language.

While the young child is trying to communicate both verbally and nonverbally with others, the thinking processes tend to be egocentric, or self-centered. Children appear to view life only from their own perspective. This can be easily documented when a child uses egocentric speech, which is talking aloud to oneself (Piaget, 1962). In this type of behavior, the child does not try to communicate with others, expects no answers, and often does not care whether anyone listens. The child is merely thinking aloud.

Vygotsky (1962) believes this type of "private speech" serves as a means of expressing and releasing tension, but it also becomes the vehicle for thought in solving problems. Hence, egocentric speech is the tool of transition from vocal to inner speech (thinking). While egocentric speech is prevalent among preschoolers, there is a decline in this behavior after age five, and it tends to disappear between seven and ten years of age.

Although normal language development in children has been extensively researched and reviewed (McCormick and Schiefelbusch, 1984; Bowerman, 1978; Bloom and Lahey, 1978), there are many problems with these data sets. Most of the studies were on very small samples and inter-rater reliability usually was not established. There has been only limited research on how infants learn to recognize various aspects of language. Further, the measurement of comprehension in young children is quite complex (Horton, 1974).

The early studies of language development were of two types: (1) longitudinal diary-like cases of the language development of individual children and (2) cross-sectional studies of the language performance of a large number of children at different age levels. These early studies, however, produced data that made it possible to specify the developmental language milestones in young children. Table 8.1 lists these milestones from infancy to five years, according to age and typical language behavior. These universals or milestones represent only gross general indices of development and should be used as such. The typical rate of development may be more variable than indicated since most developmental data have been traditionally obtained from children of middle-class professional families (Bryen and Gallagher, 1983). Furthermore, language acquisition within a particular child also is variable (Bloom, 1980).

**TABLE 8.1  Milestones in the Development of Language Ability in Young Children**

| AVERAGE AGE | QUESTION | AVERAGE BEHAVIOR |
|---|---|---|
| 3–6 months | What does he do when you talk to him? | He awakens or quiets to the sound of his mother's voice. |
| | Does he react to your voice even when he cannot see you? | He typically turns eyes and head in the direction of the source of sound. |
| 7–10 months | When he can't *see* what is happening, what does he do when he hears familiar footsteps . . . the dog barking . . . the telephone ringing . . . candy paper rattling . . . someone's voice . . . his own name? | He turns his head and shoulders toward familiar sounds, even when he cannot see what is happening. Such sounds do not have to be loud to cause him to respond. |
| 11–15 months | Can he point to or find familiar objects or people when he is asked to? | He shows his understanding of some words by appropriate behavior; for example, he points |

**TABLE 8.1  (Cont.)**

| AVERAGE AGE | QUESTION | AVERAGE BEHAVIOR |
|---|---|---|
| | *Example:* "Where is Jimmy?" "Find the ball." Does he respond differently to different sounds? | to or looks at familiar objects or people on request. He jabbers in response to a human voice, is apt to cry when there is thunder, or may frown when he is scolded. |
| | Does he enjoy listening to some sounds and imitating them? | Imitation indicates that he can hear the sounds and match them with his own sound production. |
| 1½ years | Can he point to parts of his body when you ask him to? *Example:* "Show me your eyes." "Show me your nose." | Some children begin to identify parts of the body. He should be able to show his nose or eyes. |
| | How many understandable words does he use—words you are sure *really* mean something? | He should be using a few single words. They are not complete or pronounced perfectly but are clearly meaningful. |
| 2 years | Can he follow simple verbal commands when you are careful not to give him any help, such as looking at the object or pointing in the right direction? *Example:* "Johnny, get your hat and give it to Daddy." "Debby, bring me your ball." | He should be able to follow a few simple commands without visual clues. |
| | Does he enjoy being read to? Does he point out pictures of familiar objects in a book when asked to? *Example:* "Show me the baby." "Where's the rabbit?" | Most two-year-olds enjoy being "read to" and shown simple pictures in a book or magazine and will point out pictures when you ask them to. |
| | Does he use the names of familiar people and things such as *Mommy, milk, ball,* and *hat*? | He should be using a variety of everyday words heard in his home and neighborhood. |
| | What does he call himself? | He refers to himself by name. |
| | Is he beginning to show interest in the sound of radio or TV commercials? | Many two-year-olds do show such interest, by word or action. |
| | Is he putting a few words together to make little "sentences"? *Example:* "Go bye-bye car." "Milk all gone." | These "sentences" are not usually complete or grammatically correct. |
| 2½ years | Does he know a few rhymes or songs? Does he enjoy hearing them? | Many children can say or sing short rhymes or songs and enjoy listening to records or to mother singing. |

**TABLE 8.1   (Cont.)**

| AVERAGE AGE | QUESTION | AVERAGE BEHAVIOR |
|---|---|---|
| | What does he do when the ice cream man's bell rings out of his sight or when a car door or house door closes at a time when someone in the family usually comes home? | If a child has good hearing and these are events that bring him pleasure, he usually reacts to the sound by running to look or telling someone what he hears. |
| 3 years | Can he show that he understands the meaning of some words besides the names of things? *Example:* "Make the car go." "Give me your ball." "Put the block in your pocket." "Find the big doll." | He should be able to understand and use some simple verbs, pronouns, prepositions, and adjectives, such as *go, me, in,* and *big.* |
| | Can he find you when you call him from another room? | He should be able to locate the source of a sound. |
| | Does he sometimes use complete sentences? | He should be using complete sentences some of the time. |
| 4 years | Can he tell about events that have happened recently? | He should be able to give a connected account of some recent experiences. |
| | Can he carry out two directions, one after the other? *Example:* "Bobby, find Susie and tell her dinner's ready." | He should be able to carry out a sequence of two simple directions. |
| 5 years | Do neighbors and others outside the family understand most of what he says? | His speech should be intelligible, although some sounds may still be mispronounced. |
| | Can he carry on a conversation with other children or familiar grown-ups? | Most children of this age can carry on a conversation if the vocabulary is within their experience. |
| | Does he begin a sentence with "I" instead of "me"; "he" instead of "him"? | He should use some pronouns correctly. |
| | Is his grammar almost as good as his parents? | Most of the time, it should match the patterns of grammar used by the adults of his family and neighborhood. |

From the National Institute of Neurological Diseases and Stroke, *Learning to Talk: Speech, Hearing and Language Problems in the Pre-School Child.* Washington, DC: U.S. Department of Health, Education, and Welfare, 1969.

More recent research of language development studied children's language learning from a linguistic perspective. This research demonstrates that children learn an underlying linguistic system that is regular and consistent, rather than all the sounds and possible words and sentences in a language (Bloom and Lahey, 1978; Berko, 1958; Brown and Bellugi, 1964). Instead of unitary stages of language development, the milestones thus overlap, and change appears to be continuous. Moreover, it should be emphasized that even for children without problems, learning language is hard work (Bloom, 1980).

### Linguistic Learning

Language skills can be viewed in terms of four linguistic systems: phonology, semantics, syntactics, and pragmatics. *Phonology* refers to the acoustical, or sound, systems of speech, including intonation, stress, and pause. *Phonemes* are the individual elements within a group of sounds, the units of sound such as /m/ or /ch/. As such, they do not carry meaning. *Semantics* refers to meanings of words (the word *bed*) and its referent (*the actual bed*). Unlike the other linguistic systems, semantics continues to grow and develop throughout a person's life as vocabulary increases. *Syntactics* refers to the order in which words are strung together in the formation of a phrase or sentence, the rules of grammar construction, and organization of language. A *morpheme* signifies the meaning units in a word. Whereas a phoneme is the smallest unit of sound, a *morpheme* is the smallest unit of meaning. For example, although the word *eight* has five letters, it has only two phonemes (*ā* and *t*) and one morpheme (meaning unit). *Pragmatics* refers to the way in which language is used in the environment. It signifies the purposes or functions served by language, how these purposes are related to wider interpersonal and sociocultural factors, and the effects these factors have on the use of language. These four linguistic systems are the forms (the *how*) of language, the aspects of language that are heard (Bloom, 1980). These forms must ultimately be integrated with the content of language and the use of language.

Funky Winkerbean *by Tom Batiuk, (c) 1980 Field Enterprises. Courtesy Field Newspaper Syndicate.*

## Speech Skills

Speech skills are dependent on several components: auditory perception, articulation, and voice. These components are intricately meshed in an interdependent manner to receive and produce word symbols.

*Auditory perception* is the integration of the hearing sensation with the act of listening. It is dependent on the child's ability to hear and organize the incoming stimuli into patterns, to attach significance to the sensation.

*Articulation* is dependent on auditory perception and a neuromuscular system capable of producing the various vowel and consonant sounds. Table 8.2 indicates the average age at which the motor system is capable of handling various sounds in English.

*Voice* is the actual sound and includes pitch, quality, loudness, and rhythm. When the rhythm is highly irregular (or disfluent), it is known as stuttering.

The degree to which a child's language can be understood is also developmental, progressing from babbling and approximations to normal speech. Along the way, understandability or intelligibility may be affected by omissions, substitutions, and/or distortions. For example, at 3 years Paula could not pronounce the "g" sound and said "mama" for "grandma." By age 4, she had learned the "g" sound and said "grandma." Table 8.3 shows the development of intelligibility according to chronological age.

**TABLE 8.2   Order of Phonemic Development by Age**

| CHRONOLOGICAL AGE (C.A.) | PHONEME |
|---|---|
| 3½ years | all 14 vowels, p, b, m |
| 4½ years | n, ng, w, h, t, d, k, g, all dipthongs (vowel blend) |
| 5½ years | f, v, y, th (voiced and voculars), l, wh |
| 6½ years | r, s, z, ch, j, sh, zh |
| 7 years | consonant blends (cl, dr, st, and so on) |

From C. Weiss and H. Lillywhite. *Communicative Disorders: A Handbook for Prevention and Early Intervention.* St. Louis, MO: C. V. Mosby, 1976, p. 51.

**TABLE 8.3   Development of Intelligibility**

| CHRONOLOGICAL AGE (C.A.) | PERCENT OF INTELLIGIBLE SPEECH |
|---|---|
| 18 months | 25 |
| 24 months | 60 |
| 30 months | 75 |
| 36 months | 85 |
| 42 months | 95 |
| 48 months | 100* |

*Does not mean perfectly normal speech; it means understandable speech.

From C. Weiss and H. Lillywhite. *Communicative Disorders: A Handbook for Prevention and Early Intervention.* St. Louis, MO: C. V. Mosby, 1976, p. 51.

### Nonverbal Communication

Another component of communication is nonverbal—conveying meaning without words. Egolf and Chester (1973) estimate that up to 93 percent of all communication is nonverbal. This includes such factors as gestures, facial expressions, body posture, tone and pitch of voice, visual interaction, physical attributes, and proximity. Just as other aspects of communication, it is learned and may prove to be a stumbling block for some children.

All aspects of communication skills develop through imitation, practice, and the interaction of cognitive and linguistic processes. These cognitive and linguistic processes of perception, imagery, motivation, and symbolization modify both the reception and expression of language and the intermediate organization process that must sort, code, store, and retrieve the various components of information—a very complex endeavor. In addition, researchers have yet to resolve the following issues:

1. What effect does the presence or absence of language have on mental development?
2. Are children's thoughts affected by the particular speech patterns or language forms with which they are familiar?
3. Which develops first—the nonverbal idea or the words to express it?

Even though we may not have conclusive answers to these questions, there is little doubt that cognitive development and language development are intricately related. That relationship must be taken into account when discussing the conditions that impede language development.

## CONDITIONS THAT IMPEDE NORMAL LANGUAGE DEVELOPMENT

It has been estimated that more than one million children and adults in the United States are unable to communicate orally (Diggs, 1981). Over 70 percent of all three- to five-year-old children receiving special services were classified as "speech impaired" (U.S. Department of Education, 1985). The learning of language may be disrupted for a variety of reasons, among them: (1) sensory deprivation; (2) experiential deprivation; (3) emotional disorganization; and (4) neurological dysfunction. These four causes along with their corresponding conditions are shown in Table 8.4. In each case, the symptom is the same—the child has difficulty learning language. However, the accompanying characteristics are different for each condition causing the language disorder. A *differential diagnosis* is the assessment process to determine the cause (or etiology) of the language disorder. In some cases, there are several conditions contributing to the language

**TABLE 8.4   Disruption of Language Learning**

| CAUSE | CONDITIONS |
|---|---|
| Sensory deprivation | Hearing impairment<br>Visual impairment<br>Combination (deaf–blind) |
| Experiential deprivation | Cultural deprivation, lack of opportunity<br>Cultural difference |
| Emotional disorganization | Personality disorder<br>Autism, psychosis, neurosis<br>Elective mutism |
| Neurological dysfunction | Mental retardation<br>Neuromotor disorders<br>Organic impairments<br>Childhood aphasia<br>Specific learning disabilities |

problem; these children have multiple causes for their communication disorders.

### Sensory Deprivation

The condition of auditory deprivation includes both deaf and hard-of-hearing children. Children who are deaf from birth develop certain characteristics that differentiate them from others having difficulty learning language. For example, deaf children do not babble for long because they cannot hear their own voices. Their voices have a characteristic nonmelodic quality. Deaf children frequently use and are likely to understand gestures. They attend closely to facial expressions, movements, and other visual cues and are particularly sensitive to tactile sensations and impressions. The second group of children with auditory deprivation—hard-of-hearing children—have varying degrees of hearing loss, ranging along a continuum from near deafness to near normal hearing. They may appear to be inattentive and may miss certain sounds or words in conversation.

The loss of hearing acuity is measured through two dimensions: frequency and intensity. *Frequency* is the pitch of the sound and ranges from low sounds to high-frequency sounds. To hear human speech, one must be able to respond to frequencies between 500 and 2,000 vibrations per second. *Intensity* refers to the loudness of sound and is measured in decibels (dB). Hearing impairment affects the ability to receive or hear language, but it also impairs the child's ability to use or express speech sounds. Depending on the degree of auditory loss, speaking becomes a laborious, if not impossible, task.

Children who have language disorders that are caused by, or complicated by, a hearing impairment require special training (Ruder, 1978).

Usually there is an emphasis on visual input and the use of amplification and auditory training.

Vision also plays an important role in the development of verbal communication. The eyes are used to verify what is heard, relate objects with their verbal symbols, study faces, get feedback, and develop a sense of space, distance, and proportion (Weiss and Lillywhite, 1976). A surprisingly large percentage of blind and visually impaired children have deficient speech and language, primarily in the acquisition of word concepts that are based on reference to visual experiences, abstractions, or images. For example, a blind child would have difficulty fully understanding the phrase "blowing a kiss."

### Experiential Deprivation

Experiential deprivation can impede language development for the preschool child. To learn language, one must have sufficient experiences, stimulation, and feedback. Some young children may not learn language because of social, cultural, and/or economic limitations. They may lack opportunities for language learning in their home or caregiving environment. Among the environmental factors known to adversely affect language development are multiple, closely spaced births; crowded living conditions; disruptions in consistent caregiving (too many different people caring for the child after six months of age); institutionalization (that is, orphanages); inadequate food and nutrition; and poor health care. Moreover, a lag in language development tends to widen as the child gets older. One of the purposes of Head Start is to overcome the detrimental effects of experiential deprivation and provide the child with opportunities to expand language experiences (Garber and Slater, 1983).

Language deficiencies due to experiential deprivation should not be confused with language differences. *Language differences* and *language deficiencies* are not the same. A child with a language difference has a rich language pattern but it is different from that of standard English. The child may use a dialectical variation of English. Some children use a mixture of two languages, such as English and Spanish. There are many dialects in the United States today that reflect the language of certain cultural groups. Thus, the structure of the sentence may be different, the vocabulary may be different, or the pronunciation or speech inflection may be different from that of standard English. Linguists who have studied these dialectical variations of standard English have claimed them to be complete and equal languages with predictable syntactic, semantic, and phonological systems (Labov, 1970; Shuy, 1970). When the child is in school, however, the language of instruction is usually in standard English. Recent studies show that when children use a language different from that used at school, there is a gap between the child's language and that of the school. This language gap makes school learning more difficult and contributes to educational failures (Worthington, 1985).

## Emotional Disorganization

Language deficits due to emotional disorganization are perhaps the most difficult and uncharted types of language disturbance. This type of problem has a low incidence and usually consists of a unique combination of characteristics. Children with severe emotional disorganization—such as those with infantile autism or childhood schizophrenia—are likely to have one or more of the following traits in language, speech, and communication (Prizant and Duchan, 1981; Lovaas, 1977; Wing, 1976):

1. *Mutism or elective mutism* (functionally equivalent): Children with this language disorder do not talk at all.
2. *Nonfunctional expressive language*: These children use echolalia, or gibberish.
3. *Severe receptive language dysfunction*: These children do not understand language; they do not respond to their own name or follow simple directions.
4. *Exclusive use of egocentric speech*: These children do not use words for interpersonal communications.
5. *Lack of visual contact*: These children do not establish eye contact when using language.
6. *Pronoun reversals*: These children use expressions "me want cookie" long beyond the normal stage of such usage.
7. *Lack of verbal requests*: These children do not use phrases such as "I want" or "give me."
8. *Articulation problems* in conjunction with above traits.

Before a child is diagnosed as schizophrenic or autistic, these traits must be accompanied by other behavioral characteristics (for example, perceptual impairments; social withdrawal; self-stimulating behavior, such as head banging or rocking; proprioceptive or vestibular stimulation, such as whirling or swinging), which may vary in severity (Gardner, 1977). Deviations in language development are a primary consideration in making a differential diagnosis. When such behavioral characteristics are present, the child is almost always significantly impaired in *all* aspects of the developmental process. Thus, language training alone is ineffective. Chapter 10, "Teaching Social and Affective Skills," suggests activities for dealing with the affective (psychosocial) domain in preschool children.

## Neurological Dysfunction

Language deficits not due to sensory deprivation, experiential deprivation, or emotional disorganization may be due to some degree of neurological dysfunction. Several handicapping conditions are discussed under neurological dysfunctions as separate entities. In reality, they may overlap.

*Mental retardation* was discussed in Chapter 2. Due to the relationship between language and thinking, communication skills are generally delayed in varying degrees with this group of children. The greater the degree of mental retardation, the greater the degree of language and speech disability (Fallen and Umansky, 1985). Oral language stimulation at an early age may minimize later language disabilities and reduce social and emotional problems as well.

*Neuromotor disorders,* such as cerebral palsy, are often related to language deficits. It has been estimated that about 50 percent of children with such disorders have speech and language problems due to a number of related conditions: difficulty in use of the speech apparatus itself, associated perceptual problems, and limited ability to move about which affects the experiences necessary for language development.

*Organic impairments* of the speech mechanism—such as cleft palate and lip, deformity of the jaw, tongue, or larynx (voice box)—may all cause temporary or permanent language and speech problems that need to be recognized and dealt with by the speech and language specialist.

*Childhood aphasia* is another central nervous system dysfunction that interferes with the association between the spoken symbol or word and the corresponding element of experience. It may be an input, processing, and/or output problem; that is, the child may not be able to understand speech (receptive aphasia), use speech (expressive aphasia), or use language for any purpose (central aphasia). Eisenson and Ingram (1978) report that aphasic children have perceptual problems that cause faulty discriminations and categorizations. These children learn grammatical rules more slowly. Thus, they need a vocabulary of almost 200 words before they can produce a two-word utterance, whereas a normal child combines two words with a vocabulary of only about 50 words. Moreover, aphasic children's language and speech skills develop differently from those of normal children. There is a qualitative distinction.

*Specific learning disabilities* often involve language deficits of various types. Some educators tend to avoid this term with preschool children, preferring *developmental delay* as a noncategorical term to encompass children with problems that may be attributable to more than one condition or that cannot be classified with certainty at an early age (Lerner, 1985). Regardless, according to Bloom (1980), a preschool child who is learning language slowly or with particular difficulty has a learning problem. The preschool child with a problem in learning language will likely have a learning disability in the school years.

## A CLASSIFICATION SYSTEM FOR SPEECH AND LANGUAGE DISORDERS

Although it is useful for purposes of assessment to determine the cause of the communication problem, this grouping does not provide the best classification for planning instruction. In addition to the cause, or etiology, of the problem, one must consider the severity or functional status of the child's communication problem. Whatever the cause or severity of the problem, children with deviant language need the following (McCormick and Schiefelbusch, 1984):

1. To have language learning experiences at least as rich as those provided normal language users
2. To be concerned with and talk about many of the same objects, events, and relationships that normal learners do
3. To experience the same control over their environment as their more competent peers at the same stage of development

For purposes of instruction, children with communication problems can be classified into three types: (1) nonverbal children; (2) language-disordered children; and (3) speech-impaired children. This classification cuts across causes, or etiologies.

### Nonverbal Children

This problem refers to children who have no language at all, and it is the type of communication problem that occurs least frequently. Some children from several of the handicapping conditions might be described as nonverbal; including children who are autistic, severely and profoundly hearing impaired, physically handicapped if it affects the speech mechanism, multihandicapped, and profoundly mentally retarded. Often these children are helped by learning nonverbal alternative communication systems (such as signing), rather than through oral language instruction.

### Language Disorders

A language disorder is the inability to relate linguistic symbols to experiences because of central nervous system dysfunction. It includes youngsters with childhood aphasia, some children with specific learning disabilities, and others with language problems. The child may have a *receptive language disorder* (difficulty in understanding language) or an *expressive language disorder* (difficulty in producing and using language). Further, the difficulty may be with specific linguistic systems, such as

*Disorders of semantics:* meager understanding of vocabulary (receptive language disorder) and poor ability to produce and use words (expressive language disorder)

*Disorders of syntax and morphology:* inability to comprehend connected discourse, awkward sentence construction, improper sequencing of words, omissions of words, and incorrect use of morphological rules

Often children are *delayed* in language development; that is, they do not begin to talk at the normal age. In other cases, the children do not follow an orderly pattern when learning the language code and their language is unintelligible. Figure 8.1 lists possible signs of receptive language disorders followed by possible signs of expressive language disorders.

DeHirsch (1981) suggests that early evidence of language disorders, even subtle problems, at an early age are red flags that predict later learning difficulties. Often these children have subsequent difficulty learning to read, write, do mathematics, and follow oral classroom rules and procedures. They also may become inattentive and distractible due to their poor processing of linguistic information.

**FIGURE 8.1** Signs of Possible Language Disorders

**Receptive**

1. By 6 months child does not quiet to the sound of the caregiver's voice.
2. By 11 months child does not turn head and shoulders toward familiar sounds (that is, phone ringing, footstep) even when there is nothing to be seen.
3. By 15 months the child does not understand and respond to name, "no-no," "bye-bye," and "bottle."
4. By 21 months the child does not respond correctly to "Give me that," "Sit down," "Stand up."
5. By 24 months the child does not understand and point to, on command, mouth, nose, hair, and ears.
6. By 30 months the child does not understand and demonstrate, on command, in, on, under, front, and back.
7. By 48 months the child cannot answer correctly the questions: "What do we sleep on?" "What do we sit on?" "What do we cook on?" "What is your name?" "What do you do when you are hungry?" "What do you do when you are thirsty?" (by pointing or gestures).
8. By 48 months the child cannot distinguish boy from girl, big from little, one object from two or more objects.
9. By 60 months the child cannot tell the use of book, stove, house, and key.
10. By 60 months the child cannot distinguish soft from hard, smooth from rough, and tell why we have a chair, house, dress, and window.

**Expressive**

1. By 18 months the child is not saying at least six words with appropriate meaning.
2. By 24 months the child is not combining words into phrases, such as "Go bye-bye." "Want cookie."
3. By 30 months the child is not using short sentences, such as, "Mommy see dolly," "Daddy go bye-bye."
4. By 36 months the child has not begun asking simple questions.
5. By 48 months the child's sentences are telegraphic, reversed, or confused, such as, "Me car go," "Baby loud crying," "Candy me want."
6. By 48 months the child is not using auxiliary verbs, such as, "is," "have," and "can."

7. By 60 months the child is not using the personal pronoun "I" such as "Me (instead of I) want a cookie," or uses name instead of pronoun, such as "Bobby (instead of I) want a drink."
8. By 60 months the child consistently, incorrectly uses past tenses, plurals, and pronouns, such as "Them throwed a balls."
9. By 60 months the child's expressive vocabulary is limited and shallow, fewer than 200 to 300 simple words.
10. The child's language has not improved in sentence length, complexity, and accuracy within any 6-month period after age 2.
11. The child has difficulty in self-expression, according to the age level, or is concerned or teased about the language used.

From C. Weiss and H. Lillywhite. *Communicative Disorders: A Handbook for Prevention and Early Intervention.* St. Louis, MO: C. V. Mosby, 1976, p. 176–178.

### Speech Impairment

The largest number of children with communication difficulties have speech impairments. This classification includes problems with articulation of sounds and words, stuttering, and voice disorder. Speech impairments are not considered central nervous system problems; they involve difficulties in the formation and production of the sounds needed in using oral language and speaking. Indications of speech impairments are listed in Figure 8.2.

*Articulation problems.* It is estimated that articulation disorders comprise about 60 percent of all defective speech disorders (Safford, 1978). Considered the least serious of the speech disorders, they are also the most responsive to treatment. Since the ability to articulate sounds correctly improves with maturity, some articulation problems disappear as the child develops. The speech therapist may be needed to help the child learn more precise speech patterns and correct articulation errors such as omissions, substitutions, or distortion of sounds.

*Stuttering.* The problem of stuttering is noticed so frequently during the preschool years that it is generally considered a normal speech characteristic of preschoolers. Speech specialists generally advise ignoring this behavior in preschoolers and recommend that parents not call attention to this behavior by asking the child to slow down or to begin the sentence again. If the stuttering persists for an extended period of months, then the child should be examined by a speech therapist.

*Voice disorders.* Voice problems include inappropriate intensity, pitch, or quality of the voice. The child may speak in a voice that is raspy, unusually high, or very low. In some cases, the speech therapist can help the child use a more appropriate voice. If the voice problem is due to malformation of the vocal or auditory mechanisms, surgical or prosthetic

**FIGURE 8.2** Signs of Possible Speech Impairment

1. The child uses mainly vowels in babbling or speech after twelve months of age.
2. The speech is not more than 50 percent understandable by age 24 months.
3. There are many consonant omissions by 36 months.
4. There is a predominance of vowels in the speech after age 36 months.
5. The speech is not 100 percent understandable by 48 months; this does not mean all phonemes are used correctly, just understandably.
6. The child omits most initial consonants after age 3.
7. The child omits, substitutes, or distorts any phonemes after age 7.
8. Phonemes are more than 6 months late in appearing, according to normal developmental sequence.
9. The speech has not become noticeably more understandable and more fluent in the last 6 months, up to the age of 7.
10. The child is concerned or teased about the speech at any age.
11. The child repeats, hesitates, stops, and starts over frequently.
12. The child has been dysfluent for more than 6 months.
13. The child appears to be struggling to say words, blinks eyes, and grimaces when speaking.
14. The dysfluency becomes noticeably more severe at any time.
15. The child fears speaking situations at any age.
16. The rate of speaking is too fast, too slow, jumbled, or telescoped.
17. The voice quality is nasal (talks through the nose).
18. The voice quality, pitch, or loudness is abnormal (conspicuous).
19. The voice is monotone, dysphonic, or whiney most of the time.
20. The child has persistent, recurring hoarseness or breathiness.

From C. Weiss and H. Lillywhite. *Communicative Disorders: A Handbook for Prevention and Early Intervention.* St. Louis, MO: C. V. Mosby, 1976, p. 172.

intervention followed by speech therapy is needed. One technique used by speech therapists to modify the child's voice is to use an instructional method in which the child hears his or her own voice as feedback.

## INSTRUCTIONAL STRATEGIES FOR TEACHING COMMUNICATION SKILLS

Effective language learning programs are well organized, sequential, intensive, and consistent. They usually are based on research findings and/or language learning theories.

There are three interrelated explanations of language learning, each with implications for teaching. The first explanation, *natural learning theory,* is a psycholinguistic view of language learning (Chomsky, 1968). According to this theory, children are predisposed biologically to learn and use language. That is, they are born with an innate capacity for both understanding and producing language. What the child learns is not merely a string of words through imitative learning but rather a set of transformational rules. These rules enable the child to: (1) understand an infinite variety of sentences as a listener, and (2) generate an infinite variety of novel sentences as a speaker.

The second explanation is a *behavioral theory* of language learning. According to this view, speech and language are learned systematically through imitation, or *modeling,* and encouraged through *reinforcement* (Hendrick, 1975; Safford, 1978). Thus, children learn communication skills by first imitating the specific speech characteristics in their environment that serve as speech and language models. Then, if the child's utterances, sounds, and gestures are reinforced in terms of adult attention and reaction, the language behavior is maintained. From this perspective, the goals of the teacher are to provide a good language model, encourage and reinforce desirable speech and language skills, and provide a secure atmosphere that will promote the learning of these skills. (See Chapter 10 for a fuller discussion of behavioral techniques.)

The third explanation for language learning is that the child's *cognitive development* sets the stage for language acquisition (Slobin, 1973). According to Piaget (1962), language development is related to the child's ability to manipulate the symbolic function or meaning of a concept. Thus, language will not develop until the child has reached the cognitive stage, which permits the child to represent one thing with another, to make something "stand for" something not present. The point is that language and cognition are so interrelated that language learning should not be isolated from its broad developmental context (Morehead and Morehead, 1974). For the teacher, this means that language training should go hand in hand with nonlinguistic representation systems—symbolic play with objects, role playing, imagery, and drawing. The semantic concepts that provide the basis for early language acquisition are derived directly from these linguistic and nonlinguistic experiences.

For children with severe communication problems, the internal mechanism for producing language is not intact. They are not developing and using language in the normal way. These children need direct teaching of language and the instructional use of behavioral techniques of modeling and reinforcement. An early intervention program in language should begin during early infancy or as soon as a baby's problem is identified, rather than in the middle of the second year of life (Bricker and Bricker, 1974). In addition, nonspeech systems may be necessary—not only for deaf and hard-of-hearing children, but for children who find oral language acquisition incredibly difficult. Manual systems of communication (such as signing) may be taught as oral facilitators or as a second language support system.

The language intervention program should include the following strategies:

1.  Identifying the individual child's receptive, expressive, and nonverbal communication skills that need to be developed or modified.
2.  Considering the particular propensities of each child. Some children are more inclined toward expressing personal wants and feelings and initiating social interactions—"expressive" children. Other children are more oriented toward categorizing and labeling objects—"referential" children. Awareness of these propensities enables the teacher to choose vocabulary for initial training with consideration for the child's abilities and interests (Bowerman, 1978).
3.  Allowing the child to control the interaction. The child will learn the most when the adult speech gives meaning to whatever the child is attending to. This is possible even when the child does not speak, first by attending to whatever the child is noticing at the moment and talking about it.

Further, auditory stimulation should be combined with opportunities to feel, see, and, if possible, smell objects. Combining the use of the various avenues of sense generally enhances language acquisition.

Children with severe communication problems usually require the assistance of related specialists; but they should be included in regular preschool activities as often as possible. Children with no language skills, such as autistic children, often benefit from a substitute communication method—such as some type of signing, rebus symbols, computer speech, or using a visual system to communicate in lieu of an auditory system. Research has shown these strategies to be effective with nonverbal children.

Children with more subtle communication problems may need to be identified by the classroom teacher through screening techniques and/or systematic observation in a variety of situations over a period of time. The child who is unusually quiet may never be a discipline problem, thus becoming the one most easily overlooked as a language-disordered child.

The sequence of language training should be based on two principles (Ruder, 1978):

1.  Language forms and functions that have immediate utility for the child should be trained first.
2.  Normal language development data (Tables 8.1, 8.2, 8.3; Figures 8.1, 8.2) suggest the content and sequence of a language training program.

One should keep in mind that language intervention is more effective when it occurs throughout the day rather than only during a special "language" time (Karczmarek, 1985). No language program can teach every word, phrase, or concept. Therefore, a basic goal of every program is to train for generalization by reinforcing children whenever they create new and novel linguistic utterances. The ultimate goal of language intervention is having the child use the skills taught in natural contexts appropriately and independently (Kaczmarek, 1985).

## Teaching Receptive Language Skills

*Listening* is a receptive language skill and it is a learned skill. The child must learn to listen to acquire verbal communication abilities. Listening differs from hearing (the process of receiving sound waves) because listening is an active process requiring concentration and thinking. Listening requires a child to deliberately attend to sounds so that the brain can translate, interpret, and store them for later use. Figure 8.3 illustrates the relationship of listening to other aspects of the receptive and organizing processes.

After an audiometric evaluation, an auditory discrimination program should be started. Environmental sounds are selected that are relevant to the immediate situation, interest, and experiential background of the child. In this way the child's attention is focused toward the sound through visual cues. It is often necessary to shape the attending behavior within the context of the program. This is often accomplished by increasing motivation. Sounds and their sources must be associated consistently so the child makes a connection between the two. Finally, the child's responses to sound are positively reinforced, both verbally and nonverbally.

Both teachers and parents should consciously use linguistic and nonlinguistic cues such as repetition, exaggeration, pointing, and gestures as they speak. *Motherese*, a term coined by Newport (1976), refers to a manner of speaking to young children in which the sentences are shorter, simpler, higher in pitch, and more redundant than speech to adults. Research findings also suggest it is useful to speak slower than the normal rate of 150 to 175 words per minute (Horton, 1974).

In conjunction with auditory discrimination, work should begin on gross motor imitation followed by categorization of objects by action and functional use. It is generally easier to teach the child to imitate a motor act than a verbal act. Examples of motor acts that even a ten-month-old will learn to imitate are

Waving your hand and saying 'bye-bye'
Moving your head from side to side

**FIGURE 8-3**  The Links of Receptive and Organizing Processes

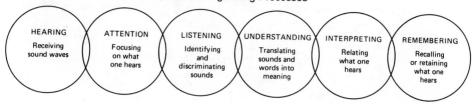

Pretending to drink from a cup (then giving the cup to the child)
Putting your hands together as in "pat-a-cake"
Hitting the table with your hand (then later varying the rhythm)

After the child masters gross motor imitation, putting all the objects that roll (ball, coin, wheel) together would precede putting all the vehicles or all the foods together. Working on one function at a time leads to faster mastery than beginning with several different functions. Other functions can be introduced after the first function is mastered in one context without decreasing performance. This allows the child to work on several functions at different levels of mastery. This procedure is known as *concurrent training*. As the child learns additional functions, he or she will generally require progressively fewer trials. Learning acceleration is caused by experience in learning and accentuates the importance of such experiences for language and cognitive development.

To encourage good listening habits, the teacher, therapist, and parent(s) should keep in mind the following guidelines:

> *Give instructions only once* so that children become trained to tune in the first time. Try not to repeat instructions. However, everything else can and should be repeated.

*Use a quiet, normal voice,* which provides a good model and requires closer listening than a loud demanding tone.

*Give short, concise, clearly stated instructions* or explanations. Children (and adults) tend to tune out long, rambling, unclear ones.

*Use a moderate rate of speech,* which is easier to follow than a rapid rate.

*Listen attentively* when a child speaks to you. Again, this serves as a good model for the child.

*Be certain you have the child(ren)'s attention* before you begin your directions. Use eye contact to verify attention. If necessary, block out visual distractions from the child(ren)'s view when speaking.

*Create quiet, calm surroundings,* which provide the most conducive environment for the development of listening skills.

*Use a sound cue* or carrier phrase, such as "ready," or snap your fingers to alert the child to "tune in." Be consistent with this cue and gradually fade it out.

*Use intonation and stress* appropriately.

The teacher needs to be flexible so that the different needs of individual children are met. A good beginning objective for improving listening skills is to help the child learn to attend for short periods of time. During listening activities, the auditory environment should be carefully structured to minimize distractions and auditory confusion. This will help the child to attend to the teacher's voice. Weiss and Lillywhite (1976) suggest "101 ways to help the child learn to talk."

Nursery rhymes offer one of the most effective listening activities for young children (Glenn and Cunningham, 1984). They are characterized by repetitive rhymes and words and obvious beginnings and endings. They provide a structured and appealing framework to help the child learn to anticipate events and to acquire gestures and vocalizations. For some children it is helpful to modify the nursery rhymes by using fewer words and/or selecting words that are more easily understood and related to the child's own environment.

### Teaching Expressive Language Skills

Listening skills are the "readiness" stage of communication skills. They lead to the expressive speech skills, using vocabulary as the bridge. Step-by-step sequential instruction is needed to help the child progress to more complex language structures. However, this must be a slow procedure for the child who has language deficits. It is necessary to control language stimuli so the child is not continuously overwhelmed. All adults caring for a given child—teacher, aide, parents, therapist—should work on the same specific language goals to achieve continuity. Isolate small elements of language to build on. The training must be concrete and experientially based, using real objects rather than pictures, so that meaning is always conveyed. Encourage approximations, reinforcing any response at first, but gradually switching to an intermittent schedule. Remember that children learn best in an accepting environment. Therefore, do not correct the child's inaccurate attempts, even when they are phonologically imperfect or semantically inappropriate.

After the child has learned to imitate gross motor acts, begin training to imitate sounds. The child who babbles is ready for these activities:

> Say a sound and if the child repeats, show pleasure and repeat again, making it a game
>
> Make a coughing sound
>
> Say "sh" and put your finger on your mouth
>
> Smack your lips to make a kissing sound
>
> Make a panting sound
>
> Add sounds that go with certain activities, such as "oh, oh," "boom," "zoom"
>
> Move to identifying and naming objects, followed by teaching the child to verbalize needs and wants.
>
> Eventually, move to pictures and more abstract concepts.

Vocabulary training should proceed from nouns to verbs, followed by adjectives and then adverbs. A model for a verbal communication skills program for language-impaired children would contain the following components (Figure 8.4).

It is always desirable to include nondelayed children in the language program. Besides serving as models for the children with delayed language, they provide data for the staff on the normal acquisition of language and cognitive processes.

Guidelines for teaching vocabulary include (Hatten and Hatten, 1975):

1. The word and object (or experience) must be presented simultaneously so the association between the sound and what it refers to becomes clear.
2. A new word must be experienced in a variety of ways before it can be meaningful.
3. Repetition is mandatory.
4. Seeing and hearing what the word is *not* also is important.

**FIGURE 8.4** Verbal Communication Skills Program

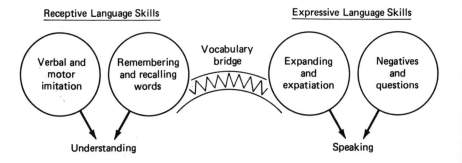

For example, hand the child an orange and say the word, "orange." The child holds it, smells it, and even tastes it after it is peeled and sectioned. At another time, possibly the regular snack time, squeeze the orange and have the child drink the juice. Next, the child can learn to select an orange from other objects: first from nonfoods, then from other foods, and finally from other fruits. Then move from the actual objects to flannel cutouts and realistic-looking pictures. Additional guidelines for encouraging expressive language include:

1. Give children enough time to express a thought.
2. Let children make their needs known; do not anticipate for the child.
3. Ask open-ended questions rather than those that require only a yes or no response.
4. Find interesting things to talk about.
5. Provide opportunities for repetition and practice.
6. Use praise and/or tangible rewards frequently.

Children normally develop syntax in language through a process of interaction between caregiver and child, which is called *expansion*. When the child utters a phrase such as "Bobby, orange," the adult responds by repeating the statement in syntactically expanded form such as, "Oh, Bobby wants an orange." The words are retained in the same order as spoken by the child, and the expansion results in a well-formed simple sentence that is appropriate to the situation (Brown and Bellugi, 1964). The technique of expansion is easy to use and is effective in helping children learn language in a natural environment, such as free-playtime (McLean and Vincent, 1984).

*Expatiation* is a form of expansion that requires the adult to react to the child's utterance by expanding it conceptually rather than linguistically. For example, if the child said "Bobby, orange," the adult might respond "I'm sorry, it's almost lunchtime." This form of expansion is more significant for the child who can mimic but has expressive delays due to concept formation problems, rather than vocabulary or syntactical problems.

Other language approaches are based on behavior modification principles and advocate a structured pattern drill; for example, *Distar Language* (Engelmann and Bruner, 1967). Repetitive behavior plays an important part in both mental growth and language development. This approach has proved to be successful for some children with emotional disturbance or environmental deprivation.

Expressive language skills can be further developed during many activities in early childhood settings—such as show-and-tell, dramatic play, group discussion, story sharing and telling, and puppetry. Puppets become the center of attention instead of the child, often enabling the child to express feelings as well as concepts.

Music—with its form, rhythm, and tonal sequences of melody—also can be used in developing communication skills (Thursby, 1977). For

instance, children can tap out rhythms using contrasting words such as fast or slow, soft or loud. They can learn verbs—such as run, jump, walk, or crawl—by responding to music. In still another activity, music can set the mood for a creative story.

### Teaching Nonverbal Communication Skills

Nonverbal communication skills also may have to be taught. If the child has intact receptive skills, a verbal explanation of gestures, laughter, and other nonverbal symbols should be presented to the child simultaneously.

Some children will never develop speech as an effective way of communicating; others may need temporary assistance until their expressive skills are adequate enough to avoid frustration in conveying their needs and expressing their ideas. Devices to help the nonverbal child communicate are known as augmentative communication systems (Shane, 1981). They range from relatively simple lap trays and story boards to sophisticated electronic devices with synthetic voice machines. For young children, the devices utilize pictures and symbols to enable two-way communication depending on the physical abilities of the child. They are usually designed for the particular needs and abilities of a child and can be modified as the child's needs and abilities change. The goal of the augmentative system is to facilitate effective interaction between nonspeaking children and the people in their environment (Bottorf and DePape, 1982). The use of computers to enhance communication is discussed in Chapter 9.

### Parent Training for Language Development

A parent-training component is a very important part of the language intervention program. Parents may need to be taught how to reinforce what is being taught in the program and how to conduct language training at home. Parents need to learn that words should be used within meaningful contexts, how to expand what the child says, how to label objects in the environment, and how to talk about objects and events or experiences as much as possible. In other words, parents should learn to talk, talk, talk! Parents can be taught in a simulated home environment so that everyday activities of the household become the curriculum.

Parents are a key component of a successful language intervention program. A parent-training program should (Horton, 1974):

1. Teach parents how to optimize their child's auditory environment
2. Teach parents how to talk to their child
3. Familiarize parents with the principles, stages, and sequence of normal language development
4. Show parents how to apply what is known about normal language development when stimulating their child
5. Teach parents strategies of behavior management

It should be remembered that parents are most effective when they function as parents and not as teachers. The program should help parents modify their communication style but always in the context of natural parent–child interactions and activities.

## MATERIALS FOR TEACHING COMMUNICATION SKILLS

Developmental language kits are commercial products designed to stimulate receptive, associative, and expressive language, as well as cognitive development of preschool children. Among them are the *Peabody Early Experience Kit—PEEK* (Dunn et al., 1976) and the *Development Kit (revised) Level P* (Dunn et al., 1981). These kits contain many concrete objects for teaching language meaning, sequenced lesson plans, colorful pictures, as well as chips that can be used in a reinforcement system. Although they can be used with any preschooler, these kits are widely used to teach language development to handicapped preschoolers (Dell, 1984). Another comprehensive set of materials is *Early Childhood Discovery Materials* (Bank Street College of Education, 1973). These materials are designed to extend and reinforce specific language skills as well as concept, perception, and motor development of preschoolers.

Some materials were developed specifically for language-impaired and language-delayed children. Among them are GOAL (Game Oriented Activities for Learning—Level 1, Language Development—Karnes, 1972), which is geared for ages three to five or older special-needs children. With over 1,500 activities within 289 lesson plans, the program is designed for small groups of 5 to 8 children. The activities are built around the processes of the Illinois Test of Psycholinguistic Abilities (ITPA): reception, association, expression, memory, and closure. The *MWM Program for Development of Language Abilities* (Minskoff, Wiseman, and Minskoff, 1972) is also based on the ITPA model. In the MWM material there are separate manuals for each of the five linguistic processes of the ITPA, and the program is organized around three language clusters: verbal, visual-motor, and readiness. In comparing these two materials (GOAL Program and MWM Program), Logan and Colarusso (1978) found that both programs, as supplements, are superior for training expressive skills but neither is more effective than a regular program for auditory reception.

There is also a language curriculum program designed for infants and toddlers (birth to three years) who have communication, physical, and mental disabilities (Reidlicht and Herzfeld, 1984). This program gives three specific activities for each month of developmental age level, and it can be implemented in class or at home.

Other special education materials include the *Clark Early Language Program* (Clark and Moses, 1981) for language- and hearing-impaired children. This material employs rebus cards. The *Communication Training Program* (Waryas and Stremel-Campbell, 1982), goes from prelanguage functions through basic semantic and syntactic structures to elaboration of grammatical constructions. There are excellent materials for stimulating oral expression, such as the *All-Purpose Photo Libraries and Story Telling Pictures*, as well as games for articulation (*Land of S, Land of R*). There are also audiotapes of familiar environmental sounds for auditory perception, auditory memory, auditory discrimination, and articulation therapy. There is a plastic speech mask that enables children to hear themselves speak just as other people hear them. These materials are distributed by DLM Teaching Resources (see Appendix C). For communication skills materials designed for use by parents, see Chapter 3.

Relatively new sources for teaching language development are microcomputer software and speech synthesizers. Some microcomputer packages are accompanied by sound so children receive both auditory and visual input (see Chapter 9). The Laureate Learning Systems programs (*First Words, First Verbs, First Categories*) (Wilson and Fox, 1982, 1983, 1985) are examples of microcomputer programs using speech synthesizers to teach language.

A note of caution must be added here. It is important that teachers not become overly dependent on kits or packaged materials. Utilize them to meet the individual needs of each child. A disadvantage of kits or "canned" programs is that they are too general in scope and may not be appropriate for an individual child's problems. However, kits do provide a structure, and they can be modified to meet a child's specific needs.

## SUMMARY

The development of communication skills is vital for every child. Not only do these skills affect how one functions in society and interacts with others, but they also affect how one thinks. A developmental hierarchy of skills has been recognized. Inner, receptive, and expressive language are components of oral communication.

Normal language development milestones have been documented by many studies of individual children and groups of children. In addition, language skills can be differentiated from speech skills just as language and speech, although closely related, can be distinguished from each other.

There are many conditions that impede normal language development.

They can be divided into four general etiological groupings—sensory deprivation, experiential deprivation, emotional disturbance, and neurological dysfunction—or they can be regrouped into classes of severity with nonverbal children as the most severe but smallest class, language-disordered children as the moderate class, and speech-impaired children as the mildest but largest class.

Teaching communication skills necessitates general knowledge of normal language development and specifics for the particular needs of the individual child. Guidelines for group and individual sessions by the teacher, aide, therapist, and/ or parent are given along with materials useful for teaching communication skills.

## REVIEW QUESTIONS

**Terms to Know**

| | |
|---|---|
| inner language | pragmatics |
| receptive language | sensory deprivation |
| expressive language | experiential deprivation |
| phonology | emotional disorganization |
| semantics | neurological dysfunction |
| syntactics | childhood aphasia |
| "motherese" | expansion |
| expatiation | concurrent learning |

1. What is the distinction between language and speech?
2. Describe the relationship of inner, receptive, and expressive language. Why is this relationship important to a teacher of language-impaired children?
3. Define the three components of speech skills: auditory perception, articulation, and voice.
4. Complete this chart:

**Conditions That Impede Normal Language Development**

| SENSORY DEPRIVATION | EXPERIENTIAL DEPRIVATION | EMOTIONAL DISORGANIZATION | NEUROLOGICAL DYSFUNCTION |
|---|---|---|---|
| 1. | 1. | 1. | 1. |
| 2. | 2. | 2. | 2. |

5. Compare, contrast, and classify language and speech problems according to etiology. Classify language and speech problems according to degree of the problem.
6. Complete this chart:

**Signs of Possible Problems**

| RECEPTIVE LANGUAGE | EXPRESSIVE LANGUAGE | SPEECH |
|---|---|---|
| 1. | 1. | 1. |
| 2. | 2. | 2. |
| 3. | 3. | 3. |
| 4. | 4. | 4. |
| 5. | 5. | 5. |

7. Johnny, age 3 years 5 months, is placed in your room on a trial basis for one week. The major presenting problem is that he is nonverbal. List five hypotheses you could check out informally. Explain how you would do each.

## REFERENCES

BANK STREET COLLEGE OF EDUCATION. (1973) *Early Childhood Discovery Materials.* Riverside, NJ: Macmillan.

BERKO, J. (1958) "The Child's Learning of English Morphology." *Word,* 14, 150–77.

BLANK, M. (1974) "Cognitive Functions of Language in the Preschool Years." *Developmental Psychology* 10, 229–45.

BLOOM, L. (1980) "Language Development, Language Disorders, and Learning Disabilities: LD." *Bulletin of the Orton Society,* 30, 115–30.

BLOOM, L. and M. LAHEY (1978) *Language Development and Language Disorders.* NY: Wiley.

BOTTORF, L. and D. DEPAPE (1982) "Initiating Communication Systems for Severely Speech Impaired Persons." *Topics in Language Disorders,* 2, 55–71.

BOWERMAN, M. (1978) "Semantic and Syntactic Development: A Review of What, When, and How in Language Acquisition." In R. Schiefelbusch (ed.) *Bases of Language Intervention.* Baltimore: University Park Press.

BRICKER, W., and D. BRICKER (1974) "An Early Language Training Strategy." In R. Schiefelbusch and L. Lloyd (eds.) *Language Perspective—Acquisition, Retardation, and Intervention.* Baltimore: University Park Press.

BROWN, R., and U. BELLUGI (1964) "Three Processes in the Child's Acquisition of Language." *Harvard Educational Review,* 34, 133–51.

BRUNER, J. (1976) "Interpreting Baby Talk." *Time,* August 23.

BRYEN, D., and D. GALLAGHER (1983) "Assessment of Language and Communication." In K. Paget and B. Bracken (eds.) *Psychoeducational Assessment of Preschool Children.* NY: Grune & Stratton.

CHOMSKY, N. (1968) *Language and Mind.* NY: Harcourt, Brace & World.

CLARK, C., and D. MOSES (1981) *Clark Early Language Program.* Allen, TX: DLM Teaching Resources.

DEHIRSCH, K. (1981) "Unready Children." In A. Gerber and D. Bryen (eds.) *Language and Learning Disabilities.* Baltimore: University Park Press.

DELL, A. (1984) "Teaching Approaches in Programs Serving Preschool Handicapped Children in North Dakota." *Journal of the Division for Early Childhood* 8 (1), 74–85.

DIGGS, C. (1981) "School Services." *Language, Speech and Hearing Services in Schools,* 4, 269–71.

DUNN, L., L. CHUN, D. CROWELL, L. DUNN, L. HALEVI, and E. YACKEL (1976) *Peabody Early Experience Kit—PEEK.* Circle Pines, MN: American Guidance Service.

DUNN, L., J. SMITH, L. DUNN, K. HORTON, and D. SMITH (1981) *Peabody Language Development Kit (revised) Level P.* Circle Pines, MN: American Guidance Service.

EGOLF, D. and S. CHESTER (1973) "Nonverbal Communication and the Disorders of Speech and Language." *ASHA,* 15, 511–18.

EISENSON, J., and D. INGRAM (1978) "Childhood Aphasia—An Updated Concept Based on Recent Research." In M. Lakey (ed.) *Readings in Childhood Language Disorders.* NY: John Wiley.

ENGELMANN, S. and E. BRUNER (1967) *Distar Language I & II.* Chicago: Science Research Associates.

FALLEN, N. and W. UMANSKY (1985) *Young Children with Special Needs.* Columbus: Chas. E. Merrill.

GARBER, H., and M. SLATER (1983) "Assessment of the Culturally Different Preschooler." In K. Paget and B. Bracken (eds.) *The Psychoeducational Assessment of Preschool Children.* NY: Grune & Stratton.

GARDNER, W. (1977) *Learning and Behavior Characteristics of Exceptional Children and Youth.* Boston: Allyn & Bacon.

GLENN, S. and C. CUNNINGHAM (1984) "Nursery Rhymes and Early Language Acquisition by Mentally Handicapped Children." *Exceptional Children,* 51 (1), 72–74.

HATTEN, J. and P. HATTEN (1975) *Natural Language.* Tucson, AZ: Communication Skill Builders.

HENDRICK, J. (1975) *The Whole Child: New Trends in Early Education.* St. Louis: C.V. Mosby,

HORTON, K. (1974) "Infant Intervention and Language Learning." In R. Schiefelbusch and L. Lloyd (eds.) *Language Perspectives—Acquisition, Retardation, and Intervention.* Baltimore: University Park Press.

KACZMAREK, L. (1985) "Integrating Language/Communication Objectives into the Total Preschool Curriculum." *Teaching Exceptional Children,* Spring, 183–89.

KARNES, M. (1972) *GOAL (Game Oriented Activities for Learning).* Springfield, MA: Milton Bradley.

LABOV, W. (1970) "The Logic of Non-standard English." In F. Williams (ed.) *Language and Poverty.* Chicago: Markham.

LEONARD, L. (1978) "Cognitive Factors in Early Linguistic Development." In R. Schiefelbush (ed.) *Bases of Language Intervention.* Baltimore: University Park Press.

LERNER, J. (1985) *Learning Disabilities: Theories, Diagnosis, and Teaching Strategies* (4th ed.) Boston: Houghton Mifflin.

LOGAN, R., and R. COLARUSSO (1978) "The Effectiveness of the MWM and GOAL Programs in Developing General Language Abilities." *Learning Disabilities Quarterly,* 1, 32–38.

LOVAAS, O. (ed.) (1977) *The Autistic Child: Language Development Through Behavior Modification.* NY: Halsted Press.

MCCORMICK, L. and R. SCHIEFELBUSCH (1984) *Early Language Intervention.* Columbus: Charles E. Merrill.

MCLEAN, M. and L. VINCENT (1984) "The Use of Expansions as a Language Intervention Technique in the Natural Environment." *Journal of the Division for Early Childhood* 9 (1), 57–66.

MINSKOFF, E., D. WISEMAN, and G. MINSKOFF (1972) *The MWM Program for Developing Language Abilities.* Ridgefield, NJ: Educational Performance Associates.

MOREHEAD, D. and A. MOREHEAD (1974) "From Signal to Sign: A Piagetian View of Thought and Language During the First Two Years." In R. Schiefelbusch and L. Lloyd (eds.) *Language Perspectives—Acquisition, Retardation, and Intervention.* Baltimore: University Park Press.

NATIONAL INSTITUTE OF NEUROLOGICAL DISEASES AND STROKE (1969) *Learning to Talk: Speech, Hearing and Language Problems in the Pre-school Child.* Washington, DC: U.S. Department of Health, Education and Welfare.

NEWPORT, E. (1976) "Motherese: The Speech of Mothers to Young Children." In N. Castellan, D. Pisoni, and G. Potts (eds.) *Cognitive Theory: Vol. II.* Hillsdale, NJ: Lawrence Erlbaum Associates.

PIAGET, J. (1962) *The Language and Thought of the Child.* NY: World Publishing.

PRIZENT, B. and J. DUCHAN (1981) "The Functions of Immediate Echolalia in Autistic Children." *Journal of Speech and Hearing Disorders,* 46, 241–49.

REIDLICHT, C., and M. HERZFELD (1984) *0–3 Years: An Early Language Curriculum.* Moline IL: Lingui Systems.

RUDER, K. (1978) "Planning and Programming for Language Intervention." In R. Schiefelbusch (ed.) *Bases of Language Intervention.* Baltimore: University Park Press.

SAFFORD, P. (1978) *Teaching Young Children with Special Needs.* St. Louis: C.V. Mosby.

SHANE, H. (1981) "Decision Making in Early Augmentative Communication System Use." In R. Schiefelbusch and D. Bricker (eds.) *Early Language: Acquisition and Intervention.* Baltimore: University Park Press.

SHUY, R. (1970) "The Sociolinguists and Urban Language Problems." In F. Williams (ed.) *Language and Poverty.* Chicago: Markham.

SLOBIN, D. (1973) "Cognitive Prerequisites for the Development of Grammar." In C. Ferguson and D. Slobin (eds.) *Studies of Child Language Development.* NY: Holt, Rinehart & Winston.

THURSBY, D. (1977) "Music Therapy for Young Handicapped Children." *Teaching Exceptional Children,* Spring, 77–78.

U.S. DEPARTMENT OF EDUCATION (1985) *To Ensure a Free Appropriate Public Education of All Handicapped Children.* Washington, DC: Government Printing Office.

VYGOTSKY, L. (1962) *Thought and Language.* Cambridge, MA: MIT Press.

WARYAS, C., and K. STREMEL-CAMPBELL (1982) *Communication Training Program.* Allen, TX: DLM Teaching Resources.

WEISS, C. and H. LILLYWHITE (1976) *Communicative Disorders: A Handbook for Prevention and Early Intervention.* St. Louis: C.V. Mosby.

WHORF, B. (1956) *Language, Thought, and Reality.* Cambridge, MA: John Wiley.

WILSON, M. and B. FOX (1982) *First Words.* Burlington, VT: Laureate Systems.

WILSON, M. and B. FOX (1983) *First Categories.* Burlington, VT: Laureate Systems.

WILSON, M. and B. FOX (1985) *First Verbs.* Burlington, VT: Laureate Systems.

WING, L. (ed.) (1976) *Early Childhood Autism.* Oxford: Pergamon Press.

WORTHINGTON, R. "Despite Warning, City Schools Slow to Silence Black English." *Chicago Tribune,* April 14, 1985, 3–4.

# NINE

# Teaching Cognitive Skills

## INTRODUCTION

"I think—therefore I exist." The inference of Descartes' oft-quoted adage is that the essence of being human is the ability to think. The process of thinking (or cognition) is involved in all forms of learning—motor, perceptual, language, and social.

Children who are handicapped or at-risk for handicapping conditions often experience difficulties with cognitive skills. They may have difficulty in the perception of objects—differentiating or comparing them. They may have difficulty in recalling or remembering what they have seen or heard. Or they may do poorly in other areas of cognition—such as forming concepts, making judgments, thinking through a sequence of events, or problem solving.

This chapter reviews the nature of cognition, several theories of how cognition develops in young children, the efficacy of early intervention on improving cognitive development, specific intervention strategies to promote cognitive growth, and the microcomputer as a tool for learning cognitive skills.

## COGNITIVE SKILLS

The term *cognitive skills* refers to the many mental abilities related to thinking and learning. Cognitive skills include such abilities as knowing and recognizing, developing concepts, organizing ideas, remembering, prob-

CASE EXAMPLE—JULIA: COGNITIVE DISABILITIES

Julia, age 4, appears to act without thinking. Her motor and language abilities are in the average range. However, her behavior often is impulsive rather than planned and thoughtful. She acts in such haste and so inappropriately that she is not careful about her own safety; in her haste to get a toy, for example, she often knocks over a block structure that other children are working on. She is easily distracted by sights and sounds in the room; and once she is put off track, she cannot bring her attention back to the task at hand. Julia often seems to forget directions. For example, when she is sent to another room to get something, she may leave and then reappear shortly to ask what she was supposed to get.

Julia rushes through a task without any attention to detail. She appears unable to think through the problem by herself. She does not evaluate or monitor her own progress during the work. Sometimes, she does not even realize when the work is completed. When given a problem to solve, such as putting a puzzle together, she usually says, "I can't do that" and seems unable to put forth a concerted effort to solve the problem. At the most, she pays attention for a minute or two. When she tires of one activity, she moves on to another. Sometimes she covers a great many activities in a short time, as different things attract her attention. Julia appears unable to control and direct her thinking.

lem solving, labeling and naming, understanding cause-and-effect relationships, drawing inferences, developing rules and generalizations, and making judgments and evaluations. *Cognition* is a pervasive term in that it occurs in all areas of learning. Preschool children need cognitive skills for learning in every phase of the early childhood curriculum—self-help, motor, language, perceptual, preacademic, social, and reasoning activities.

Because thinking and cognition are an integral part of all aspects of human learning and behavior, it is difficult to examine them as an entity apart from other kinds of learning. Cognitive abilities develop during all of the individual's life, beginning with infancy and early childhood. For example, when infants recognize the nipple or their mother's face, this is a perceptual skill and evidence of a growing ability "to know." Other evidence of the development of cognitive skills in young children can be observed: the young child playing at putting pots and pans inside each other; the child realizing that pushing a button or bell results in a ringing noise or buzz; a 15-month-old trying to feed a cup of milk to the child in a picture; or the youngster who looks for the horse in back of the television set as the horse on the screen rides off in the sunset. Closely related to the development of cognitive skills is the learning of language which cannot be separated from cognitive and concept development. The 4-year-old who refers to the "two girls with the same face" in her class shows she has developed the concept of "twins" even though she doesn't know the word to express this concept.

To illustrate the baby's growing cognitive abilities, we can observe Aaron's developing cognitive skills over a period of time through his reaction to a common object—a set of keys. As a newborn, he responds to the auditory stimulus of the keys, turning his head when the keys are rattled. At a few months of age, the moving keys attract the infant's attention and he stares at them and then visually tracks the keys as they are slowly moved. A few months later, the baby reaches for the keys and later hits them to make them move. Still later, he holds the keys and then explores them by putting the keys in his mouth. As he learns to release objects from his grasp, he enjoys dropping the keys from his high chair, and a little later, throwing the keys on the floor. His first movements in crawling and his steps in walking are to obtain the set of keys. At 16 months, he tries to insert the key in a keyhole, imitating what he has observed others doing. By this stage, the concept of keys has been formed and the word is added to his vocabulary, first understanding it when others say it (receptive) and later actually saying the word himself (expressive). Thus, a common object such as a set of keys can be used to stimulate a variety of cognitive functions over a period of time—auditory perception, visual perception, memory, perceptual–motor skills, cause and effect, concepts, relationships, labeling. It is important that the child-care provider be aware of and offer such opportunities to stimulate learning and cognitive development.

## THEORIES OF COGNITIVE DEVELOPMENT

There are several theories regarding how cognitive abilities develop in children. As noted in the discussion of curriculum in Chapter 6, the curriculum of the early childhood program is guided by an underlying theory of learning and cognitive development. Three major theories are discussed here: (1) maturational, (2) cognitive-emphasis, and (3) behavioral. Many programs combine elements of each theoretical approach.

### Maturational Theories   *Gesell*

The maturational theory suggests that the development of cognition is the direct result of a normal process of maturation and will occur in the normal course of events without direct teaching. This view is reflected in the enrichment curriculum, as discussed in Chapter 6. The emphasis is on the "whole child"; and intellectual development is considered along with the child's physical, social, and emotional growth. The purpose of the preschool environment is to provide opportunities for the child's natural growth processes to unfold by offering a learning environment that is enriching, encouraging, and nurturing. The implication is that the teacher does not have to actively promote cognitive development; the child will naturally develop cognitive skills given enough time. Many early childhood programs relfect this view of cognitive development.

## Cognitive-Emphasis Theories   Piaget

These theories stress the development of cognitive skills and thinking in young children. As noted in Chapter 6, the cognitive-emphasis curriculum emphasizes activities designed to develop abilities such as perception, discrimination, memory, concept formation, problem solving, and decision making. The ideas of the Swiss psychologist Jean Piaget (1952) provide the foundation for this theoretical approach to cognitive development.

*Piaget's theories of cognitive development.*   Jean Piaget devoted his lifetime to studying how children develop cognitive abilities. One of Piaget's important insights about children is that they do not think like adults but pass through distinct stages of development that are characterized by particular types of thinking.

**Stages in cognitive growth.**   A key feature of the Piagetian theory is the concept of sequential stages of cognitive development. Each child progresses through each of these stages in a common sequential manner. While age levels are attached to each stage, these are only approximations of the age at which each stage is reached. Some children master a particular stage earlier; others later. Certain cognitive behaviors are manifested at each stage, and the teacher can determine the child's stage of development by examining the tasks that a child is able to perform consistently.

1. *Sensorimotor period: Birth to two years of age* During this stage, the child learns through sense and movement and by interacting with the physical environment. By moving, touching, hitting, biting, and so on, and by physically manipulating objects, the child learns about the properties of space, time, location, permanence, and causality. (This period is discussed in greater detail in Chapter 7.)

2. *Preconceptual thought period: Ages two to four years* Speech begins during this period, and the child makes rapid progress in learning the names of objects and using speech to communicate ideas. During this period, the child masters an increasingly larger set of concepts and further differentiates cognitive processes. The learning is accomplished by imitation, symbolic play, drawings, mental images, and verbal evocation of events. The child's thinking is dominated largely by the world of perception. (This period is discussed further in Chapter 8.)

3. *Intuitive thought period: Ages four to seven years* This stage is an extension of the preconceptual thought period. It is characterized by the mastery of more complex forms of language. In addition, laws of physics and chemistry—such as conservation of number, mass, and the like—are brought under control.

4. *Concrete operations period: Ages seven to twelve years* It is in this stage that the child develops the ability to think through relationships, to perceive consequences of acts, and to group entities in a logical fashion. Children are now better able to systematize and organize their thoughts. These thoughts, however, are still shaped in large measure by previous experiences, and they are dependent upon concrete objects that the children have manipulated or understood through the senses. Children can now deal with aspects of logic, including classes, number, relations, and reversibility.

5. *Formal operations period: Ages eleven to fifteen years* This stage reflects a major transition in the thinking process. At this stage, instead of observations directing thought, thought now directs observations. The individual now has the capacity to work with abstractions, theories, and logical relationships without having to refer to the concrete. The formal operations period provides a generalized orientation toward problem-solving activity.

**How cognitive structures develop (Schemata).** Piaget contends that children learn through action. From the moment of birth, the child is the active interpreter of the environment. The child builds what Piaget calls an internal *schemata,* or an inner construct of the world. This schemata becomes the basis for further thought. The concepts of *assimilation* and *accommodation* are central to Piaget's theory of cognitive development.

**Assimilation and accommodation.** *Assimilation* is the process by which children take into their models of thinking the awareness of aspects of the environment. Through the process of assimilation, children build their knowledge base by adding new information gained through experience. That is, children incorporate new experiences into their already existing schemata, or cognitive structures.

In *accommodation* children revise their internal schemata to fit their observations when confronted with something they cannot understand. Through the process of accommodation, children integrate new information by reorganizing their current cognitive structure. The child focuses on the new features of the situation and changes the internal schemata, or cognitive structure, accordingly.

In other words, the child adapts to the environment and structures knowledge in two complementary ways—assimilation and accommodation. Let us take the example of a young child picking up a ball. The process of assimilation of a grasping technique already mastered will help the child in picking up the ball. The child also will accommodate to the new features of this ball by modifying his or her cognitive structure. In accommodation there is an expansion of the existing internal cognitive structure. Cognitive development results from a succession of these expansions in the internal cognitive structures. Cognitive development is cumulative and interactional.

*Cognitive learning strategies.* There has been much recent interest in how a child's cognitive approach to learning influences the effectiveness of that learning. Cognitive style refers to the child's general behavior and attitude when presented with a learning task. Analysis of the child's cognitive style of learning provides insight into the child's learning difficulties (Karnes, Johnson, Cohen, and Shwedel, 1985; Meichenbaum, 1977; Torgesen, 1982).

Efficient learners appear to have a different cognitive style from inefficient learners. Efficient learners are able to channel their thinking processes in order to facilitate learning. They are actively involved in the learning process; they have persistence; and they work independently at solving a problem and at learning something.

In contrast, inefficient learners are passive in their approach to learning, waiting for the teacher to take charge and direct them as to what they should do. That is, they do not know how to go about the task of learning. As a consequence, inefficient learners become passive and dependent learners—in a style that has been referred to as "learned helplessness" (Torgesen, 1982). This analysis suggests that teachers help children develop learning strategies so that they can control and direct their own thinking and learning. A cognitive learning strategies theory is also espoused by Reuven Feuerstein (1980), who suggests using the technique of *instrumental enrichment* to help children develop cognitive strategies needed for learning (Messerer, Hunt, Meyers, and Lerner, 1984).

Cognitive learning strategies focus on *how* children learn rather than *what* they learn. In short, the teacher's role is to help children learn how to learn.

Although most research with cognitive learning strategies has been conducted with older children, the concept has application for preschoolers as well. For example, Karnes et al. (1985) found a relationship between "task persistence" and achievement in preschool at-risk children.

### Behavioral Theories   Skinner

Another view and approach to cognitive development is offered by behavioral theorists. The directed-teaching curriculum and the procedure of task analysis, as discussed in Chapter 6, are based on behavioral theories. Behavorial theory suggests that the child's learning and mental abilities can be shaped through direct teaching of specific skills. Behavorial approaches are used to increase desirable behavior and also to reduce inappropriate and undesirable behaviors (Bijou and Baer, 1979; Gagné, 1985; Bloom, 1978).

A central concept of behavioral theory is that human activity can be modified through a procedure known as *behavior modification*. A specific change in the child's observable behavior can be brought about through a systematic arrangement of environmental events. If a pleasurable event (a reinforcer) follows the occurrence of a behavior, it increases the likelihood that the child will engage in that behavior again. Therefore, finding workable reinforcers is important.

In using a behavioral approach, the teacher must (1) carefully and systematically observe and tabulate the occurrence of specific events that *precede* the behavior of interest and those that *follow* the behavior of interest and (2) manipulate those events to effect a desired change in the child's behavior. For example, Dennis whines and points to a ball when he wants it (stimulus event); Mother gives Dennis the ball (subsequent event). If the ball is not given to Dennis unless he says the word "ball," getting the ball becomes the reinforcement for saying the word, "ball." Reinforcements that are positive and immediate are most effective in promoting the desired behavior. Young children usually respond well to reinforcements such as hand clapping, praise ("good girl") a hug, or an approving smile. Behavioral management strategies include imitation, modeling, and reinforcements.

In the behavioral approach, the teacher takes a direct and active role in deciding upon the skills to be learned and in teaching them. Learning is not left to chance or maturation. The skills selected for learning are observable and countable. Often there is an emphasis on the learning of pre-academic skills: counting, knowing colors, shapes, letters, words, numbers, and basic concepts. *Task analysis* (discussed in Chapter 6) is an important process for analyzing the skill to be learned. Here is a summary of the steps in a behavioral approach using task analysis:

1. State objectives to be achieved and skills to be learned in terms of the child's performance.
2. Analyze the skill to be learned in terms of specific subskills.
3. List the subskills to be learned in a sequential order.
4. Determine which of these tasks the child knows and which the child does not know.
5. Teach through direct instruction. Do not make assumptions about the child's ability to acquire the skill.
6. Teach one subskill at a time. When that subskill has been learned, teach the next subskill.
7. Evaluate the effectiveness of the instruction in terms of whether the student has learned the skill. This often requires charting or event recording to document instructional changes.

To illustrate how a skill is broken into subskills, take the skill of putting on a t-shirt (Hayden and Smith, 1978). The objective can be broken down into the following smaller steps:

Lay the shirt flat on a table with the label-side up and the bottom toward the child.
Put both arms inside the shirt.
Move both arms along the sides of the shirt to the armholes.
Push arms through the armholes.
Lift the shirt up so the neck hole is on top of the head.
Pull the neck hole down over the head.
Pull the bottom of the shirt down from the armpits to the chest.
Pull the bottom of the shirt down from the chest to the waist.

Considering how many motions it takes to put on a t-shirt, it is easy to understand why a child would have difficulty with this task. One effective way to teach this skill is through *backward chaining*. The teacher does all the steps and requires the child to do the last step. When that is learned, the child is reinforced for his or her behavior. Then the child does the last two steps. This kind of teaching continues until the child can perform all of the subskills of the entire task.

### Integrating Theories of Cognitive Development

Most early childhood special education programs integrate ideas from all of the theoretical approaches to cognitive development. They provide for the development of the "whole child" and create an environment that encourages exploration, growth, and maturation. They also provide activities designed to promote cognitive development. In addition, they directly teach specific skills, including preacademic skills.

## IMPACT OF EARLY INTERVENTION ON COGNITIVE DEVELOPMENT

The underlying premise of early childhood special education is the belief that programmatic intervention can enhance cognitive development for at-risk and handicapped children. The conviction is that what the teacher does in the classroom and what the parent(s) do at home is effective in helping children learn, in improving cognitive growth, and in helping children manage the world about them. Fortunately, research is bearing out this assumption (Bricker, 1986; U.S. Department of Education, 1985; Edmiaston and Mowder, 1985; Strain, 1984; Reynolds, Egan, and Lerner, 1983). Early intervention does pay off. The research shows that (Edmiaston and Mowder, 1985):

1. Early childhood intervention with handicapped and at-risk preschool children is more effective than no intervention.
2. Early childhood intervention is effective across handicapping conditions.
3. The positive effects of early childhood intervention last over time.
4. Early childhood intervention with handicapped children is cost-effective.

In this section, we provide a summary of the accumulating evidence that early intervention does help children learn and develop better cognitive skills (Reynolds, Egan, and Lerner, 1983). Three kinds of efficacy studies are reviewed: (1) the early studies; (2) the HCEEP studies; and (3) recent longitudinal studies.

### Early Studies

Until the mid-1960s, there were few programs serving young handicapped and high-risk children. All that parents could find were a few private agencies or clinics and some state institutions. Virtually no public school programs were available for parents or their preschool children. During this era, however, several experiments set the stage for later work by demonstrating that the intellectual functioning of young children can improve dramatically under stimulating environmental conditions.

An early theory that was widely accepted, as set forth by Goddard (1916), was that intellectual functioning was largely inherited and that training would not affect a child's intellectual ability. This view was challenged by researchers who conducted experiments to show the crucial importance of the early childhood years to the development of thinking skills and cognitive growth.

Hunt (1961) in his famous work *Intelligence and Experience* disputed the notion that intelligence, or cognitive ability, is a fixed entity and argued that a person's intellectual level can be changed by environmental experiences. Bloom (1964) supplied further evidence to show how critical the early years are to cognitive growth. Finding that 80 percent of the child's cognitive development is completed by age four, Bloom warned that waiting until the child reaches age six is perhaps too late. Research studies that demonstrated improvement in the cognitive abilities of retarded babies who were placed in favorable environmental conditions gave further evidence of the impact of early intervention on cognitive growth.

Skeels and Dye (1939) reported on an experiment in Iowa in which thirteen children less than three years of age were removed from an orphanage and placed in an institution for mental defectives. These infants were placed, only one to a ward, with adolescent mentally retarded girls who gave them attention and training. There was also a comparison group that remained in the orphanage and received no special training or care. Two years later both groups were tested, and the babies who had received a great deal of attention and stimulation from the retarded girls in the institution increased their scores on intelligence tests an average of 27.5 points. The children who remained in the orphanage in an unstimulating environment experienced an average decrease of 26.2 points in their intelligence test scores. In follow-up studies three years later, the experimental children had retained their accelerated rate of development in foster homes, while the orphanage children retained their decreased intellectual performance (Skeels, 1942). In a follow-up study twenty-one years later, all of the 25 subjects were located. Skeels (1966) found that the thirteen children in the experimental group were all self-supporting. Not one of them was in an institution. Of the twelve in the contrast group, one had died and four were wards of institutions. In terms of education, the experimental group had completed a median of 12th grade; four subjects had a college education. The contrast group completed a median of third grade.

Kirk (1958, 1965) conducted an experiment on effects of preschool education on the mental and social development of young mentally retarded children. Two preschool groups were organized—one in the community and the other in an institution. Children who received the two years of preschool education increased in both mental and social development and retained the increase to age eight. Those who did not receive preschool education dropped in both their IQ and SQ (social quotient).

A program designed to increase academic skills in young children from low socioeconomic status (SES) homes was conducted by Bereiter and Engelmann (1968). They taught fifteen four-year-old children with a series of deliberately planned lessons involving demonstrations, drill, exercise, and problems. At the beginning of the instruction these children were a year or more retarded in language and cognitive abilities; but within nine months, they progressed to normal levels as assessed with language and IQ tests. Moreover, after instruction the children scored at the second-grade level in arithmetic and at the first-grade level in reading.

### HCEEP Studies

The great majority of programs for preschool handicapped children today are the result of the federally funded model or demonstration projects known as HCEEP (Handicapped Children's Early Education Programs). (See Chapter 1 for a discussion of the legislation supporting HCEEP.) The HCEEP programs vary widely in purpose, curriculum, handicaps served, age groups, and activities (Cook and Armbruster, 1983). Twenty-one of these projects were approved by the Joint Dissemination Review Panel as projects of excellence (White, Mastropieri, and Castro, 1984). To illustrate the diversity, three successful and widely disseminated HCEEP programs are briefly described.

The Portage Project (Shearer and Shearer, 1976) was a home-based program. The project staff traveled to the child's home to help parents learn how to work with their children in the home setting. Located in a rural area of Wisconsin, this project has been successfully disseminated in many other sites.

The PEECH (Precise Early Education for Children with Handicaps) project was a cognitive/psycholinguistic model program for multihandicapped children aged three to five. Nonhandicapped children also were enrolled to provide an opportunity for the handicapped children to interact with nonhandicapped peers. The children attended preschool classes for half-day (2½ hour) sessions daily. The teachers spent the remainder of the day on other activities, such as work with parents, curriculum planning, case conferences, and IEP writing. The results of the project showed that social and academic progress persisted into the elementary grades. There was significant language growth, the children were successfully mainstreamed, and there was increased parent involvement. The program was successfully replicated in twenty sites in a cost-effective manner (Karnes, Kokotovic, and Shwedel, 1982).

Another widely disseminated HCEEP project is INREAL (INclass REActive Language) (Weiss, 1981; *DEC Communicator*, 1984). The goal of this project was to improve the language and learning skills of three- to five-year-old language-handicapped and bilingual children. The project emphasized the learning style relationship between the child's individual levels of cognitive, communicative, social, and motor development. INREAL is described as a child-centered program using a natural conversational milieu. The teacher uses a communicative interaction rather than a didactic model of teaching.

Overall, HCEEP has been successful in stimulating the development of early childhood special education programs in the public schools. It has demonstrated the implementation of programs based on a variety of philosophical approaches and diverse settings (urban, suburban, and rural).

### Recent Longitudinal Studies

Several longitudinal studies show impressive long-term effects of early intervention for high-risk children. Two follow-up studies, in particular, have received wide publicity: the Head Start longitudinal study (Lazar and Darlington, 1979) and the Perry Preschool Program study (Schweinhart and Weikart, 1980; Berrueta-Clement, Schweinhart, Barnett, Epstein, and Weikart, 1984).

An unusual opportunity to investigate the impact of early intervention on cognitive growth and later adjustment came with the Head Start programs. Head Start was funded by the federal government in 1964 as part of the War on Poverty. The intent of Head Start was to provide compensatory educational experiences for preschoolers who might otherwise come to school unprepared and unmotivated to learn. Over 800 children who had taken part in Head Start or similar programs were evaluated some fifteen years later. The data collected in this follow-up study revealed impressive and very encouraging information, which demonstrated that early intervention is effective (Lazar and Darlington, 1979). The following questions were asked to evaluate the early intervention experience after a long period:

1.   Was the student placed in a special education class during schooling or in a regular class?
2.   Was the student left back a grade or more?
3.   Did the student finish school by the age of eighteen?

The follow-up data revealed that Head Start participants did significantly better on all these measures than did the control children. Moreover, the study showed that Head Start programs were cost-effective. That is, society saved money by providing preschool education since the investment reduced costs for special education and grade retention later.

Another important longitudinal study, the Perry Preschool Program, was carried out by the High/Scope Educational Research Foundation of Ypsilanti, Michigan (Schweinhart and Weikart, 1981; Clements, et al.,

1984). The preschool children selected for this project had test scores showing low cognitive ability and came from the bottom 20 percent in terms of economic income. The Perry Preschool Program had a cognitive emphasis curriculum. When the participants were tested at ages fifteen and nineteen, the positive effects were impressive. These students were more committed to school and doing better in school than peers who did not have the preschool experiences. Scores were higher on reading, arithmetic, and language achievement tests at all grade levels. Moreover, there was a 50 percent reduction in the need for special educaton services. These students also had less deviant and delinquent behavior, and parents reported that they received greater satisfaction from their children.

In summary, the longitudinal evidence demonstrates that early intervention for handicapped and high-risk preschoolers is effective in improving cognitive skills, behavior, attitude toward school, and academic achievement. In terms of cost–benefit analysis, the schools get their money back with interest because there is less need for special education services and a decrease in the retention rate, thereby reducing the time that children spend in public school. Further, upon completion of schooling, the students are more likely to be gainfully employed—to be taxpayers rather than tax receivers—and to be citizens who contribute to society.

## INTERVENTION STRATEGIES FOR TEACHING COGNITIVE SKILLS

Classroom activities should be planned with the child's developmental stage of cognitive growth in mind. Furth and Wachs (1975, pp. 43–47) specify six characteristics of curriculum activities that enhance cognitive growth. They view it as a way to teach thinking.

1. *The activity of thinking is worthwhile in itself.* Thinking skills are not developed in the child as a means to accomplish something else but as an end in itself.

2. *The structured activities are to enhance the child's developing intelligence, not to take away the individual freedom that is a condition of healthy psychological growth.* Both the teacher and the child initiate activities. The teacher plans and prepares the activities for the child, but at the same time the child has the freedom to participate or not participate and has individuality of style and timing in responding to the task.

3. *The activities are developmentally appropriate so as to challenge the child's thinking but not too difficult so as to invite failure.* The teacher's task is to know the general type of activities that are appropriate for the child's cognitive stage. The activities must be difficult enough to challenge the child's thinking. However, if they are too difficult, this leads to failure and a psychologically unhealthy use of low-level thinking.

4. *The child is involved in and focuses his or her attention on the activity and not on the teacher as the source of knowledge.* It is the child who initiates intellectual growth. The teacher can only provide the occasion, prompt, facilitate, and encourage.

5. *Activities are performed by each individual child with a group of peers with whom he or she relates socially and cooperatively.* A small group of children provides an

effective atmosphere for cognitive learning. Children learn from imitation and are encouraged by successful activities of others.

6. *Teachers provide the model of a thinking person for the child.* The teacher must be free from rigid regulations and take the initiative within the general structure. The teacher can influence a child's developing intelligence by providing occasions and opportunities and by serving as a model of a thinking person to imitate.

### Instructional Strategies

There is a common body of preschool activities, regardless of the theoretical basis of that curriculum. They commonly include the pre-academic skills of colors, shapes, numbers, letters, parts of wholes, the function and use of objects, and the use of speech parts. Most of the curriculum approaches recognize that the child must learn to make comparisons, classify and categorize, build vocabulary, reason and make judgments. Appropriate cognitive skills objectives often include the following kinds of activities:

1. *Classification activities:* ability to group objects that have similarities. There are three subgroups:
   a. *relational classification:* grouping objects on the basis of function (for example, put together all of the things we can drink).
   b. *descriptive classification:* grouping on the basis of common attributes (for example, put together all of the red items or round items).
   c. *generic classification:* grouping items on the basis of general classes or categories (for example, put together all of the furniture or fruit).
2. *Seriation activities:* putting things or events in order or sequence. There are several subgroups:
   a. *ordinal sizes:* for example, *big, bigger, biggest; small, smaller, smallest; short, shorter, shortest.*
   b. *ordinal positions*: first, last, middle, third.
   c. *ordinal patterning:* copying a sequence of beads.
   d. *time sequences*: for example, arranging pictures that tell a story into the correct time sequence.
3. *Spatial relations:* the relationship of the child to the space in the outer world. There are several subgroups:
   a. *body awareness and body concepts:* naming and identifying parts of the body, moving parts of the body.
   b. *position:* developing concepts such as *on, off, into, over, under, next to, on top of.*
   c. *direction:* directional concepts such as *up, down, forward, backward.*
   d. *distance:* concepts such as *near, far, close to, far from.*
4. *Temporal relations:* These activities are related to time. Subgroups are:
   a. *beginning and end of time intervals:* such as *now, start, stop, end.*
   b. *ordering of events:* planning and evaluation concepts such as *first, last, next, again.*
   c. *different time lengths:* such as *a short time, a long time, a longer time.*

### Specific Intervention Activities

*Teaching concepts.* *Conceptualization* refers to the intellectual process needed to group diverse things according to common properties. The ideas resulting from this process are called *concepts.* While concepts may deal with concrete things, they are in themselves abstractions. For example, the concept of *roundness* develops from many concrete experiences with round objects—plates, balls, oranges, Frisbees. Round objects are concrete; they can be touched, seen, and so on. The idea of *round,* however, exists only in the mind. The brain creates it. It is an abstraction—not a reality.

The concepts of the shape *round* and the color *red* are easier than more complex concepts such as *weather* or *time.* Still more difficult are concepts such as *sharing, fairness* or *loyalty.* As the concept gets further away from a basis of concrete experience, it becomes more difficult. Thus, the curriculum must give the child many concrete opportunities to develop concepts. The handicapped child may have much more difficulty than the normal child in developing concepts needed for further learning. If there is a physical disability, the child may not have the opportunity to have the primary experience. For example, the blind child would have difficulty developing the concept of *color,* such as "red." Preschool children with special needs frequently have difficulty in being able to recall concepts. For handicapped children, therefore, greater direct experience for concept development is needed wherever possible.

**Concept of color: red.** Associate the color red with an object the child is familiar with, such as catsup. If the new object is the color of catsup, it is red. Show the child a bottle of catsup. Group together objects and drawings that are red. Start with two objects (later three objects) of various colors. Ask, "Is this red?" Later on, after other colors have been taught, ask the child to identify the color when three colors are presented at one time. Have the child select which objects fit which color.

**Teaching spatial relations.** Spatial relationships such as *on, in, between, under, in front of, next to* are often difficult for handicapped children to understand. Use a box and an object to help the child. Place the object (such as a block) *in* the box, and say, "The block is *in* the box." The child is then asked to place the object *in* the box. The teacher places the object in the box and asks, "Where is the block?" Similar activities are used to teach other spatial relations. First each is taught in an isolated fashion; later directions can be mixed. After the action, the teacher should verbalize it to reinforce the concept.

**Teaching numbers.** Number concepts such as *more, less, first, last* are important and should be included in the curriculum. To teach *one more,* have the child build a tower and then add one more block to it. Then one more, and so on. Using a pasting activity, ask the child to paste one more flower. At snack time, ask the child to take one more cracker. During a working period, ask the child to add one more bead to a chain. In other words, provide many opportunities to have direct experience with the cognitive skill being taught.

*Teaching classification skills.* Classification involves grouping or sort-ing of objects according to some rule or principle. Children can be grouped into boys and girls or into big and small or into brunettes, blonds, and redheads. Children often have much difficulty with classification. They confuse the thing with the class. That is, they confuse the physical object with the class to which it belongs. They also have difficulty with the language of classification and with the fact that an object can belong to two or more classes. For example, one child could not see that a plate could be called "round," since it was a plate. When children were asked if the moon could be called "cow," they said no because it does not give milk. Handicap-ped children in particular need many experiences in sorting and classify-ing.

*Matching games.* Have several pairs of matching objects. Place one of a pair in front of the child. Ask the child to "find one like this."

*Sorting games.* Have two containers and several objects. Ask the child to put the red items in one container and the blue items in the other. Do the same thing with shapes and textures. Later ask the child to sort objects without the container—on a piece of paper or simply on two sides of a table. Then have the child select his or her own sorting principles.

*Classifying games.* Make nine geometrical cutouts: three triangles, three circles, three squares each of blue, yellow, and red. Have children sort them. At first they will classify by color, later by shape. The principle

taught is that the way one classifies is arbitrary. Other objects that can be used are buttons, silverware, pictures, or toys.

*Teaching sequencing.* This cognitive skill involves recognizing the sequential order of things. The item is correctly placed when it takes into account the neighboring items and the sequence or pattern that the items form within the whole. There can be a sequence to auditory activities, visual activities, and movement activities. There also is a sequence to events.

*Bead stringing.* One type of sequential activity is copying a bead pattern using different shapes or colors of beads. Bead patterns can be placed on a transparency to use this activity with a group of children.

*Auditory pattern games.* A series of rhythm patterns can be made by clapping, tapping, or using a drum, where the child is asked to copy the pattern.

*Time*

*Story sequence.* A child repeats a story by highlighting the sequence of events in the story. Three or four pictures that illustrate the sequence can be used, and the child places these in appropriate order (top to bottom or left to right) and then relates the story. Cartoons or comic strips can be cut apart and used for this purpose. Children need to be taught the relationship from one picture frame to the next. Flannel board cutouts also are useful in helping the child order the events of the story.

*Arranging.* The child is given several objects and asked to arrange them in a sequence. For example, four circles or sticks can be arranged from biggest to smallest or longest to shortest.

*Guessing or discovery games.* Logical thinking involves reasoning and predicting. Some games help the child experience this process. Riddles are an activity children enjoy. "I am thinking of an object that is white, long, breaks easily, and leaves its mark on a chalkboard." When telling or reading a story, ask the child to guess what will happen next. Then check out the event to see if the child was correct. Use an ordered series with a pattern and have the child tell which one comes next.

*Creative thinking.* Many of the activities and lessons in education are designed to teach a specific concept or skill. These lessons may be thought of as lessons to teach *convergent* thinking because the child must close in on a particular point established by the teacher. The contrast to this type of lesson are those that teach *divergent* thinking. These are open-ended lessons in which the child is encouraged to expand the thinking process into areas beyond those determined by the teacher. Play and dramatics can encourage this type of activity. They are more self-directed than activities designed for convergent thinking. Nevertheless, this is an important part of the cognitive curriculum and one that should not be neglected.

*Toy library.*    A toy library of games and play ideas and materials is suggested by Johnson (1978). Such a resource would give teachers, aides, parents, grandparents, and others who work with children the opportunity to borrow materials and games for use with children. Two organizations that lend toys and educational materials for young children are:

U.S. Toy Library Association, 5940 West Touhy, Chicago, IL 60648.

National Lekotek Center, 2100 Ridge Ave., Evanston, IL 60204.

## THE MICROCOMPUTER AS A TOOL FOR LEARNING

Because the microcomputer is revolutionizing so many aspects of our lives, it is predicted that it will soon become as handy and useful as a pencil. The microcomputer has literally exploded on the special education scene and has the potential for changing many of the traditional ways we have been teaching in special education (McCann and Kelemen, 1984; Brinker and Lewis, 1982: Rosegrant, 1985). The technology of the microcomputer rep-

resents the most revolutionary innovation yet developed in the field of special education. Much more than a mere technological addition to our teaching tools, it holds the potential to dramatically expand the horizons of exceptional children. The computer is a tool to teach cognitive skills. Seymour Papert (1980), the developer of LOGO, a programming language for young children, sees the computer as a means to develop cognitive skills. He stated that his interest was in the invention of "objects-to-think-with."

> My central focus is not on the machine but on the mind . . . .The role I give to the computer is that of a *carrier* of cultural "germs" or "seeds" whose intellectual products will not need technology support once they take root in an actively growing mind.

The microcomputer has the power to help ordinary people do extraordinary things. For the exceptional child, however, the microcomputer allows extraordinary children do ordinary things. Thus, it is even more urgent for handicapped children to have access to the microcomputer than nonhandicapped children. The number of burdensome tasks that the microcomputer can perform is of greater use to the handicapped than to any other population. It is not only a tool that can help them learn, but it also can remove overwhelming hurdles, allowing them an access to learning. It can bring voice and communication to the nonvocal child, Braille and speech synthesis to the blind child, communication with others through telecommunications to the deaf child, and new learning opportunities for the mentally retarded. It also can overcome attention deficits and distractibility for the learning disabled, extend movement and motor control through adaptive devices for the physically handicapped, and offer new creative challenges for the gifted child. In short, the microcomputer can bring equality to the handicapped child by meeting the special needs that may be present as a result of the handicap (Behrmann, 1984; Cain, 1984; Hagen, 1984).

In addition to meeting their unique special needs, the microcomputer offers exceptional children the exciting uses that all children have with this new educational tool. They have access to programs for (1) drill and practice; (2) word processing; (3) telecommunications; (4) tutorials; (5) creativity; and (6) problem solving. For the special education teacher, there are other microcomputer applications, such as developing and managing IEPs, word processing, scoring and interpreting tests, and authoring programs to create individualized lessons.

There are many exciting applications of microcomputer technology for young at-risk and handicapped children. The computer can creatively present colors, differences (such as *larger* or *smaller*), concepts such as *above/*

*below* and *left/right,* shape and letter recognition, counting, matching, and sequencing. Several of these applications are reviewed here. (Table 9.1 at the end of this chapter lists: (1) microcomputer demonstration and research projects geared for special-needs preschoolers; (2) useful peripherals and adaptive devices; and (3) software designed for young children.)

The following discussion of microcomputers is divided into two sections: (1) special adaptive devices and applications for handicapped children and (2) the uses of regular microcomputer programs for young handicapped and at-risk children.

### Special Adaptations and Applications for Young Handicapped Children

The following microcomputer adaptive devices are specially designed to help physically handicapped, nonverbal, hearing impaired, and visually impaired children.

*Adaptive devices for physically handicapped children.*    Physically handicapped children who have little control over their environment often develop a sense of helplessness that turns into an ingrained attitude, making later learning more difficult. Through the microcomputer, along with various kinds of adaptive devices, physically handicapped children can gain control of their environment. Even if they have very little movement, they can indicate a choice through adaptive devices such as special keyboard additions, switches, touch tablets, eyebrow controls, and head and hand controls. The computer's immediate feedback lets the child know that something has happened and that the child's actions caused it. For some children, this may be the first time that they have been able to control the play situation to successfully take charge of the environment without help from others. The child can make sounds and music, move toys about the room, hear a voice speak, draw pictures, play games, and learn.

The field of rehabilitation medicine has developed a number of devices using prosthetic technology that assist in overcoming physical limitations. Microimplants connected to nerves and electrode-connected microcomputers have shown that damage due to certain neurological and spinal diseases and injuries can be overcome, permitting the disabled to have motor control over their bodies.

*Technology for the nonverbal child.*    Some handicapped children are unable to talk because of various disabling conditions—such as cerebral palsy, deafness, autism, and other physical or emotional conditions. Communication devices make oral language and communication possible for these children. They learn to use electronic "talking personal computers" in a range of ways—to express basic needs, to communicate with others, and to create complex language productions. Thus, they can express basic needs ("I need to go to the toilet"), indicate a choice ("I want a cheese-burger and a coke"), hold an interactive discussion with others, or compose a poem or story. The technological devices that produce speech have become small and portable. They include speech synthesiers (ECHO and Type 'n' Talk), Touch Talker with Minspeak, Epson SpeechPAC, Vois, and Talking Blissapple. One ten-year-old boy who had never been able to express ideas through speech before gratefully said the simple word T-H-A-N-X to his teacher with his talking personal computer.

*Deaf and hearing-impaired children.* Children with a hearing loss can use the microcomputer in much the same way as all children. There are, however, some specialized uses designed for deaf children. They can use the talking personal computer devices. Software is available for teaching lip reading, sign language, and finger-spelling. Telecommunications via the microcomputer provides opportunities to communicate and use language in a meaningful way using modems and bulletin boards.

*Blind and partially sighted children.* The speech synthesizer is par-ticularly useful for blind children. The computer reads the written language for them. There are Braille keyboards and Braille printers. There are also special word processing programs. For partially sighted children who need large print, there are programs that increase the size of the type of the screen and on the printed copy.

## Uses of Regular Computer Programs by Young Exceptional Children

Many of the microcomputer programs designed for nonhandicapped young children are very effective with handicapped and at-risk pre-schoolers. The characterisics of microcomputer programs make their use particularly advantageous for youngsters with learning disabilities, mental retardation, and behavior disorders. The programs can be motivating, they can reduce attention problems, they can be adjusted to go more slowly if necessary, and they have infinite patience and will nonjudgmentally review the work as often as the child wants or needs it repeated. Following are some of the ways the young special-needs child can use the microcomptuer.

*Play and games.* As discussed in chapter 10, play is the work of childhood. Through play children come to an understanding of the phys-ical and social properties of life in their society. Many handicapped chil-dren do not have normal opportunities for play. Playing games with the microcomputer is a genuine opportunity and a unique experience. They can compete with each other or with themselves.

*Drill and practice.* The computer is an excellent tool for review, rein-forcement, and practice. Computers have the patience and endurance to offer repeated drill and practice sessions. In drill and practice programs, the children should already have been taught the basic concept or skill. Young children can use these programs to review shapes, letters, numbers, colors, words, and so on.

*Tutorial programs.*   Tutorial programs actually teach a skill or area of knowledge. They offer children who need repeated instruction the opportunity to have a skill retaught many times. A good tutorial program provides constant feedback, alternative pacing, motivation, reinforcement, and possibly sound and color. Examples of skills taught young children could be parts of the face or body, shapes, concepts, words, or telling time.

*Word processing.*   Word processing software has proved to be a tremendous boon to the teaching of writing for all ages. It is also effective in teaching writing to primary-age children. For the child who cannot use a pencil easily it is especially helpful. Word processing makes the arduous task of revising, rewriting, and correcting much easier. The writer can make additions, correct, and delete freely until the screen shows exactly what the writer wants. At that point, the writer simply tells the computer to print and quickly receives a printed copy. The printed copy can be further revised, corrected, and reedited. The new changes and corrections are typed and shown on the screen. When satisfied with the corrected version, the writer instructs the computer to print again to obtain a revised printed copy. Several word processing programs are especially geared for young children (Magic Slate, Bank Street Writer). There also are programs to teach young children keyboard and typing skills (Typing Tutor, Type Hype).

*Problem solving and creativity.*   Perhaps one of the most exciting and creative uses of the microcomputer is in problem solving and learning to program. LOGO is a programming language that can be learned and used at many levels of complexity. A young child can do some fascinating graphics programs within a few minutes of being introduced to LOGO. LOGO

**TABLE 9.1   Microcomputer Technology Sources**

---

**Demonstration Projects and Informational Sources for Young Children With Special Needs**

*Project ACTT:* Activating Children Through Technology. Western Illinois University; 17 Horrabin Hall; Macomb, IL 61455
*Purpose:* To develop, implement, and demonstrate an innovative microcomputer curriculum model using affordable and practical microcomputer hardware and software. The primary target population is children age birth to six years, who demonstrate moderate to severe handicaps.

*Project M.U.S.E.:* Microcomputer Use in Special Education. Western Illinois University, 27 Horrabin Hall, Macomb, IL 61455
*Purpose:* To train special education teachers to use microcomputers in their classrooms. Also, to identify, evaluate, and catalog hardware and software that is designed for, or can be modified for use with, handicapped children.

*LAUSD/UCLA Microcomputer Project:* UCLA Intervention Program; 1000 Veteran Ave., Rm. 23–10; Los Angeles, CA 90024
*Purpose:* To see what young handicapped children can do with the computer. They are also networking with special education teachers in the schools and providing a resource for parents.

*National Lekotek Center;* 2100 Ridge Ave., Evanston, IL 60204
*Purpose:* To teach young handicapped children to play using microcomputer software games. (Lekotek is an organization dedicated to encouraging learning through play for handicapped young children through toy-lending and parent-counseling.)

*Closing the Gap:* P.O. Box 68; Henderson, MN 56044
A newspaper containing timely and useful information on computers for the handicapped.

### Special Hardware

| Products | Sources |
|---|---|
| Adaptive Firmware Card | Adaptive Peripherals, Inc. |
| ECHO II | Street Electronics |
| Koala Pad | Koala Technologies Corporation |
| Muppets Keyboard | Koala Technology |

### Software for Young Children With Special Needs

The most widely used microcomputer in the schools is the Apple II series (II +, IIe, or IIc). The software and hardware listed here is for the Apple II series.

| Software | Publisher |
|---|---|
| Apple LOGO | Apple Computer, Inc. |
| Blissymbols: Blissymbol Concepts | MECC |
| Children's Carrousel | Dynacomp |
| Color Me | Versa Computing |
| DIAL-LOG | DIAL, Inc. |
| Dragon's Keep | Sierra on Line |
| Early Learning Games | Learning Tools, Inc. |
| Facemaker | Spinnaker |
| First Words | Laureate Learning Systems |
| First Categories | Laureate Learning Systems |
| Hodge Podge | Artworx Software |
| Juggle's Rainbow | The Learning Company |
| Motor Training Games | Computers to Help People |
| Stickybear programs | Xerox Educational Publications |

employs a "turtle," a small shape that can be moved about the screen leaving a line in its path. The child can create colorful and complex designs. The child sets up problems and solves them through the graphics of LOGO, which offers quick visual feedback to let the child know whether he or she made the right decisions. (LOGO is also a powerful and complex computer language for the more advanced student.) Young children also can create graphics using the Koala pad, the joy stick, or the keyboard.

## SUMMARY

Cognitive skills are a collection of mental abilities related to thinking activities. They include knowing, recognizing, developing concepts, organizing ideas, remembering, problem solving, labeling, relating cause and effect, drawing inferences, and developing rules and generalizations. All areas of the preschool curriculum require cognitive abilities.

There are several theories explaining the process of cognitive development in young children. The *maturational theory* holds that cognitive skills will develop through maturation given sufficient time. The *cognitive-emphasis theories* analyze the process of the development of cognitive skills and suggest intervention experiences that will promote the development of these cognitive abilities. The *behavioral theories* examine ways to structure the environment to reinforce desired behavior. The behavioral approach utilizes the methods of behavior management and task analysis.

Research studies show that a child's cognitive abilities can be stimulated through early intervention programs. Three types of research studies show the efficacy of early intervention: the early studies, HCEEP studies, and recent longitudinal studies.

Intervention strategies for teaching cognitive skills were suggested.

The microcomputer is an innovative and useful learning tool for young handicapped and at-risk children. There are special adaptations of the computer for various handicapping conditions. Standard microcomputer programs for young children also are used successfully with special-needs preschoolers.

## REVIEW QUESTIONS

**Terms To Know**

cognitive skills
assimilation
accommodation
Piaget
Piaget's stages of cognitive growth

maturational theory
software
HCEEP
hardware

1. Describe some cognitive skills evident in the young child's behavior.
2. What are Piaget's stages of cognitive growth?
3. Discuss the ways cognitive abilities develop from a maturational, cognitive-emphasis, and behavioral viewpoint.

4. How can a microcomputer be used with young handicapped and at-risk children? With a young gifted child?
5. Conduct a task analysis of a cognitive skill appropriate for teaching a young child.
6. Discuss the research findings on the efficacy of early childhood intervention.

## REFERENCES

BEHRMANN, M. (1984) *Handbook of Microcomputers in Special Education.* San Diego, CA: College-Hill Press.

BEREITER, C. and S. ENGELMANN (1968) *Teaching Disadvantaged Children in the Preschool.* Englewood Cliffs, NJ: Prentice-Hall.

BERRUETA-CLEMENT, J., L. SCHWEINHART, S. BARNETT, A. EPSTEIN, and D. WEIKART (1984) *Changed Lives.* Ypsilanti, MI: High/Scope Educational Foundation.

BIJOU, W. and D. BAER (1979) "Child Development I: A Systematic and Empirical Theory." In B. Suran and J. Rizzo (eds.) *Special Children: An Integrative Approach.* Glenview, IL: Scott, Foresman.

BLOOM, B. (1964) *Stability and Change in Human Characteristics.* NY: Wiley.

BLOOM, B. (1978) "New Views of the Learner: Implications for Instruction and Curriculum." *Educational Leadership,* 35, 563–75.

BRICKER, D. (1986) *Early Education of At-Risk and Handicapped Infants, Toddlers, and Preschool Children.* Glenview, IL: Scott, Foresman.

BRINKER, R. and M. LEWIS (1982) "Making the World Work with Microcomputers: A Learning Prosthesis for Handicapped Infants." *Exceptional Education,* 49, 163–70.

CAIN, E. (1984) "The Challenge of Technology: Educating the Exceptional Child for the World of Tomorrow." *Teaching Exceptional Children,* 16, 238–42.

COOK, R., and V. ARMBRUSTER (1983) *Adapting Early Childhood Curricula.* St. Louis: Mosby.

DEC COMMUNICATOR (1984) 19 (3).

EDMIASTON, R. and B. MOWDER (1985) "Early Intervention for Handicapped Children: Efficacy Issues and Data for School Psychologists." *Psychology in the Schools,* 22 (April), 171–78.

FEUERSTEIN, R. (1980) *Instrumental Enrichment: An Intervention Program for Cognitive Modifiability.* Baltimore: University Park Press.

FURTH, H. and H. WACHS (1975) *Thinking Goes to School.* NY: Oxford University Press

GAGNÉ, R. (1985) *Conditions of Learning.* NY: Holt, Rinehart & Winston.

GOODARD, H. (1916) *Feeblemindedness: Its Causes and Consequences.* NY: Macmillan.

HAGEN, D. (1984) *Microcomputer Resource Book for Special Education.* Reston, VA: Reston Publishing Co.

HARE, B. and M. HARE (1977) *Teaching Young Handicapped Children.* NY: Grune & Stratton.

HAYDEN, A. and R. SMITH (1978) *Mainstreaming Preschoolers: Children with Learning Disabilities.* U.S. Department of Health and Human Services, Head Start Bureau. Washington, DC: Government Printing Office.

HUNT, J. (1961) *Intelligence and Experience.* NY: Ronald Press.

JOHNSON, S. (1978) "A Toy Library for Developmentally Disabled Children." *Teaching Exceptional Children,* 11, 22–26.

KARNES, M., L. JOHNSON, T. COHEN, and A. SHWEDEL (1985) "Facilitating School Success Among Mildly and Moderately Handicapped Children by Enhancing Task Persistence." *Journal of the Division for Early Childhood,* 9 (2), 136–50.

KARNES, M., A. KOKOTOVIC, and A. SHWEDEL (1982) "Transporting a Model Program for Young Handicapped Children: Issues, Problems, and Efficacy." *Journal of the Division for Early Childhood,* 6, 42–51.

KIRK, S. (1958) *Early Education of the Mentally Retarded.* Urbana, IL: University of Illinois Press.

KIRK, S. (1965) "Diagnostic, Cultural and Remedial Factors in Mental Retardation." In S. Osler and R. Cooke (eds.) *Biosocial Basis of Mental Retardation.* Baltimore: Johns Hopkins Press.

LAZAR, I. (1979) "Does Prevention Pay Off?" *The Communicator.* Council for Exceptional Children, Division of Early Childhood, 1979, Fall, 1–7.

LAZAR, I., and R. DARLINGTON (1979) *Lasting Effects After Preschool.* Publication No. (OHDD) 80-30179. Washington, DC: Government Printing Office. U.S. Department of Health and Human Services. Office of Human Development Services, Administration for Children, Youth and Family.

McCANN, S. and E. KELEMAN (1984) "Microcomputers: New Directions and Methods for the Preparation of Special Education Personnel." *Teacher Education and Special Education,* 7 (3), 178–84.

MEICHENBAUM, D. (1977) *Cognitive Behavior Modification.* NY: Plenum.

MESSERER, J., E. HUNT, G. MEYERS, and J. LERNER (1984) "Feuerstein's Instrumental Enrichment: A New Approach for Activating Intellectual Potential in Learning Disabled Youth." *Journal of Learning Disabilities,* 17, 321–25.

PAPERT, S. (1980) *Mindstorms.* NY: Basic Books.

PIAGET, J. (1952) *The Origins of Intelligence in Children.* M. Cook (trans.) NY: International University Press.

REYNOLDS, L., R. EGAN and J. LERNER (1983) "Efficacy of Early Identification of Preacademic Deficits: A Review of the Literature." *Topics in Early Childhood Special Education,* 3, 47–56.

ROSEGRANT, T. (1985) "Using the Microcomputer as a Tool for Learning to Read and Write." *Journal of Learning Disabilities,* 18, 113–14.

SCHWEINHART, L. and D. WEIKART (1980) *Young Children Grow Up: The Effects of the Perry Preschool Program on Youths Through Age 15.* Monographs of the High/Scope Educational Research Foundation.

SHEARER, D. and M. SHEARER (1976) "The Portage Project: A Model for Early Childhood Intervention." In T. Tjossem (ed.) *Intervention Strategies for High Risk Infants and Young Children.* Baltimore: University Park Press.

SKEELS, H. (1942) "A Study of the Effects of Differential Stimulation on Mentally Retarded Children: A Follow-up Study." *American Journal of Mental Deficiency,* 46, 340–50.

SKEELS, H. (1966) *Adult Status of Children with Contrasting Early Life Experiences.* Monographs of the Society for Research in Child Development. Chicago: University of Chicago Press, 31.

SKEELS, H. and H. DYE (1939) *A Study of the Effects of Differential Stimulations on Mentally Retarded Children.* Proceedings and Addresses of the Sixty-Third Annual Session of the American Association on Mental Deficiency. 44, 114–30.

STRAIN, P. (1984) "Efficacy Research with Young Handicapped Children: A Critique of the Status Quo." *Journal of the Division for Early Childhood,* 9 (1), 4–10.

TORGESEN, J. (1982) "The Learning Disabled Child as an Inactive Learner: Educational Implications." *Topics in Learning and Learning Disabilities,* 2, 45–52.

U.S. DEPARTMENT OF EDUCATION (1985) *To Assure the Free Appropriate Public Education of All Handicapped Children.* Seventh Annual Report to Congress on the Implementation of the Education of the Handicapped Act. Washington, DC: Government Printing Office.

WEISS, R. (1981) "INREAL Intervention for Language Handicapped and Bilingual Children." *Journal of the Division for Early Childhood,* 4, 40–51.

WHITE, K., M. MASTROPIERI, and G. CASTO (1984) "An Analysis of Special Education Early Childhood Projects Approved by the Joint Dissemination Review Panel." *Journal of the Division for Early Childhood,* 9 (1), 11–26.

# TEN

# Teaching Social and Affective Skills

## INTRODUCTION

Children are whole beings. That is, a child is not comprised of separate and discrete components to be identified as language abilities, cognitive abilities, emotional development, or social skills. Rather, these components are all integrated; to emphasize the completeness, the term *whole child* is used. Yet, for purposes of study and curriculum development, it is useful to

---

CASE EXAMPLE—ELAINE: SOCIAL PERCEPTION PROBLEMS

Elaine is a five-year-old with a social disability. Elaine was judged to have an IQ in the high–superior range and was able to read simple stories. However, the kindergarten teacher frequently called Elaine's mother to school to complain about Elaine's disruptive social behavior. She was bossy, did not seem to understand the word *no*, shouted and cried frequently, pushed others to be first in line, and then kissed and hugged her classmates to gain affection. In desperation, her mother tried to arrange social situations by inviting another child to their house to play with her daughter. Elaine would become so excited that she would run around without direction. Within a short time, the friend would tearfully beg to go home, and Elaine was in tears because she did not know what went wrong. On one occasion when she was invited to a birthday party, Elaine's behavior was so disturbing that her mother was phoned to request that she be taken home early.

divide the child's activities into separate areas of behavior. This chapter attends to the affective domain—the emotional, social, behavioral, and psychodynamic side of the young child. It is the psychosocial area of development that can be the most debilitating for the child and the most painful for the parent. The topics of this chapter include the types of social, emotional, and behavioral problems of young children; psychosocial development in young children; and intervention strategies in the areas of life skills, play, behavior, and social skills.

*emotions are called Affective skills*

## SERIOUS SOCIAL, EMOTIONAL, AND BEHAVIORAL PROBLEMS IN YOUNG CHILDREN

In terms of total life functioning, psychosocial problems may be far more debilitating than academic dysfunction. Children who have good social skills and get along well with the teacher and their classmates, come across as positive, cooperative, constructive, and interested individuals. They are likely to do well in school—even though they have shortcomings in certain academic skills. However, children who come across as hostile, disruptive, aggressive, and disturbing to the teacher and their classmates are likely to get into trouble in school (Good and Brophy, 1978).

*impairs learning*

Most children display behavioral problems at times. It is important, however, to distinguish between children who are seriously emotionally disturbed and children who are within the normal range of behavior responses but display such behaviors occasionally. Young children may have temporary or mild problems of a social or behavioral nature, often triggered by a specific event that occurs in the environment, in the family, or in the classroom. Parents and teachers can help these children deal with their problems and develop more socially acceptable behaviors.

Young children with serious social, emotional, or behavioral problems display a wide range of maladjustive behaviors. Children who are seriously emotionally disturbed show inappropriate behaviors frequently and over a long period of time. They will require the services of specialists in the fields of psychodynamics and mental health for assessment and treatment. The Head Start definition of children with serious emotional disturbance includes the following conditions: dangerously aggressive toward others; self-destructive, severely withdrawn, and noncommunicative; hyperactive to the extent that is affects adaptive behavior; severely anxious, depressed; or phobic, psychotic, or autistic (Lasher, Mattick and Perkins, 1978).

*can be emotional reaction*

### Aggressive Behavior

*A hyperactive child can't control himself at all*

*don't have inner control to do what he should*

Aggressive behavior is any behavior that occurs without provocation, which is designed to hurt other people or destroy property in the environment. A child is considered disturbed when his or her typical ways of reacting to others are by forceful and uncontrolled physical aggression (hitting, biting, scratching, kicking) and/or by verbal aggression (shouting, screaming, cursing, name-calling). Some aggressive children will respond with sudden anger only to particular situations, such as when they cannot have a toy. Others will explode more at times of stress, such as when they are tired or have been confined to a small space for a long time. Still others seem to use aggression as their major means of communication.

These children appear to be angry deep down inside and suspicious or hateful toward people in general. Many aggressive children are quite destructive. They may rip books, pull dolls apart, or break crayons into bits. They also may be very demanding and impatient. They may play with other children for a while and then suddenly push them out of the way or grab their toys. They may disturb others, interrupt or interfere with their play, and refuse to cooperate with the teacher (Lasher et al., 1978).

Often, aggressive behavior is a way of covering up an inner sense of fear, vulnerability, and inferiority. It is theorized that aggressive children are actually fearful of their own aggression. They may appear confused and anxious in the midst of an attack on another child because they desperately want to escape from the situation and hide their lack of self-control (Lasher et al., 1978). Immediate events triggering aggressive responses include overstimulation, seeing violence among adults, inadequate space for motor activity, growing up in an aggressive environment (Rutter, 1981; Caldwell, 1979). Teachers and parents should try to identify situational or environmental factors that provoke aggressive behavior and try to change the situation if possible. Also, it may be possible to provide suitable outlets for aggressive behavior; for example, a punching bag or a strenuous physical activity.

### Withdrawn Behavior

Withdrawal is one of the symptoms of severe social or emotional disability. Some children are uncomfortable when people and activities get too close to them. Often, withdrawn children have a favorite spot in the classroom, usually away from activity areas and frequently on the floor. They do not interact regularly with other children and adults, instead they react by moving away when someone gets too close. Withdrawn children appear disinterested in and unaware of most of what goes on. They seem to have few interests and frequently need self-comfort in the form of self-stimulating behaviors—thumb-sucking, rocking, masturbating, or pulling on their hair or ears (Lasher et al., 1978).

Some preschool children also appear to be depressed and seem unhappy about something. It is not always clear to themselves or others why they are so sad. They often daydream, and they startle and cry easily. Some can be comforted and cheered by playing for a while. Most depressed children have fluctuating moods and will become sad and extremely quiet many times during the day.

The shy child should not be viewed as having a serious emotional problem. Shy children are simply slow or hesitant to interact with others. They need to develop good self-feelings and have teachers and parents accept their natural shy temperament. These children need more opportunities to build successful social experiences and self-confidence. Given enough time and a nurturing environment, a shy child will warm-up to other children and eventually mix with peers in age-appropriate play situations.

### Anxious Behavior

All children go through periods of strong fears and anxieties. However, some children are so anxious for such a long time that they can hardly think of anything else. They may be thinking of the terrible things that could happen to them or others in their family. If a child's fears reach such an extent, they are called *phobias.* For example, some children develop a fear, or phobia, about going to school. They worry that something bad will happen to Mother and that she will not come back to take him or her home. The phobia may become so overpowering that the child will even refuse to go to school. The child is considered emotionally disturbed when the fear, or phobia, persists over a long time and becomes limiting to the extent that it prevents the child from performing his or her daily routine (Lasher et al., 1978).

Anxious children look worried; little things bother them, and they cry frequently. Some will wet or soil themselves; some will get stomachaches or headaches. Some have nervous self-stimulating behaviors; they might bite their nails, repeatedly rub their hands together, or blink their eyes. Some bang their heads against the floor or walls when they are upset. Anxious children are overly cautious, afraid of making a mistake, and are often viewed as "perfectionists" by teachers and parents. They may refuse to stop an activity until it is completed to their satisfaction (Lasher et al., 1978; Knoblock, 1983).

Anxious children do best in routine and structured situations. They are upset when given too much leeway and freedom as to what to do. It is important to reassure anxious children about what will happen, that all will be well. Explain early what is expected of them and reassure them that you are confident in their abilities to do what others can do. It is important for them to know that when they make a mistake you understand and accept them.

### Hyperactivity and Attentional Deficits

Most children have a high energy level and are very active. However, hyperactive children have an activity level way beyond what is considered normal. These children seem to have an inner drive and are constantly on the move. They cannot wait for explanations or their turn and they seldom pause long enough to relax or to watch or listen to what is going on. They tend to rush without purpose into situations. They often have awkward gross and fine motor skills, continually falling, breaking things, and dropping things. They have an extremely short attention span, and they are easily distracted by auditory and visual stimuli in the environment. Because of their difficulty in concentrating and attending, they may have trouble learning preacademic skills—such as letters, sounds, or words.

Hyperactive children need a carefully structured environment that will reduce distracting stimuli. Behavior modification techniques also have proved to be successful in helping hyperactive children gain better control, reduce hyperactive behaviors, increase attention, and learn preacademic skills.

### Psychotic Behavior

Childhood psychotic disorders present a very special challenge to both parents and the child care-givers. Conditions include autism and childhood schizophrenia. These emotional and behavioral disorders are very severe, calling for the services of highly trained specialists in psychosocial disorders. Children with autistic-like behaviors have problems in the way they perceive the world, in the sequence and rate at which they achieve certain developmental milestones, in speech and language development, in formal relationships with other people, and in the way they use their bodies. They develop in atypical ways and display bizarre behaviors. These children may not talk at all, they may echo or repeat what others have said, or they may use a private language not understood by others. Often, they completely avoid eye and physical contact with others or even seem unaware of the existence of others. They may use their bodies in strange ways, pacing in circles or rocking back and forth. They may engage in head banging, rubbing themselves, or even biting or hitting themselves (Knoblock, 1983; Lasher et al., 1978; Orwitz and Ritvo, 1976).

Although there is an overlap of symptoms among the childhood psychoses, child psychiatrists suggest that there are necessary and sufficient symptoms to distinguish between infantile autism and schizophrenia (DSM-III, 1980). As noted in Chapter 2, autism has been reclassified in PL 94-142 under the category "other health-impaired."

Symptoms of *infantile autism* are

1. *Severe withdrawal*
2. *Severe impairment in verbal and nonverbal communication:* the child may be mute or use jargon, or words, with or without echolalia.
3. *Bizarre responses to the environment:* this includes either abnormal stereotyped preoccupations and/or complex ritualistic behaviors.

All of these symptoms must have developed prior to thirty months of age.

_Schizophrenics look any or look sick_ [handwritten annotation]

_Schizophrenia,_ on the other hand, is distinguished by the presence of a formal thought disorder. Since this can be documented usually by language, it is often not diagnosable until after thirty months of age. [handwritten annotation: mechanical]

### Social Perception Difficulties

[handwritten annotations: misinterpret / what happens / gets mixed messages from home / speech]

Although not considered one of the conditions of serious emotional disturbance in the Head Start definition, many young children have social perception problems. A deficit in social skills implies a lack of sensitivity to people and poor perception of social situations. Social imperception often is viewed as a type of learning disability. These children do poorly in the kinds of independent activities expected of other children of the same chronological age; they are inept in judging moods and attitudes of others, they are insensitive to the atmosphere of a social situation, they display inappropriate social behaviors, and they often make inappropriate remarks. Social deficits affect almost every aspect of a child's life and can lead to serious emotional problems (Kronick, 1981; Bryan, Pearl, Donahue, Bryan, and Pflaum, 1983).

This social insensitivity may be a source of the handicapped child's difficulty with peers and parents. In general, such children are not liked by others and often are ignored when attempting to initiate a social interaction (Bryan et al., 1983). Children with social imperception difficulties may have to be directly taught how to be sensitive to the subtle social cues given by others and how to interact in a social situation.

Most children naturally pick up social skills simply through observation and daily living. But the child with a deficit in social skills needs conscious effort and specific intervention to learn about the social world, its nuances, and its silent language. Methods of intervention for the young child with social perception difficulties include activities to develop self-perception and body image; activities to develop sensitivity to the feelings of others; learning appropriate ways of acting in social situations through modeling, role-playing, and peer-mediated instruction; and developing independent and self-help skills (Odom, 1985; Strain, 1984; Beckman, 1983). Strain, Hayson, and Jamieson (1985) found that the use of normal preschoolers as peer agents with autistic preschoolers was effective in improving social interaction of the autistic children.

## THEORIES OF PSYCHOSOCIAL DEVELOPMENT

Psychologists have long tried to understand the psychodynamics of personality development. What are the forces that mold each individual's unique behavioral responses? Several theories of psychosocial development as they pertain to young children are reviewed in this section.

## Attachment

*[handwritten: 1ˢᵗ theory psycho-social level]*

*[handwritten margin: can cause psychosocial problem]*

Attachment refers to the special relationship that develops early between the infant and the mother. It begins with an instinctive tie of the infant to the mother. The "bonding" process develops as the mother provides the source of all pleasure for the infant by satisfying the baby's instinctual needs, such as eating and caressing (Bowlby, 1969). At the same time, the infant satisfies many needs within the mother. Thus, there is a dyadic partnership between the infant and the mother in the attachment as they satisfy each other's basic needs. Mothers, fathers, or caregivers do things that the infant likes (smile, talk, coo, hold). Reciprocally, the infant does things that the caregiver likes (smile, kick, wave, babble, cling, follow). Each becomes dependent upon the other and interacts with the other in a mutual communication game. This process is important because it establishes a first social relationship for the child (Bailey and Wolery, 1984). The infant who is handicapped or at-risk and spends the initial early weeks or months in a hospital setting may miss these important social beginnings.

### Temperament Styles in Young Children

Young children display different styles of behavior, called *temperament* by Thomas and Chess (1977). For example, some babies are alert and responsive; others are irritable or passive. Distinctive and individual personalities in infants can be reliably observed and recorded, and set the stage for the child's later reactions to the world.

Thomas and Chess (1977) identified ten categories of temperament as the underlying style, or pattern, of a child's behavior: *Activity level* refers to the child's level of activity; some children are active, while others are passive. *Rhythmicity* refers to the child's regularity of behavior; that is, does the child's sleeping patterns, bowel movements, and so on occur with predictable regularity each day. *Approach/withdrawal* refers to the child's outgoingness; that is, does the child tend to easily approach or to withdraw from new people and situations? *Adaptability* refers to the child's ability to adjust to new situations. *Intensity of reaction* refers to the child's level of reaction to stimuli; that is, does the child generally respond vigorously or somewhat indifferently. *Threshold of responsiveness* refers to the degree of stimulation needed to evoke a response. A child with a low responsive threshold responds quickly. *Quality of mood* refers to general disposition. Is the child usually in a whiny bad mood or in a good mood? *Distractibility* refers to the degree to which the environmental stimuli can divert the child's attention. *Attention span* refers to the child's ability to focus on a particular task. *Persistence* deals with the child's tendency to stick with a task until it is completed, despite frustrations and obstacles. Research indicates that infants and young children with certain types of temperament patterns are more likely to display behavior disorders later in childhood (Thomas and Chess, 1977; Ludlow, 1981).

*Interaction patterns between child and parent.* An infants' range of social and affective behaviors affects how others in their environment react to them. A mother (or caregiver) responds differently to children of different temperaments, and these responses may lead to different social developmental outcomes. For example, the caregiver's interaction with a child who is responsive and outgoing will be different than the child who is not very responsive and tends to withdraw (Brooks-Gunn and Lewis, 1982). Further, what is considered a difficult temperament by one caregiver is not necessarily viewed as difficult by another. Therefore, the interaction resulting from the characteristics of the caregiver and the temperament of the young child is probably a better predictor of future behavior problems than only consideration of the child's temperament (Thurman and Widerstrom, 1985). Thus, an important dimension affecting the development of the child's social and affective behaviors is the interactive process between child and parent.

Children with handicapping conditions may lack certain normal behavioral responses. Physically handicapped babies may lack some reflexes; blind children may appear less interested because of reduced visual input; hearing-impaired babies may appear as rejecting because they do not respond to sound; and neurologically impaired children may not have normal reflexes and exhibit high activity levels. These basic traits and responses make it more difficult for parents to establish basic interaction patterns with handicapped and at-risk infants and to overcome the influence of conditions that hinder development.

*Children react to teacher's moods and personalities*

### Psychosocial Development: Erik Erikson

The ideas of Erik Erikson (1963) provide the basis for one widely used model of preschool education that emphasizes the child's psychosocial development. Erikson's theories of psychosocial development are based on Freud's psychoanalytic theory, but they go further and take into account the social and cultural factors that influence the child's behavior.

Erikson sees the personality of the individual developing through a series of interrelated stages. Each stage of personality growth has a critical period of development. These critical stages become a series of turning points that contain both desirable qualities and dangers. The positive and negative features result in a conflict that must be resolved in a positive way if further conflicts also are to be resolved. A brief review of Erikson's stages of psychosocial development follows. The first three stages usually take place during the preschool years. *go thru developmental process psychosocially*

*Trust vs mistrust stage: birth to one year.* It is during this early period that the infant learns to trust the world. Trust is learned when the infant experiences consistency, continuity, and sameness of experience. In this way, the needs of the infant are met, and the child learns to think of the world as a safe and dependable place. The danger of this stage is that suspicion and fear is learned if these early experiences are undependable, inconsistent, unsafe, and if the early care is inadequate. Then the child learns to approach the world with fear and suspicion.

*Autonomy vs. shame and doubt stage: two to three years of age.*   In the next psychosocial stage of the Erikson theory, the child gains some degree of independence. This autonomy develops when parents and teachers permit children to do what they are capable of—to do it at their own pace and in their own way. Of course, the child still needs careful supervision, but the freedom to perform independently enhances the child's sense of autonomy. The danger during this stage occurs when the parents and teachers do not permit children to do things by themselves. The adults become impatient or they are overly critical, reprimanding or shaming the child for unacceptable behavior. Rather than developing autonomy, then, the child learns self-doubt and shame. Teachers and parents must tread the fence between too little and too much control.

*Initiative vs. guilt stage: four to five years of age.*   The child now has the physical and language abilities for initiating activity and for exploring the physical world, for being active and on the move. Children need the freedom to explore and experiment and to have questions answered in order to foster the quality of initiative. The danger during this stage lies in the restricting of the initiative, in an attitude that the child's activities are pointless or a nuisance. At this period, also, the child develops a concept of right and wrong. The punishment or disapproval of actions may lead to an oppressive feeling of guilt—which can continue throughout life.

*Stages beyond the preschool level.*   There are several stages of Erikson's psychosocial development that go beyond the preschool years: *industry versus inferiority,* six to eleven years of age; *identity versus role con- ~~unsure~~ fusion,* twelve to eighteen years of age; still other stages refer to young adulthood, middle age, and old age.

## PLAY: AN IMPORTANT LEARNING ACTIVITY

Play is a natural activity of children. Children need to play, and play serves an essential role in the young child's development.

### The Role of Play in Child Growth

*They learn by being active.*

The spontaneous and creative activities of play make invaluable contributions toward the child's learning of cognitive, language, motor, and social skills. The child learns in a natural way about color, shapes, textures,

forms, sizes, rules, and people. An endless variety of materials—blocks, paints, sand, toys, clay, boxes, balls, and the like—can be used. The child learns motor skills by playing with balls, skates, ropes, tricycles, wagons, playground equipment, and sewing. Cognitive skills are developed through games, dolls, and creative activities. Social and communication skills are nurtured through group activities with another child or through group games, such as playing house or playing Superman. The essence of play is that it is child-originated and child-oriented and that the child's own intrinsic absorption in mastery provides the energy for the learning experience (Newson and Newson, 1979).

Early childhood educators understand the value of play for the young child and the need to provide play opportunities, including uninterrupted time. In fact, the right to play richly, joyously, and freely has been called the precious right and necessity of early childhood—one that must be carefully guarded.

Play can be classified into two general types: *spontaneous play* and *directed play*. *Spontaneous play* is initiated by the child. It is not consciously influenced by the desire of adults. It is free and without adult-set goals or objectives. The children solve their problems to their own satisfaction. This free, child-oriented, spontaneous type of play can provide the key for intellectual development.

*Directed play* is structured, initiated, or planned by others—such as adults, parents, or teachers. The tendency in education today is for more controlled educational, or directed, play. We have turned the child's instinctive need for spontaneous play into planned and directed educational play. The aim, or goal, of this directed play is determined by the adult, and the value of the play activity is assessed by what is learned. Many early childhood educators decry this trend, fearing that it has resulted in an overcapitalization of the child's innate desire for play. They fear an exploitation of the child's natural instinct for play. There is at present a difference of opinion between those educators who feel that children would benefit from more spontaneous play and those who believe that learning is enhanced by more directed and structured play.

### Play and the Handicapped Child

Play activities are as essential for the young handicapped and at-risk child as for the nonhandicapped. However, its importance and role in the curriculum are often neglected. The handicapped child needs play experiences and activities. The teacher must plan for appropriate opportunities and an environment appropriate to the handicapped child. Handicapped children do not appear to learn as easily as the nonhandicapped through spontaneous play and, therefore, need more directed and structured play.

Beckman (1983) observed free-play situations between handicapped and nonhandicapped preschoolers and found that the amount of interaction varied as a function of the severity of the handicap and age. The older preschoolers and children with mild handicaps displayed more social interaction during free play. Odom (1981) observed moderate and severe mentally retarded preschoolers during free play and found a significant correlation between play behavior and the child's developmental level. Kohl, Beckman, and Swenson-Pierce (1984) found that adult-directed play increased handicapped preschoolers' functional use of toys.

## Functions of Play for Handicapped Children

Play has four major functions for the young handicapped child (Beers and Wehman, 1985):

1. *To facilitate growth of desirable behaviors in motor, language, cognitive, and social skills* The play activities can help the child develop gross and fine motor skills through physical activities. Language skills can be developed through communication and expressive activities in group games. Social skills are developed through cooperative group work. Cognitive skills, problem solving, concepts, creative activities are developed through games and thinking play.

2. *To reinforce instructional activity* Once a skill is learned, play provides a means for practicing and reinforcing that skill in a way that provides pleasure and fun for the child. Children enjoy the practicing and perfecting of a skill when it is viewed as play.

3. *To inhibit socially inappropriate behavior* When children are actively involved in a play activity, they inhibit behaviors that are considered socially unacceptable. Research shows that there is a significant reduction in self-stimulating behaviors through the acquisition of play skills. Behaviors such as self-inflicting aggression, stereotypical rocking behavior, and bizarre vocal sounds are decreased or eliminated through play.

4. *To provide pleasure or joy* Play provides pleasure, joy, fun, and a diversion from daily routines for people of all ages. Handicapped children are no exception and are even more in need of the pleasures of playing with toys and games. Severely handicapped children may need direct instruction in how to play or to use free time. Mildly handicapped children will be able to enjoy many leisure activities without precise training and direction.

## Play Problems of Young Handicapped Children

The value of spontaneous play in learning and child growth has been extolled by early childhood educators. The problem is that many handicapped children fail to develop play activities by themselves in a spontaneous manner. The more severe the handicapping condition, the less likely the child is to develop play behavior without external stimulation and direction. Many handicapped children must be taught to play; they need external cues, direct instruction, and careful supervision. Strategic arrangements of play materials also may be needed.

Handicapped children need special toys and play materials. Their toys must be more durable than those needed by the nonhandicapped because with slowly emerging skills, the child will use the toy over a longer period of time than the normal child. Also, the child may be stronger and larger than the nonhandicapped child when the toy is used.

Many recreation specialists are not trained to understand the unique behaviors and needs of handicapped children. For example, they may not understand the lack of spontaneity with toys that is characteristic of many handicapped young children. What frequently occurs when young handicapped children are introduced to a roomful of toys is repetitive and nonfunctional actions with playthings. In such a situation, the nonhandicapped child would play with the toys by beating the drum, blowing the horn, and bouncing the ball. The developmentally delayed child, however, may hit the horn repetitively on the floor until it breaks. Therefore, teachers in early childhood special education must have a specialized set of skills combining competencies in recreational therapy with competencies in early childhood and special education and behavior management techniques. This includes a thorough understanding and working knowledge of reinforcement theory, modeling, shaping behavior, and methods of behavior recording and monitoring. These techniques are discussed later in this chapter.

### Kinds of Play

There are four categories of play for the young handicapped or at-risk child (Beers and Wehman, 1985): (a) *exploratory play;* (b) *toy play;* (c) *social play;* and (d) *structured game play.* These four types are somewhat hierarchical in nature, although they may be overlapping as well. The four categories are useful in assessing the child's present level of play behavior and in planning a play curriculum.

1. *Exploratory play* In this kind of play, the child explores the environment by engaging in motor, sensory, and searching behavior.
2. *Toy play* In this type of play, the child interacts with toys and other play material. The child pushes, pulls, puts together, takes apart, throws, or pounds a toy.
3. *Social play* In this type of play, the child interacts with other individuals—an adult, parent, teacher, or another child. The child learns to cooperate and communicate. The child also learns psychosocial skills by sharing, taking turns, planning, and interacting. This type of play may be a way of integrating nonhandicapped and handicapped preschoolers. Guralnick (1980) found that nonhandicapped and mildly handicapped children interacted with each other during free play more frequently than expected.
4. *Game play* This type of play is considered the highest and most complex level of the play skills sequence. Rules are set forth in games that must be followed. Playing a game requires cooperation and communication. The child must learn to both win and lose. Care should be taken that the rules are simple enough for the child to understand. Computer games can be effective with young children (Strain and Kachman, 1984).

One of the best examples of the success of play for the handicapped is the annual Special Olympics for the handicapped events. In these events, handicapped youngsters have the chance to participate at the local, state, and national level in athletic events that are limited to handicapped children. The Special Olympics events gain in popularity each year and are enjoyed by all participants.

There are several organizations that lend toys to young handicapped children.

*Toy libraries for handicapped young children* Contact U.S. Toy Library Association; 5940 West Touhy; Chicago, IL 60648 and National Lekotek Association; 2100 Ridge Ave.; Evanston, IL 60204.

## BEHAVIOR MANAGEMENT

The ideas developed in behavioral psychology and the field of applied behavior analysis are employed in many preschool and special education programs. Among the techniques developed from these fields are those known as behavior modification. *Behavior modification* can be described as a systematic arrangement of environmental events to produce a specific change in observable behavior (Allen, 1980).

Behavior modification requires the teacher to (1) carefully and systematically observe and tabulate the occurrence of behaviors of concern and (2) alter the environment so that there is a desired change in the child's behavior.

There are several specific strategies that are used in behavior management: reinforcement, modeling, shaping, and methods of behavior recording and monitoring.

### Reinforcement

An event that follows a behavior and has the effect of controlling that behavior is considered a *reinforcer*. It helps the teacher shape behavior toward the desired responses by rewarding correct behaviors and purposefully ignoring incorrect or irrelevant behaviors. Harlan and Leyser (1980) found that Head Start teachers gave more criticism and less encouragement to emotionally disturbed children than they gave to all other handicapped children. Thus, an intensive effort to change teacher attitudes and help them employ positive reinforcement techniques was essential. Commonly used reinforcers include candy, gummed stars, verbal praise, and smiling faces.

For example, if Jason puts away his art materials with the other children at the end of the free-play period, the teacher can reinforce him verbally by saying. "Good work, Jason," or nonverbally, by giving him a hug. If Jason does not clean up, the teacher ignores his behavior. Or if Mark begins to make inappropriate shouting or screaming sounds during snack time, the teacher can assist in reducing these undesirable behaviors by turning Mark's chair around, away from the food and other children, until the sounds are stopped. Immediate and consistent use of reinforcers is very important for long-term gains.

## Modeling

The term *modeling* is used in behavior management to show an example of the behavior that the teacher wishes the child to acquire. The hope is that the child will observe and imitate this desired behavior. The model could be an adult, teacher, parent, or another child. For example, if Sarah watches another child playing with a new toy that makes pleasant sounds, she will imitate that play behavior when given that same toy. Several researchers have reported that the modeling tactic has been successful in improving psychosocial skills. Children learned to share toys with classmates, engage in appropriate physical contact, and make complimentary remarks to each other (O'Leary and O'Leary, 1977; Strain, 1984).

## Shaping Behavior

*actually doing an action w/child*

Shaping behavior means the reinforcement of successful approximations of a desired act. It can be used when the child simply does not respond or when the child begins to make a mistake.

For example, if Pam refuses to hang up her coat, the teacher thinks through the successive steps needed for Pam to hang up her coat. The teacher starts with the first step and rewards Pam if she performs that act. Then each step along the way is rewarded. For example, walking to the coat hook, picking up the coat, finding the loop, and so on.

### Methods of Behavior Recording and Monitoring

Behavior management methods stress the importance of objective recording of the child's behavior as the basis for judging whether behavior has changed. The teacher could use a checklist, a graph, a chart, simple counting, and the like. There are two general ways of measuring observations. One is by *frequency*. For example, the teacher measures how often Jennifer has a temper tantrum. The other is by *duration*. The teacher measures how long Scott remains isolated from the other children in his group.

It is important for teachers to keep accurate, objective records in order to establish a baseline. The *baseline* is a frequency or duration measure prior to the implementation of behavior management.

Once a system of behavior management is put into operation, the teacher should record changes in the events. Specific target behaviors can be identified and recorded as they occur. Intervention then is based on a systematic analysis of what the teacher sees the child doing. Behavior management procedures are useful both for eliminating undesirable psychosocial behaviors and establishing desirable behaviors. In behavior monitoring, it is important to establish small steps to observe and record. This serves to simplify complex behaviors and to monitor what is occurring.

## INTERVENTION STRATEGIES FOR TEACHING PSYCHOSOCIAL SKILLS

While the normal child is able to learn social skills through daily living and observation, the child with difficulties in the affective realm needs specific teaching to learn about the social world. This child must be helped to understand the nuances of the social world and the meaning of silent language in interactions with people. Just as children must be taught academic skills—reading, writing, spelling, arithmetic—they also must be taught to learn to live with and around other people. Just as we must use different methods to teach school subjects, so we have to use different methods to teach children how to get along with others.

*Show and tell.* A well-known activity with preschool and primary teachers is the activity of Show and Tell (sometimes cynically referred to as "Bring and Brag"). The child is simply asked to bring something to show or share with the group. The activity puts the child in the limelight, and the child has a few minutes to experience being the focus of the group. The child could bring a new toy, a Mickey Mouse hat, talk about a trip, show a tooth that fell out, or show something for a pet. Children like to bring their "show-and-tell" item in a paper bag to deepen the suspense or surprise. Behind each article is something very personal, of value to the self. For the child who is too shy or frightened to speak before a group, merely showing the article would be a first step. Later the child might be asked to talk about the item in one sentence. The show-and-tell activity can be developmental with children learning to express more of themselves over time.

*About me.*   In this activity children have the opportunity to reveal themselves to others—their likes, dislikes, fears, hopes, and dreams. The children sit in a comfortable group—possibly a circle—and take turns telling something about themselves. They might tell about their favorite television show, book, color, food, toy, or pet. Another discussion could concern things they dislike, or what they would like to do, or the dreams they have had.

*Building self-worth with pictures.*   Take polaroid pictures of children or have them take pictures of each other. Make posters or pages of a book with each child's picture. Have the child sit in the center of the group, with his or her picture. The other children can dictate a sentence about the child to put with the picture. For example:

Jean shares toys with others.
Tom listens at story time.
George told us about his trip to the circus.
Mary watered all the plants today.

Another way of using pictures is to take slides of the children engaged in activities at school. Show the slides and discuss the activities.

*The outerspace man.*   Have the children pretend that a spaceship from another planet landed in the school yard. Have the children discuss what the spaceman will look like. Then have the children draw a large picture of this person and give him a name. Ask one child or the teacher to sit behind the poster and become the voice of the outerspace man. Ask questions such as: "The people from the planet Crypton want to know what you enjoy about living on Earth. What do you think the Crypton people would enjoy about living on Earth? What do you think the Crypton people would enjoy doing or seeing? What should people from Crypton be careful about here on Earth?" This activity might be too advanced for those children with major language or cognitive handicaps. However, it would work well with gifted preschoolers.

*Pictures and feelings.*   Give each child a magazine and ask them to cut out one picture of a person showing emotion. The picture should show how a person feels—happy, sad, angry, thoughtful, worried, frightened. Paste the picture on a separate piece of paper. Discuss each picture. How does this person feel? What do you think might have made the person feel that way? How should you treat a person who feels this way? This activity gives the children the opportunity to discuss the feelings and emotions of others and ways to detect these feelings, as well as how to react to them in an objective way.

*Relax and remember.*   In this activity, the children are asked to relax their bodies, to close their eyes, and to see things in their mind's eye. They are asked to conjure up memories of places, things, and feelings. They are asked to see, taste, hear, and feel. Some items could be

| | |
|---|---|
| tasting a peanut butter sandwich | hearing a bird singing |
| splashing in a pool on a hot day | blowing up a balloon |
| walking through dry leaves in the fall | hearing thunder |
| feeling the warm sunshine | taking a bubblebath |
| biting into a crunchy apple | smelling a flower |
| walking in snow drifts | cutting an onion |
| smelling freshly baked cookies | |

*The wonders of nature.*   Children can be helped to become attuned to the wonders of nature. One passes over things every day that can be quite beautiful. The *nature walk* is an activity to help children become aware of the wonders in the world. The children can be taken out of doors and asked to be very quiet as they walk to find *one* object that causes them to wonder. The object could be a leaf or a rock or a twig. The group can share what they find. Children can explain what they see of wonder in their object.

## SUMMARY

The affective domain refers to the psychosocial skills of the preschool child—the social and emotional aspects of development. Preschoolers can have serious social, emotional, and behavioral problems. Behavior problems include aggressive behavior, anxiety, hyperactivity, and attention deficits.

Childhood psychoses include the conditions of autism and schizophrenia. Some children exhibit social perceptional difficulties and do poorly in social situations. There are a number of theories of psychosocial development in young children.

*Attachment* refers to the close bonding relationship between infant and mother. *Temperament* refers to the individual and distinctive personality styles observed in infants and young children. Erikson's theories of a child's psychosocial development through a series of interrelated stages provide another concept of the developing personality.

Play activity serves an important role in child development. Through play children learn motor, cognitive, language, sensory, and social skills. The nonhandicapped child learns many of these skills through spontaneous play. Handicapped children, however, may need carefully planned and directed activities to learn how to play. For the handicapped child, play facilitates growth of desired behaviors, reinforces instructional activity, inhibits inappropriate behavior, and provides pleasure. The kinds of play include exploratory play, toy play, social play, and game play.

Behavior management techniques are an important intervention strategy for young handicapped and at-risk children. The techniques include reinforcement, modeling, shaping behavior, recording and monitoring behavior.

A wide variety of activities can be used by the teacher to help the child develop psychosocial skills.

## REVIEW QUESTIONS

**Terms to Know**

temperament
behavior management
reinforcement
modeling

bonding
spontaneous play
directed play
attention deficit

1. Describe a serious psychosocial problem a preschool child might have.
2. Describe three temperaments displayed by infants.
3. What is the value of play for handicapped and at-risk preschoolers?
4. What is the theory underlying behavior management?
5. Give an example of reinforcement, modeling, and shaping behaviors.
6. What is the difference between *spontaneous play* and *directed play*?

## REFERENCES

ALLEN, K. (1980) *Mainstreaming in Early Childhood Education.* Albany, NY: Delmar.

BAILEY, D. and M. WOLERY (1984) *Teaching Infants and Preschoolers with Handicaps.* Columbus, OH: Charles E. Merrill.

BECKMAN, P. (1983) "The Relationship Between Behavioral Characteristics of Children and Social Interaction in an Integrated Setting." *Journal of the Division for Early Childhood,* 7, 69–77.

BEERS, C. and P. WEHMAN (1985) "Play Skill Development." In M. Fallen and W. Umansky (eds.) *Young Children with Special Needs.* Columbus, OH: Charles E. Merrill, 403–40.

BOWLBY, J. (1969) *Attachment.* NY: Basic Boosk.

BROOKS-GUNN, J. and M. LEWIS (1982) "Temperament and Affective Interaction in Handicapped Infants." *Journal of the Division for Early Childhood,* 5, 31–41.

BRYAN, T., R. PEARL, M. DONAHUE, J. BRYAN, and S. PFLAUM (1983) "The Chicago Institute for the Study of Learning Disabilities." *Exceptional Education Quarterly,* 4(1), 1–23.

CALDWELL, B. (1979) "Aggression and Hostility in Young Children." In L. Adams and B. Gorelick (eds.) *Ideas that Work with Young Children* (Vol. 2) Washington, DC: National Association for the Education of Young Children.

DSM-III. (1980) *Diagnostic and Statistical Manual.* Washington, D.C., American Psychiatric Association.

ERIKSON, E. (1963) *Childhood and Society*. NY: W.W. Norton.

GOOD, T. and J. BROPHY (1978) *Looking in Classrooms*. NY: Harper & Row.

GURALNICK, M. (1980) "Social Interactions Among Preschool Children." *Exceptional Children*, 46 (4), 248–53.

HARLAN, J. and Y. LEYSER (1980) "Head Start Teachers' Use of Verbal Encouragement." *Exceptional Children* 46 (4), 290–91.

KNOBLOCK, P. (1983) *Teaching Emotionally Disturbed Children*. Boston: Houghton, Mifflin.

KOHL, F., P. BECKMAN, and A. SWENSON-PIERCE (1984) "The Effects of Directed Play on Functional Toy Use and Interactions of Handicapped Preschoolers." *Journal of the Division for Early Childhood*, 8 (2), 114–18.

KRONICK, D. (1981) *Social Development of Learning Disabled Persons*. San Francisco, CA: Jossey-Bass.

LASHER, M., I. MATTICK, and F. PERKINS (1978) *Mainstreaming Preschoolers: Children with Emotional Disturbance*. U.S. Department of Health & Human Services, Office of Human Development Services, Head Start Bureau. Washington, DC: Government Printing Office.

LUDLOW, B. (1981) "Parent–Infant Interaction Research: The Argument for Earlier Intervention Programs." *Journal of the Division for Early Childhood*, 3, 34–41.

NEWSON, J. and F. NEWSON (1979) *Toys and Playthings*. NY: Pantheon Books.

ODOM, S. (1981) "The Relationship of Play to Developmental Level in Mentally Retarded Preschool Children." *Education and Training of the Mentally Retarded*, 4, 136–41.

ODOM, S. (1985) "Social Skills Instruction for Handicapped Preschool Children." *DEC Communicator*, 11 (2), 4.

O'LEARY, K., and S. O'LEARY (1977) *Classroom Management: The Successful Use of Behavior Modification*. NY: Pergamon.

ORWITZ, E. and E. RITVO (1976) *Autism*. NY: Halstead Press.

RUTTER, M. (1981) "Socio-emotional Consequences of Day Care for Preschool Children." *Journal of Child Psychology and Psychiatry*, 51, 4–29.

STRAIN, P. (1984) "Social Behavior Patterns of Non-Handicapped Developmentally Disabled Friend Pairs in Mainstreamed Preschools." *Analysis and Intervention in Developmental Disabilities*, 4, 15–28.

STRAIN, P., M. HAYSON and B. JAMIESON (1985) "Normally Developing Preschoolers as Intervention Agents for Autistic-like Children: Effects on Class Deportment and Social Interaction." *Journal of the Division for Early Childhood*, 9 (2), 105–15.

STREIN, W. and W. KACHMAN (1984) "Effects of Computer Games on Young Children's Cooperative Behavior: An Exploratory Study." *Journal of Research and Development in Education*, 18 (1), 40–43.

THOMAS, A. and S. CHESS (1977) *Temperament and Development*. NY: Bruner/Mazel.

THURMAN, S., and A. WIDERSTROM (1985) *Young Children with Special Needs: A Developmental and Ecological Approach*. Boston: Allyn & Bacon.

# APPENDIX A

## Chart of Normal Development: Infancy to Age Six

The chart of normal development on the next few pages presents children's achievements from infancy to six years of age in five areas:

Motor skills (gross and fine motor)
Communication skills (understanding language and speaking)
Cognitive skills
Self-help skills
Social skills

In each skill area, the age at which each milestone is reached *on the average* also is presented. This information is useful if you have a child in your class who you suspect is seriously delayed in one or more skill areas.

However, it is important to remember that these milestones are only average. From the moment of birth, each child is a distinct individual and develops in his or her unique manner. No two children have ever reached all the same developmental milestones at the exact same ages.

# Chart of Normal Development

| MOTOR SKILLS | | COMMUNICATION SKILLS | |
| --- | --- | --- | --- |
| Gross Motor Skills | Fine Motor Skills | Understanding of Language | Spoken Language |

## 0–12 months

| | | | |
| --- | --- | --- | --- |
| Sits without support.<br>Crawls.<br>Pulls self to standing position and stands unaided.<br>Walks with aid.<br>Rolls a ball in imitation of adult. | Reaches, grasps, puts object in mouth.<br>Picks things up with thumb and one finger (pincer grasp).<br>Transfers object from one hand to other hand.<br>Drops and picks up toy. | Responds to speech by looking at speaker.<br>Responds differently to aspects of speaker's voice (for example, friendly or unfriendly, male or female).<br>Turns to source of sound.<br>Responds with gesture to *hi, bye-bye,* and *up,* when these words are accompanied by appropriate gesture.<br>Stops ongoing action when told *no* (when negative is accompanied by appropriate gesture and tone). | Makes crying and non-crying sounds.<br>Repeats some vowel and consonant sounds (babbles) when alone or when spoken to.<br>Interacts with others by vocalizing after adult.<br>Communicates meaning through intonation.<br>Attempts to imitate sounds. |

## 12–24 months

| | | | |
| --- | --- | --- | --- |
| Walks alone.<br>Walks backward.<br>Picks up toys from floor without falling.<br>Pulls toy, pushes toy.<br>Seats self in child's chair.<br>Walks up and down stairs (hand held).<br>Moves to music. | Builds tower of 3 small blocks.<br>Puts 4 rings on stick.<br>Places 5 pegs in peg-board.<br>Turns pages 2 or 3 at a time.<br>Scribbles.<br>Turns knobs.<br>Throws small ball.<br>Paints with whole arm movement, shifts hands, makes strokes. | Responds correctly when asked *where* when question is accompanied by gesture.<br>Understands prepositions *on, in,* and *under.*<br>Follows request to bring familiar object from another room.<br>Understands simple phrases with key words (for example, *Open the door. Get the ball.*)<br>Follows a series of 2 simple but related directions. | Says first meaningful word.<br>Uses single words plus a gesture to ask for objects.<br>Says successive single words to describe an event.<br>Refers to self by name.<br>Uses *my* or *mine* to indicate possession.<br>Has vocabulary of about 50 words for important people, common objects, and the existence, nonexistence, and recurrence of objects and events (for example, *more* and *all gone*). |

| COGNITIVE SKILLS | | SELF-HELP SKILLS | SOCIAL SKILLS |
|---|---|---|---|

## 0–12 months

| | | | |
|---|---|---|---|
| Follows moving object with eyes. | Imitates gestures and actions (for example, shakes head no, plays peek-a-boo, waves bye-bye). | Feeds self cracker. | Smiles spontaneously. |
| Recognizes differences among people; responds to strangers by crying or staring. | | Holds cup with two hands; drinks with assistance. | Responds differently to strangers than to familiar people. |
| Responds to and imitates facial expressions of others. | Puts small objects in and out of container with intention. | Holds out arms and legs while being dressed. | Pays attention to own name. |
| Responds to very simple directions (for example, raises arms when someone says, come, and turns head when asked, Where is daddy?). | | | Responds to no. |
| | | | Copies simple actions of others. |

## 12–24 months

| | | | |
|---|---|---|---|
| Imitates actions and words of adults. | Recognizes difference between you and me. | Uses spoon, spilling little. | Recognizes self in mirror or picture. |
| Understands and follows simple, familiar directions (for example, Give me the cup. Show me your doll. Get your shoes). | Has very limited attention span. | Drinks from cup with one hand, unassisted. | Refers to self by name. |
| | Accomplishes primary learning through own exploration. | Chews food. | Plays by self; initiates own play. |
| Responds to words or commands with appropriate action (for example, Stop that. Get down). | | Removes shoes, socks, pants, sweater. | Imitates adult behaviors in play. |
| | | Unzips large zipper. | Helps put things away. |
| Is able to match two similar objects. | | Indicates toilet needs. | |
| Looks at storybook pictures with an adult, naming or pointing to familiar objects on request (for example, What is that? Where is the baby?). | | | |

| MOTOR SKILLS | | COMMUNICATION SKILLS | |
|---|---|---|---|
| Gross Motor Skills | Fine Motor Skills | Understanding of Language | Spoken Language |

**24–36 months**

| | | | |
|---|---|---|---|
| Runs forward well. | Strings 4 large beads. | Points to pictures of common objects when they are named. | Joins vocabulary words together in two-word phrases. |
| Jumps in place, two feet together. | Turns pages singly. | | |
| Stands on one foot with aid. | Snips with scissors. | Can identify objects when told their use. | Gives first and last name. |
| | Holds crayon with thumb and fingers, not fist. | Understands question forms *what* and *where*. | |
| Walks on tiptoe. | | | Asks *what* and *where* questions. |
| Kicks ball forward. | Uses one hand consistently in most activities. | Understands negatives *no, not, can't,* and *don't.* | Makes negative statements (for example, *Can't open it.*). |
| | Imitates circular, vertical, horizontal strokes. | Enjoys listening to simple storybooks and requests them again. | Shows frustration at not being understood. |
| | Pains with some wrist action; makes dots, lines, circular strokes. | | |
| | Rolls, pounds, squeezes, and pulls clay. | | |

**36–48 months**

| | | | |
|---|---|---|---|
| Runs around obstacles. | Builds tower of 9 small blocks. | Begins to understand sentences involving time concepts (for example, *We are going to the zoo tomorrow*) | Talks in sentences of three or more words that take the form agent-action-object (*I see the ball*) or agent-action-location (*Daddy, sit on chair*). |
| Walks on a line. | Drives nails and pegs. | | |
| Balances on one foot for 5 to 10 seconds. | Copies circle. | | |
| Hops on one foot. | Imitates cross. | Understands size comparatives, such as *big* and *bigger.* Understands relationships expressed by *if . . . then* or *because* sentences. | Tells about past experiences. |
| Pushes, pulls, steers wheeled toys. | Manipulates clay materials (for example, rolls balls, snakes, cookies). | | |
| Rides (that is, steers and pedals) tricycle. | | | Uses *s* on nouns to indicate plurals. |
| Uses slide without assistance. | | Carries out a series of 2 to 4 related directions. | Uses *ed* on verbs to include past tense. |
| Jumps over 15 cm. (6″) high object, landing on both feet together. | | Understands when told, *Let's pretend.* | Refers to self using pronouns *I* or *me.* |
| Throws ball overhead. | | | Repeats at least one nursery rhyme and can sing a song. |
| Catches ball bounced to him or her. | | | Speech is understandable to strangers, but there are still some sound errors. |

| COGNITIVE SKILLS | | SELF-HELP SKILLS | SOCIAL SKILLS |
|---|---|---|---|

## 24–36 months

Responds to simple directions (for example, *Give me the ball and the block. Get your shoes and socks*).

Selects and looks at picture books, names pictured objects, and identifies several objects within one picture.

Matches and uses associated objects meaningfully (for example, given cup, saucer, and bead, puts cup and saucer together).

Stacks rings on peg in order of size.

Recognizes self in mirror, saying, *baby,* or own name.

Can talk briefly about what he or she is doing.

Imitates adult actions (for example, housekeeping play).

Has limited attention span; learning is through exploration and adult direction (as in reading of picture stories).

Is beginning to understand functional concepts of familiar objects (for example, that a spoon is used for eating) and part/whole concepts (for example parts of the body).

Uses spoon, little spilling.

Gets drink from fountain or faucet unassisted.

Opens door by turning handle.

Takes off coat.

Puts on coat with assistance.

Washes and dries hands with assistance.

Plays near other children.

Watches other children; joins briefly in their play.

Defends own possessions.

Begins to play house.

Symbolically uses objects, self in play.

Participates in simple group activity (for example, sings, claps, dances).

Knows gender identity.

## 36–48 months

Recognizes and matches six colors.

Intentionally stacks blocks or rings in order of size.

Draws somewhat recognizable picture that is meaningful to child if not to adult; names and briefly explains picture.

Asks questions for information: *why* and *how* questions requiring simple answers.

Knows own age.

Knows own last name.

Has short attention span. Learns through observing and imitating adults and by adult instruction and explanation. Is very easily distracted.

Has increased understanding of concepts of the functions and grouping of objects (for example, can put doll house furniture in correct rooms) part/whole (for example, can identify pictures of hand and foot as parts of body).

Begins to be aware of past and present (for example, *Yesterday we went to the park. Today we go to the library.*).

Pours well from small pitcher.

Spreads soft butter with knife.

Buttons and unbuttons large buttons.

Washes hands unassisted.

Blows nose when reminded.

Uses toilet independently.

Joins in play with other children; begins to interact.

Shares toys; takes turns with assistance.

Begins dramatic play, acting out whole scenes (for example, traveling, playing house, pretending to be animals).

| MOTOR SKILLS | | COMMUNICATION SKILLS | |
|---|---|---|---|
| Gross Motor Skills | Fine Motor Skills | Understanding of Language | Spoken Language |

## 48–60 months

| | | | |
|---|---|---|---|
| Walks backward toe-heel. | Cuts on line continuously. | Follows three unrelated commands in proper order. | Asks *when, how,* and *why* questions. |
| Jumps forward 10 times without falling. | Copies cross. | Understands comparatives, such as pretty, prettier, and prettiest. | Uses modals, such as *can, will, shall, should,* and *might.* |
| Walks up and down stairs alone, alternating feet. | Copies square. | | Joins sentences together (for example, *I like chocolate chip cookies and milk.*) |
| | Prints a few capital letters. | | |
| Turns somersault. | | Listens to long stories but often misinterprets the facts. | Talks about causality by using *because* and *so.* |
| | | Incorporates verbal directions into play activities. | Tells the content of a story but may confuse facts. |
| | | Understands sequencing of events when told them (for example, *First we have to go to the store, then we can make the cake, and tomorrow we will eat it*). | |

## 60–72 months

| | | | |
|---|---|---|---|
| Runs lightly on toes. | Cuts out simple shapes. | Demonstrates pre-academic skills. | There are few obvious differences between child's grammar and adult's grammar. |
| Walks on balance beam. | Copies triangle. | | |
| Can cover 2 meters (6'6") hopping. | Traces diamond. | | Still needs to learn such things as subject-verb agreement and some irregular past tense verbs. |
| Skips on alternate feet. | Copies first name. | | |
| Jumps rope. | Prints numerals 1 to 5. | | |
| Skates. | Colors within lines. | | Can take appropriate turns in a conversation. |
| | Has adult grasp of pencil. | | Gives and receives information. |
| | Has handedness well established (that is, child is left- or right-handed). | | Communicates well with family, friends, or strangers. |
| | Pastes and glues appropriately. | | |

| COGNITIVE SKILLS | | SELF-HELP SKILLS | SOCIAL SKILLS |
|---|---|---|---|

## 48–60 months

Plays with words: creates own rhyming words, says or makes up words having similar sounds.

Points to and names 4 to 6 colors.

Matches pictures of familiar objects (for example, shoe, sock, foot; apple, orange, banana).

Draws a person with 2 to 6 recognizable parts, such as head, arms, legs; can name or match drawn parts to own body.

Draws, names, and describes recognizable picture.

Rote counts to 5, imitating adults.

Knows own street and town.

Has more extended attention span; learns through observing and listening to adults, as well as through exploration; is easily distracted.

Has increased understanding of concepts of function, time, part/ whole relationships. Function or use of objects may be stated in addition to names of objects.

Time concepts are expanding. Can talk about yesterday or last week (a long time ago), about today, and about what will happen tomorrow.

Cuts easy foods with a knife (for example, hamburger patty, tomato slice).

Laces shoes.

Plays and interacts with other children.

Dramatic play is closer to reality, with attention paid to detail, time, and space.

Plays dress-up.

Shows interest in exploring sex differences.

## 60–72 months

Retells story from picture book with reasonable accuracy.

Names some letters and numerals.

Rote counts to 10.

Sorts objects by single characteristics (for example, by color, shape, or size—if the difference is obvious).

Is beginning to use accurately time concepts of *tomorrow* and *yesterday*.

Uses classroom tools (such as scissors and paints) meaningfully and purposefully.

Begins to relate clock time to daily schedule.

Attention span increases noticeably; learns through adult instruction; when interested, can ignore distractions.

Concepts of function increase as well as understanding of why things happen; time concepts are expanding into an understanding of the future in terms of major events (for example, Christmas will come after two weekends).

Dresses self completely.

Ties bow.

Brushes teeth unassisted.

Crosses street safely.

Chooses own friend(s).

Plays simple table games.

Plays competitive games.

Engages in cooperative play with other children involving group decisions, role assignments, fair play.

From Human Development Services. *Mainstreaming Preschoolers: Children with Speech and Language Impairments*. Project Head Start. U.S. Department of Health & Human Services. Head Start Bureau, 1978, pp. 161–67.

271

# APPENDIX B

# Tests for Screening and Diagnosing Young Children

Appendix B lists the names and brief descriptive information of the most recent commercially available and highly regarded tests that are designed for young children. All are individually administered unless the name of the instrument is followed by an asterisk (*), which indicates group administration. Appendix B is divided into two sections: Part I, Screening Tests, and Part II, Diagnostic Tests. Addresses of the publishers are listed in Appendix C.

## PART I: SCREENING TESTS

| | |
|---|---|
| **Name:** | **Boehm Test of Basic Concepts-Revised*** |
| **Author(s):** | Boehm, A.E. |
| **Publisher:** | Psychological Corporation |
| **Copyright Date:** | 1985 |
| **Administrator:** | Professional (teacher, diagnostician) |
| **Age Range:** | 3–5 Yrs; Grades K–2 |
| **Purpose:** | Measures children's mastery of concepts considered necessary for achievement in the first years of school. Concepts tested include those of space (location, direction, orientation, and dimension), time, and quantity (number). Also available in Spanish. |
| **Testing Time:** | 15–30 Minutes (depending on level) |
| **Type(s) of Response:** | Nonverbal (using booklet and pencil) |

| | |
|---|---|
| **Name:** | **Bracken Basic Concept Scale (Level 1)*** |
| **Author(s):** | Bracken, B. |
| **Publisher:** | Charles E. Merrill |
| **Copyright Date:** | 1984 |
| **Administrator:** | Professional |
| **Age Range:** | 2–6 To 8–0 |
| **Purpose:** | Measures the receptive knowledge of basic concepts (letter identification, numbers/counting, comparisons, shapes, direction/position, social/emotional, size, texture/material, quantity, and time/sequence) to determine which children may need a diagnostic assessment. Two 30-item equivalent forms are available. |
| **Testing Time:** | 5–10 minutes |
| **Type(s) of Response:** | Nonverbal |

| | |
|---|---|
| **Name:** | **Comprehensive Identification Process (CIP)** |
| **Author(s):** | Zehrbach, R. |
| **Publisher:** | Scholastic Testing Service |
| **Copyright Date:** | 1976 |
| **Administrator:** | Professional (teacher, diagnostician) and/or nonprofessional (parent) |
| **Age Range:** | 2–6 To 5–6 |
| **Purpose:** | Identifies children who may need special medical, psychological, or educational assistance before they enter school. Test assesses eight areas of development: fine motor, gross motor, cognitive–verbal, speech–expressive language, hearing, vision, social–affective, and medical. |

**Testing Time:** 30 minutes
**Type(s) of Response:** Verbal, nonverbal

**Name:** **Denver Developmental Screening Test-Revised (DDST-R)**
**Author(s):** Frankenburg, W., et al.
**Publisher:** Ladoca Publishing Foundation
**Copyright Date:** 1981
**Administrator:** Professional (teacher, diagnostician) or trained paraprofessional
**Age Range:** 1 mo. to 6–0
**Purpose:** Identifies children with delays in the areas of fine motor–adaptive, gross motor, personal–social, and language development. Responses are scored as normal, questionable, or abnormal.
**Testing Time:** 20 minutes
**Type(s) of Response:** Verbal, nonverbal, rater

**Name:** **Developmental Indicators for the Assessment of Learning-Revised (Dial-R)***
**Author(s):** Mardell-Czudnowski, C. and D. Goldenberg
**Publisher:** Childcraft Education Corporation
**Copyright Date:** 1983
**Administrator:** Professional (teacher, diagnostician) or trained paraprofessional
**Age Range:** 2–0 to 5–11
**Purpose:** For identifying children with potential learning problems or potential giftedness. Areas measured include motor, concepts, language and social–emotional development. Also included is a parent questionnaire. Computer program available.
**Testing Time:** 25–30 minutes
**Type(s) of Response:** Verbal, nonverbal, rater

**Name:** **Development Profile II**
**Author(s):** Alpern, G., T. Ball, and M. Shearer
**Publisher:** Psychological Development Publications
**Copyright Date:** 1980
**Administrator:** Professional (teacher, diagnostician)
**Age Range:** Birth to 9 years
**Purpose:** Designed to use interview technique to quickly screen large populations and to clinically assess individual children's developmental competencies in the areas of physical, self-help, social, academic, and communication development. Test contains enough information to construct individual programs and to provide pre/post evaluative information.
**Testing Time:** 20–40 minutes
**Type(s) of Response:** Rater

**Name:** **Developmental Test of Visual–Motor Integration (VMI)***
**Author(s):** Beery, K. and N. Buktenica
**Publisher:** Modern Curriculum Press
**Copyright Date:** 1967, 1982

**Administrator:** Professional (teacher)
**Age Range:** 2–0 to 15–0
**Purpose:** To screen children who may have potential visual, perceptual, or motor behavior problems. Test requires that children reproduce various geometric figures which are arranged in order of increasing difficulty.
**Testing Time:** 10 minutes
**Type(s) of Response:** Nonverbal

**Name:** **Early Screening Inventory (ESI)**
**Author(s):** Meisels, S. and M. Wiske
**Publisher:** Teachers College Press
**Copyright Date:** 1983
**Administrator:** Professional (teacher, diagnostician) or nonprofessional
**Age Range:** 4–0 to 6–0
**Purpose:** Evaluates children's perceptual, cognitive, language, and motor development. Information from a medical examination, parent questionnaire, and vision and hearing screening is used in conjunction with results from the screening inventory.
**Testing Time:** 15–20 minutes
**Type(s) of Response:** Verbal, nonverbal, rater

**Name:** **Expressive One-Word Picture Vocabulary Test (EOWPVT)**
**Author(s):** Gardner, M.
**Publisher:** Academic Therapy Publications
**Copyright Date:** 1979
**Administrator:** Professional
**Age Range:** 2–0 to 12–0
**Purpose:** Assesses expressive verbal intelligence and identifies possible speech defects or learning disorders. It is also designed to estimate a bilingual child's fluency in English, readiness for kindergarten, and appraise definitional and interpretational skills.
**Testing Time:** 20 minutes
**Type(s) of Response:** Verbal

**Name:** **Florida Kindergarten Screening Battery (FKSB)**
**Author(s):** Satz, P. and J. Fletcher
**Publisher:** Psychological Assessment Resources
**Copyright Date:** 1982
**Administrator:** Professional (teacher)
**Age Range:** Kindergarten
**Purpose:** This battery of three tests (recognition–discrimination; finger localization; alphabet recitation) is administered along with the Peabody Picture Vocabulary Test–Revised (PPVT–R) and the Developmental Test of Visual–Motor Integration (VMI) to identify those children at high risk for later reading difficulties.
**Testing Time:** 20 minutes
**Type(s) of Response:** Verbal, nonverbal

|                       |                                                                                                                                                                                                                                                                                    |
| --------------------- | ---------------------------------------------------------------------------------------------------------------------------------------------------------------------------------------------------------------------------------------------------------------------------------- |
| **Name:**             | **Goodenough–Harris Drawing Test\***                                                                                                                                                                                                                                               |
| **Author(s):**        | Goodenough, S. and D. Harris                                                                                                                                                                                                                                                        |
| **Publisher:**        | Psychological Corporation                                                                                                                                                                                                                                                          |
| **Copyright Date:**   | 1963                                                                                                                                                                                                                                                                               |
| **Administrator:**    | Professional (diagnostician)                                                                                                                                                                                                                                                       |
| **Age Range:**        | 3 to 15 years                                                                                                                                                                                                                                                                      |
| **Purpose:**          | Group or individual test that assesses cognitive and intellectual maturity through a person's drawing. Value of test is its use as part of a battery of tests. Subtests include Draw-a-Man, Draw-a-Woman, and Draw Oneself.                                                          |
| **Testing Time:**     | 5–15 minutes                                                                                                                                                                                                                                                                       |
| **Type(s) of Response:** | Nonverbal                                                                                                                                                                                                                                                                       |

|                       |                                                                                                                                                                                                                                                                                                     |
| --------------------- | --------------------------------------------------------------------------------------------------------------------------------------------------------------------------------------------------------------------------------------------------------------------------------------------------- |
| **Name:**             | **Hannah–Gardner Test of Verbal and Nonverbal Language Functioning**                                                                                                                                                                                                                              |
| **Author(s):**        | Hannah, E. and J. Gardner                                                                                                                                                                                                                                                                           |
| **Publisher:**        | Lingua Press                                                                                                                                                                                                                                                                                        |
| **Copyright Date:**   | 1978                                                                                                                                                                                                                                                                                                |
| **Administrator:**    | Professional or paraprofessional                                                                                                                                                                                                                                                                    |
| **Age Range:**        | 3–6 to 5–6                                                                                                                                                                                                                                                                                          |
| **Purpose:**          | Assesses development in language-based areas vital for school performance: vision perception, auditory perception, conceptual development, and linguistic development (receptive and expressive). Also available in Spanish.                                                                          |
| **Testing Time:**     | 25–35 minutes                                                                                                                                                                                                                                                                                       |
| **Type(s) of Response:** | Verbal, nonverbal                                                                                                                                                                                                                                                                                |

|                       |                                                                                                                                                                       |
| --------------------- | ------------------------------------------------------------------------------------------------------------------------------------------------------------------- |
| **Name:**             | **Home Screening Questionnaire**                                                                                                                                      |
| **Author(s):**        | Coons, C., et al.                                                                                                                                                     |
| **Publisher:**        | Ladoca Publishing Foundation                                                                                                                                          |
| **Copyright Date:**   | 1981                                                                                                                                                                  |
| **Administrator:**    | Nonprofessional (parent)                                                                                                                                              |
| **Age Range:**        | Birth to 3; 3–0 to 6–0                                                                                                                                                |
| **Purpose:**          | Screens the quality of a child's home environment. Suspect results must be followed by an evaluation of the home by a trained professional.                           |
| **Testing Time:**     | 15–20 minutes                                                                                                                                                         |
| **Type(s) of Response:** | Rater                                                                                                                                                              |

|                       |                                                                                                                                                       |
| --------------------- | ----------------------------------------------------------------------------------------------------------------------------------------------------- |
| **Name:**             | **Joseph Preschool and Primary Self-concept Screening Test**                                                                                          |
| **Author(s):**        | Joseph, J.                                                                                                                                            |
| **Publisher:**        | Stoelting Company                                                                                                                                     |
| **Copyright Date:**   | 1979                                                                                                                                                  |
| **Administrator:**    | Professional                                                                                                                                          |
| **Age Range:**        | 3–6 to 9–11                                                                                                                                           |
| **Purpose:**          | Assesses self-concept levels using a forced-choice self-report format and a set of 27 picture cards.                                                   |
| **Testing Time:**     | 5–7 minutes                                                                                                                                           |
| **Type(s) of Response:** | Nonverbal                                                                                                                                          |

|                       |                                                                     |
| --------------------- | ------------------------------------------------------------------- |
| **Name:**             | **Learning Accomplishment Profile (LAP) and Infant Lap (LAP-I)**    |
| **Author(s):**        | Sanford, A.                                                         |

**Publisher:** Kaplan School Supply
**Copyright Date:** 1974
**Administrator:** Professional (teacher) or nonprofessional (parent)
**Age Range:** Birth to 6–0
**Purpose:** Developmental checklists for assessment and planning individual prescriptive programs in six areas of development: gross motor, fine motor, social skills, self-help skills, language, and cognition.
**Testing Time:** Nontimed
**Type(s) of Response:** Verbal and nonverbal

**Name:** **McCarthy Screening Test (MST)**
**Author(s):** McCarthy, Dorothea
**Publisher:** Psychological Corporation
**Copyright Date:** 1978
**Administrator:** Professional (teacher, diagnostician) or trained paraprofessional
**Age Range:** 4–0 to 6–5
**Purpose:** Measures a variety of abilities that are important in achieving success in school. Some of the six subtests are reported as predictive in identifying children with learning disabilities or perceptual difficulties.
**Testing Time:** 20 minutes
**Type(s) of Response:** Verbal, nonverbal

**Name:** **Metropolitan Readiness Tests (MRT), Level I***
**Author(s):** Nurss, J. and M. McGauvran
**Publisher:** Psychological Corporation
**Copyright Date:** 1976
**Administrator:** Professional (teacher)
**Age Range:** Grades K–1
**Purpose:** Measures basic prereading skills with seven subtests: auditory memory, rhyming, letter recognition, visual matching, school language and listening, quantitative language, and copying (optional).
**Testing Time:** 80–100 minutes (4–7 sittings)
**Type(s) of Response:** Nonverbal (using booklet and pencil)

**Name:** **Minneapolis Preschool Screening Instrument (MPSI)**
**Author(s):** Lichtenstein, R.
**Publisher:** Minneapolis Public Schools
**Copyright Date:** 1980
**Administrator:** Professional (teacher, diagnostician) or trained paraprofessional
**Age Range:** 3–7 to 5–4
**Purpose:** Measures skills in various areas (motor, concepts, language) which are combined into a single score to determine referrals for further assessment.
**Testing Time:** 10–15 minutes
**Type(s) of Response:** Verbal, nonverbal, rater

**Name:** **Motor-free Visual Perception Test (MVPT)**
**Author(s):** Colarusso, R., and D. Hammill
**Publisher:** Academic Therapy Publications

**Copyright Date:** 1972
**Administrator:** Professional (teacher, diagnostician) or nonprofessional (parent)
**Age Range:** 4–0 to 8–0
**Purpose:** Measures a child's visual–perceptual abilities without involving a motor component. Subtests include visual discrimination, figure–ground, spatial relations, visual closure, and visual memory.
**Testing Time:** 10 minutes
**Type(s) of Response:** Nonverbal

**Name:** **Peabody Picture Vocabulary Test-Revised (PPVT-R)**
**Author(s):** Dunn, L. and L. Dunn
**Publisher:** American Guidance Service
**Copyright Date:** 1981
**Administrator:** Professional
**Age Range:** 2–5 to adult
**Purpose:** Provides an estimate of a subject's verbal ability by measuring hearing vocabulary; measures receptive language.
**Testing Time:** 10–20 minutes
**Type(s) of Response:** Nonverbal

**Name:** **Photo Articulation Test (PAT)**
**Author(s):** Pendergest, K., J. Dickey, A. Soder, and J. Selmar
**Publisher:** Academic Therapy Publications
**Copyright Date:** 1984
**Administrator:** Unrestricted
**Age Range:** 3–0 to 12–0
**Purpose:** Assesses the child's ability to articulate the consonants, vowels, and common blends of American English.
**Testing Time:** 5 minutes
**Type(s) of Response:** Verbal

**Name:** **Preschool Behavior Rating Scale**
**Author(s):** Barker, W. and A. Doeff
**Publisher:** Child Welfare League of America
**Copyright Date:** 1980
**Administrator:** Professional (teacher)
**Age Range:** 3–0 to 5–ll
**Purpose:** Rates coordination, receptive and expressive language, environmental adaptation, and social relations to indicate typical and atypical preschool behavior.
**Testing Time:** 5–10 minutes
**Type(s) of Response:** Rater

**Name:** **Preschool Language Assessment Instrument**
**Author(s):** Blank, M., S. Rose, and L. Berlin
**Publisher:** Grune & Stratton
**Copyright Date:** 1978
**Administrator:** Professional
**Age Range:** 3–0 to 6–0
**Purpose:** Assesses four levels of language, ranging from simple demands for labeling to complex demands for reasoning and problem solving. Allows the teacher to match instruction to the child's level of understanding. Also available in Spanish.

**Testing Time:** 20 minutes
**Type(s) of Response:** Verbal, nonverbal

**Name:** Preschool Language Scale
**Author(s):** Zimmerman, I.L., V. Steiner, and R. Pond
**Publisher:** Charles E. Merrill
**Copyright Date:** 1969, 1979
**Administrator:** Professional (diagnostician)
**Age Range:** 1–6 to 7–0
**Purpose:** Measures children's language development. Scale consists of two main parts—auditory comprehension and verbal ability. A Spanish (Mexican-American) translation also is available.
**Testing Time:** 20 minutes
**Type(s) of Response:** Verbal, nonverbal

**Name:** Preschool Screening System*
**Author(s):** Hainsworth, P. and R. Hainsworth
**Publisher:** Early Recognition Intervention Systems
**Copyright Date:** 1980
**Administrator:** Professional, Nonprofessional (Parent)
**Age Range:** 2–6 to 5–9
**Purpose:** Parent developmental questionnaire and quick screening survey to provide information about a child's language, visual, perceptual, motor, and body-awareness skills.
**Testing Time:** 15–20 minutes
**Type(s) of Response:** Verbal, nonverbal, rater

**Name:** Receptive Expressive Emergent Language Scale (REEL)
**Author(s):** Bzoch, K.R., and R. League
**Publisher:** Tree of Life Press
**Copyright Date:** 1972
**Administrator:** Professional
**Age Range:** 1 month to 3 years
**Purpose:** Measures children's language development in the first three years of life. Test covers the areas of receptive, expressive, and inner language.
**Testing Time:** 25 minutes
**Type(s) of Response:** Rater

**Name:** Revised Child Behavior Checklist
**Author(s):** Achenbach, T.
**Publisher:** University of Vermont
**Copyright Date:** 1982, 1983
**Administrator:** Parent
**Age Range:** 4–0 to 16–0
**Purpose:** Checklist of 138 items that provides a profile of behavioral deviancy (eight or nine scales) based on factor analytic findings.
**Testing Time:** 15 minutes
**Type(s) of Response:** Rater

**Name:** Slosson Intelligence Test (SIT)
**Author(s):** Slosson, R.
**Publisher:** Slosson Educational Publications
**Copyright Date:** 1963, 1981

| | |
|---|---|
| **Administrator:** | Professional (diagnostician, teacher) |
| **Age Range:** | 2–0 to 18–0 |
| **Purpose:** | A quick measure of general intelligence ability. |
| **Testing Time:** | 10–20 minutes |
| **Type(s) of Response:** | Verbal, nonverbal |

| | |
|---|---|
| **Name:** | **Test for Auditory Comprehension of Language-Revised (TACL-R)** |
| **Author(s):** | Carrow-Woolfolk, E. |
| **Publisher:** | DLM Teaching Resources |
| **Copyright Date:** | 1985 |
| **Administrator:** | Professional |
| **Age Range:** | 3–0 to 7–11 |
| **Purpose:** | Measures a child's auditory comprehension of language structure. It encompasses word classes and relations, grammatical morphemes, and elaborated sentence constructions. |
| **Testing Time:** | 10–20 mintues |
| **Type(s) of Response:** | Nonverbal |

| | |
|---|---|
| **Name:** | **Test of Early Language Development (TELD)** |
| **Author(s):** | Hresko, W., D. Reed, and D. Hammill |
| **Publisher:** | Pro–Ed |
| **Copyright Date:** | 1981 |
| **Administrator:** | Professional |
| **Age Range:** | 3–0 to 7–11 |
| **Purpose:** | Yields information about the form and content of a child's language skills, as well as development of receptive and expressive language. |
| **Testing Time:** | 15–20 minutes |
| **Type(s) of Response:** | Verbal, nonverbal |

| | |
|---|---|
| **Name:** | **Tree/Bee Test of Auditory Discrimination** |
| **Author(s):** | Fudala, J. |
| **Publisher:** | Academic Therapy Publications |
| **Copyright Date:** | 1978 |
| **Administrator:** | Professional (diagnostician, special education teacher) |
| **Age Range:** | 3–0 to 8–11 |
| **Purpose:** | Surveys auditory discrimination of words, phrases, words–in–story comprehension, word pairs, same–different comparisons, pointing to words, and letter discrimination. There are four equivalent forms. |
| **Testing Time:** | 10 minutes |
| **Type(s) of Response:** | Nonverbal |

## PART II: DIAGNOSTIC TESTS

| | |
|---|---|
| **Name:** | **Adaptive Behavior Scale for Infants and Early Childhood (ABSI)** |
| **Author(s):** | Leland, H., M. Shoaee, D. McElwain, and R. Christie |
| **Publisher:** | Nisonger Center |
| **Copyright Date:** | 1980 |

| | |
|---|---|
| **Administrator:** | Professional (teacher or attendant) or nonprofessional (parent) |
| **Age Range:** | Birth to 6–0 |
| **Purpose:** | A behavior rating scale for assessing how well an infant or young child copes with environmental demands, in order to obtain a clear view of the child's strengths and weaknesses across developmental domains. |
| **Testing Time:** | Untimed |
| **Type(s) of Response:** | Rater |

| | |
|---|---|
| **Name:** | **Arizona Basic Assessment and Curriculum Utilization System (ABACUS)** |
| **Author(s):** | McCarthy, J., K. Lund, J. Glatke, and S. Vaughn |
| **Publisher:** | Love Publishing Company |
| **Copyright Date:** | 1985 |
| **Administrator:** | Professional |
| **Age Range:** | 2–0 to 5–11 |
| **Purpose:** | A home–school program that assesses, programs, and monitors the progress of handicapped children in five areas: body management, self-care, communication, preacademic, and socialization. |
| **Testing Time:** | Untimed |
| **Type(s) of Response:** | Verbal, nonverbal, rater |

| | |
|---|---|
| **Name:** | **Basic School Skills Inventory-Diagnostic** |
| **Author(s):** | Hammill, D. and J. Leigh |
| **Publisher:** | Pro–Ed |
| **Copyright Date:** | 1983 |
| **Administrator:** | Professional |
| **Age Range:** | 4–0 to 6–11 |
| **Purpose:** | A norm-referenced and criterion-referenced measure of daily living skills, spoken language, reading readiness, and classroom behavior. Contains 110 items. |
| **Testing Time:** | Untimed |
| **Type(s) of Response:** | Rater |

| | |
|---|---|
| **Name:** | **Batelle Developmental Inventory (BDI)** |
| **Author(s):** | Batelle Memorial Institute |
| **Publisher:** | DLM Teaching Resources |
| **Copyright Date:** | 1978 |
| **Administrator:** | Professional |
| **Age Range:** | Birth to 8–0 |
| **Purpose:** | Assesses five domains (personal–social, adaptive, motor, communication, cognitive) by means of observations of the child in natural settings, parent interviews, and a structured test format (a 10 to 30 minute screening component also is available separately). Developed for planning and designing educational programs and for program evaluation. |
| **Testing Time:** | Varies |
| **Type(s) of Response:** | Verbal, nonverbal, rater |

| | |
|---|---|
| **Name:** | **Bayley Scales of Infant Development (BSID)** |
| **Author(s):** | Bayley, N. |
| **Publisher:** | Psychological Corporation |

| | |
|---|---|
| **Copyright Date:** | 1969 |
| **Administrator:** | Professional (diagnostician); test to be given with the mother present |
| **Age Range:** | 2 months to 2—6 |
| **Purpose:** | Mental and motor scales that provide an evaluation of infants' early mental and psychomotor development. Scales are to be used in conjunction with the infant behavior record in order to obtain information regarding a qualitative aspect of infant behavior. |
| **Testing Time:** | 45 minutes |
| **Type(s) of Response:** | Nonverbal |

| | |
|---|---|
| **Name:** | **Bracken Basic Concept Scale (Level 2)** |
| **Author(s):** | Bracken, B. |
| **Publisher:** | Charles E. Merrill |
| **Copyright Date:** | 1984 |
| **Administrator:** | Professional |
| **Age Range:** | 2–6 to 8–0 |
| **Purpose:** | Assesses the child's functioning in eleven conceptual categories (color, letter identification, number/counting, comparisons, shape, direction/position, social/emotional, size, texture/material, quantity, and time/sequence). |
| **Testing Time:** | 20–30 minutes |
| **Type(s) of Response:** | Nonverbal |

| | |
|---|---|
| **Name:** | **Brigance Diagnostic Inventory of Early Development** |
| **Author(s):** | Brigance, A. |
| **Publisher:** | Curriculum Associates |
| **Copyright Date:** | 1978 |
| **Administrator:** | Professional and paraprofessional |
| **Age Range:** | 1 month to 6 years |
| **Purpose:** | Criterion-referenced test that integrates assessment–diagnosis with record keeping, setting of objectives, and instructional planning. Areas assessed include psychomotor skills, self-help, speech and language, general knowledge and comprehension, reading, printing, and math. |
| **Testing Time:** | Untimed |
| **Type(s) of Response:** | Nonverbal, verbal |

| | |
|---|---|
| **Name:** | **Carrow Elicited Language Inventory** |
| **Author(s):** | Carrow-Woolfolk, E. |
| **Publisher:** | DLM Teaching Resources |
| **Copyright Date:** | 1974 |
| **Administrator:** | Professional (diagnostician) |
| **Age Range:** | 3–0 to 7–11 |
| **Purpose:** | Yields performance data on the child's control of grammar. Inventory provides a means of identifying language problems by determining specific linguistic structures with which child has difficulty. |
| **Testing Time:** | 20–30 minutes |
| **Type(s) of Response:** | Verbal |

| | |
|---|---|
| **Name:** | **CID Preschool Performance Scale** |
| **Author(s):** | Geers, A. and H. Lane |
| **Publisher:** | Stoelting Company |
| **Copyright Date:** | 1984 |
| **Administrator:** | Professional |
| **Age Range:** | 2–0 to 5–6 |
| **Purpose:** | Assesses hearing-impaired or language-impaired children by means of six subtests (manual planning, manual dexterity, form perception, perceptual-motor skills, preschool skills, and part/whole relations) which are nonverbal both in instruction and response. |
| **Testing Time:** | Varies |
| **Type(s) of Response:** | Nonverbal |

| | |
|---|---|
| **Name:** | **Columbia Mental Maturity Scale** |
| **Author(s):** | Burgemeister, B., L. Blum, and I. Lorge |
| **Publisher:** | Psychological Corporation |
| **Copyright Date:** | 1972 |
| **Administrator:** | Professional (diagnostician or teacher) |
| **Age Range:** | 3–6 to 10–0 |
| **Purpose:** | Test originally developed for use with cerebral-palsied and deaf children. It is a pictorial classification test that requires subject to identify the drawing that does not belong. Also available in Spanish. |
| **Testing Time:** | 15–20 minutes |
| **Type(s) of Response:** | Nonverbal |

| | |
|---|---|
| **Name:** | **Developmental Sentence Analysis (DSA)** |
| **Author(s):** | Lee, L. |
| **Publisher:** | Northwestern University Press |
| **Copyright Date:** | 1974 |
| **Administrator:** | Professional |
| **Age Range:** | 3–0 to 6–11 |
| **Purpose:** | Measures expressive syntax in spontaneous speech by scoring 100 different intelligible and spontaneous utterances taken from a child's conversations with an adult. |
| **Testing Time:** | Varies |
| **Type(s) of Response:** | Verbal |

| | |
|---|---|
| **Name:** | **Goldman–Fristoe–Woodcock Auditory Skills Test Battery** |
| **Author(s):** | Goldman, R., M. Fristoe, and R. Woodcock |
| **Publisher:** | American Guidance Service |
| **Copyright Date:** | 1976 |
| **Administrator:** | Professional (teacher) |
| **Age Range:** | 3–8 to adult |
| **Purpose:** | Evaluates individual's ability to discriminate speech and sounds under both quiet and distracting noise conditions. Subtests include an auditory selective attention test, diagnostic auditory discrimination tests, auditory memory tests, and sound–symbol tests. |
| **Testing Time:** | 60 minutes |
| **Type(s) of Response:** | Verbal |

|   |   |
|---|---|
| **Name:** | Goodman Lock Box |
| **Author(s):** | Goodman, J. |
| **Publisher:** | Stoelting Company |
| **Copyright Date:** | 1981 |
| **Administrator:** | Professional |
| **Age Range:** | 2–6 to 5–6 |
| **Purpose:** | An objective observation of play with implications for cognitive functioning and perceptual-motor deficits. This technique is particularly useful for nonverbal and/or uncooperative children. Test yields three scores, on competence, organization, and aimless actions. |
| **Testing Time:** | 6.5 minutes |
| **Type(s) of Response:** | Nonverbal |

|   |   |
|---|---|
| **Name:** | Head Start Measures Battery (HSMB) |
| **Author(s):** | Bergan, J., et al. |
| **Publisher:** | Head Start Bureau |
| **Copyright Date:** | 1984 |
| **Administrator:** | Professional (teacher) or trained paraprofessional |
| **Age Range:** | 3–0 to 5–11 |
| **Purpose:** | A set of six path-referenced tests designed to assess cognitive and social development of children enrolled in Head Start programs, for use in institutional program management. Areas covered are language, math, nature and science, perception, reading, and social development. Both English and Spanish versions are within one manual. |
| **Testing Time:** | 50–75 minutes |
| **Type(s) of Response:** | Verbal, nonverbal |

|   |   |
|---|---|
| **Name:** | Home (Home Observation for Measurement of the Environment) Inventory |
| **Author(s):** | Caldwell, B. and R. Bradley |
| **Publisher:** | Dorsey Press |
| **Copyright Date:** | 1984 |
| **Administrator:** | Professional |
| **Age Range:** | Birth to 3–0; 3–0 to 6–0 |
| **Purpose:** | Observation and interview procedure for evaluating a child's environment and quality of stimulation during a home visit. There are six subscales in the 0–3 version: emotional and verbal responsivity of motor; avoidance of restriction and punishment; organization of the physical and temporal environment; provision of appropriate play materials; maternal involvement with the child; and opportunities for variety in daily stimulation. The 3–6 version has eight subtests: stimulation through toys, games and reading materials; language stimulation; physical environment—safe, clean and conducive to development; pride, affection and warmth; stimulation of academic behavior; modeling and encouragement of social maturity; variety of stimulation; physical punishment. |
| **Testing Time:** | Untimed |
| **Type(s) of Response:** | Rater |

| | |
|---|---|
| **Name:** | **Illinois Test of Psycholinguistic Abilities (ITPA)** |
| **Author(s):** | Kirk, S., J. McCarthy, and W. Kirk |
| **Publisher:** | University of Illinois Press |
| **Copyright Date:** | 1971 |
| **Administrator:** | Professional |
| **Age Range:** | 2–6 to 10–0 |
| **Purpose:** | Based on a three-dimensional model of communication that stresses skills in auditory, visual, and motor areas. One purpose is to see the strengths and weaknesses of individual children, compared to themselves, in the twelve subtests. |
| **Testing Time:** | 50–60 minutes |
| **Type(s) of Response:** | Verbal, nonverbal |

| | |
|---|---|
| **Name:** | **Infant Psychological Development Scales (IPDS)** |
| **Author(s):** | Uzgiris, I. and J. Hunt |
| **Publisher:** | University of Illinois Press |
| **Copyright Date:** | 1975 |
| **Administrator:** | Professional |
| **Age Range:** | 2 weeks to 2–0 |
| **Purpose:** | Covers the equivalent of Piaget's Sensorimotor Phase. It was developed to assess the functioning within the various parts of that phase. A manual (Dunst, 1980) providing record forms, age norms, and guidelines for intervention activities is published by Pro–Ed. |
| **Testing Time:** | 40–60 minutes |
| **Type(s) of Response:** | Verbal, nonverbal |

| | |
|---|---|
| **Name:** | **Kaufman Assessment Battery for Children (K-ABC)** |
| **Author(s):** | Kaufman, A. and N. Kaufman |
| **Publisher:** | American Guidance Service |
| **Copyright Date:** | 1983 |
| **Administrator:** | Professional |
| **Age Range:** | 2–6 to 12–6 |
| **Purpose:** | Assesses the ability to solve problems using simultaneous and sequential mental processes as a measure of intelligence and compares results with a separate scale of acquired knowledge as a measure of achievement. There are seven to eleven subtests for preschool children. The nonverbal scale was designed to assess deaf, language-impaired and/or non-English speaking children. |
| **Testing Time:** | 35–85 minutes |
| **Type(s) of Response:** | Verbal, nonverbal |

| | |
|---|---|
| **Name:** | **Learning Accomplishment Profile Diagnostic Assessment Kit (LAP-D)** |
| **Author(s):** | Sanford, A. et al. |
| **Publisher:** | Kaplan School Supply |
| **Copyright Date:** | 1975 |
| **Administrator:** | Professional (teacher) |
| **Age Range:** | Birth to 6 years |
| **Purpose:** | Criterion-referenced diagnostic assessment in five areas of development: motor, social, self-help, language, cognition. |

|                         |                                                                                                                                                                                                                                                                      |
|-------------------------|---------------------------------------------------------------------------------------------------------------------------------------------------------------------------------------------------------------------------------------------------------------------|
| **Testing Time:**       | 60 minutes                                                                                                                                                                                                                                                          |
| **Type(s) of Response:**| Verbal, nonverbal, rater (parent)                                                                                                                                                                                                                                   |

|                         |                                                                                                                                                                                                                                                                      |
|-------------------------|---------------------------------------------------------------------------------------------------------------------------------------------------------------------------------------------------------------------------------------------------------------------|
| **Name:**               | **Leiter International Performance Scale (LIPS)**                                                                                                                                                                                                                     |
| **Author(s):**          | Leiter, R.                                                                                                                                                                                                                                                          |
| **Publisher:**          | Stoelting Company                                                                                                                                                                                                                                                   |
| **Copyright Date:**     | 1948, 1980                                                                                                                                                                                                                                                          |
| **Administrator:**      | Professional                                                                                                                                                                                                                                                        |
| **Age Range:**          | 2 to 18 years                                                                                                                                                                                                                                                       |
| **Purpose:**            | A response to efforts of constructing a test applicable across cultures. A distinctive feature of the test is the almost complete absence of instructions—either spoken or pantomime. It was designed to cover a wide range of functions and is appropriate for many handicaps and a non-biased assessment. |
| **Testing Time:**       | Untimed/about 45 minutes                                                                                                                                                                                                                                            |
| **Type(s) of Response:**| Nonverbal                                                                                                                                                                                                                                                           |

|                         |                                                                                                                                                                                                                                                                      |
|-------------------------|---------------------------------------------------------------------------------------------------------------------------------------------------------------------------------------------------------------------------------------------------------------------|
| **Name:**               | **McCarthy Scales of Children's Abilities (MSCA)**                                                                                                                                                                                                                   |
| **Author(s):**          | McCarthy, D.                                                                                                                                                                                                                                                        |
| **Publisher:**          | Psychological Corporation                                                                                                                                                                                                                                           |
| **Copyright Date:**     | 1972                                                                                                                                                                                                                                                                |
| **Administrator:**      | Professional                                                                                                                                                                                                                                                        |
| **Age Range:**          | 2–6 to 8–6                                                                                                                                                                                                                                                          |
| **Purpose:**            | Consists of eighteen tests grouped into six overlapping scales (verbal, perceptual–performance, quantitative, general cognitive, memory, and motor).                                                                                                                 |
| **Testing Time:**       | 50–75 minutes                                                                                                                                                                                                                                                       |
| **Type(s) of Response:**| Verbal, nonverbal                                                                                                                                                                                                                                                   |

|                         |                                                                                                                                                                                                                                                                      |
|-------------------------|---------------------------------------------------------------------------------------------------------------------------------------------------------------------------------------------------------------------------------------------------------------------|
| **Name:**               | **Neonatal Behavioral Assessment**                                                                                                                                                                                                                                  |
| **Author(s):**          | Brazelton, T.                                                                                                                                                                                                                                                       |
| **Publisher:**          | J.B. Lippincott Company                                                                                                                                                                                                                                             |
| **Copyright Date:**     | 1976                                                                                                                                                                                                                                                                |
| **Administrator:**      | Professional (usually medical)                                                                                                                                                                                                                                      |
| **Age Range:**          | Birth to 1 month                                                                                                                                                                                                                                                    |
| **Purpose:**            | A psychological scale for the newborn infant. It allows for the assessment of the infant's capabilities along the dimension of adjusting to the environment and gaining mastery of physiological equipment.                                                           |
| **Testing Time:**       | 20–30 minutes                                                                                                                                                                                                                                                       |
| **Type(s) of Response:**| Nonverbal                                                                                                                                                                                                                                                           |

|                         |                                                                                                                                                                                                                                                                      |
|-------------------------|---------------------------------------------------------------------------------------------------------------------------------------------------------------------------------------------------------------------------------------------------------------------|
| **Name:**               | **Parent and Teacher Temperament Questionnaire**                                                                                                                                                                                                                    |
| **Author(s):**          | Thomas, A., S. Chess and S. Korn                                                                                                                                                                                                                                    |
| **Publisher:**          | Brunner/Mazel                                                                                                                                                                                                                                                       |
| **Copyright Date:**     | 1977                                                                                                                                                                                                                                                                |
| **Administrator:**      | Professional (teacher) and nonprofessional (parent)                                                                                                                                                                                                                 |
| **Age Range:**          | 3–0 to 7–0                                                                                                                                                                                                                                                          |
| **Purpose:**            | Rating scale to assess the temperament of a child. Parent version consists of 72 items in nine temperament categories, rated on a seven-point scale from "hardly ever" to "almost always." The teacher version has 64 items.                                          |
| **Testing Time:**       | Untimed                                                                                                                                                                                                                                                             |
| **Type(s) of Response:**| Rater                                                                                                                                                                                                                                                               |

| | |
|---|---|
| **Name:** | **Peabody Developmental Motor Scales (PDMS)** |
| **Author(s):** | Folio, M. and R. Fewell |
| **Publisher:** | DLM Teaching Resources |
| **Copyright Date:** | 1983 |
| **Administrator:** | Professional, trained paraprofessional |
| **Age Range:** | Birth to 83 months |
| **Purpose:** | Individually administered standardized test to measure gross and fine motor skills of children. PDMS was developed to meet the programming needs of handicapped children in physical education. Items are classified into five skill categories: (1) reflexes, (2) balance, (3) non-locomotor, (4) locomotor, and (5) receipt and propulsion of objects. Fine motor items are classified into four skill categories: (1) grasping, (2) hand use, (3) eye–hand coordination, and (4) manual dexterity. |
| **Testing Time:** | 45–60 minutes |
| **Type(s) of Response:** | Nonverbal |

| | |
|---|---|
| **Name:** | **Scales of Independent Behavior (SIB)** |
| **Author(s):** | Bruininks, R., R. Woodcock, R. Weatherman, and B. Hill |
| **Publisher:** | DLM Teaching Resources |
| **Copyright Date:** | 1984 |
| **Administrator:** | Professional |
| **Age Range:** | Infancy to adult |
| **Purpose:** | Assesses functional independence and adaptive behavior in motor skills, social and communication skills, personal living skills, and community living skills. It can be used alone or in conjunction with the Woodcock–Johnson Psychoeducational Battery. |
| **Testing Time:** | 45–50 minutes |
| **Type(s) of Response:** | Rater |

| | |
|---|---|
| **Name:** | **Scales of Socio–Emotional Development** |
| **Author(s):** | Lewis, M. and L. Michalson |
| **Publisher:** | Plenum Press |
| **Copyright Date:** | 1983 |
| **Administrator:** | Professional |
| **Age Range:** | Birth to 3–0 |
| **Purpose:** | An observational procedure for assessing the social–emotional functioning (fear, anger, happiness, affiliation and competence) of a child in a program with other children. |
| **Testing Time:** | One day |
| **Type(s) of Response:** | Rater |

| | |
|---|---|
| **Name:** | **Sequenced Inventory of Communication Development-Revised (SCID-R)** |
| **Author(s):** | Hendrick, D., E. Prather, and A. Tobin |
| **Publisher:** | University of Washington Press |
| **Copyright Date:** | 1984 |
| **Administrator:** | Professional (diagnostician) |
| **Age Range:** | 4 months to 4–0 |
| **Purpose:** | Measures children's abilities in the areas of expressive language (which includes imitation, initiating, and syntactic structures of verbal output); articulation; and receptive language (which includes behavioral items that test sound |

and speech discrimination, awareness, and understanding).

**Testing Time:** 30–75 minutes
**Type(s) of Response:** Verbal, nonverbal, rater

**Name:** **Smith–Johnson Nonverbal Performance Scale**
**Author(s):** Smith, A. and R. Johnson
**Publisher:** Western Psychological Services
**Copyright Date:** 1975
**Administrator:** Professional (diagnostician)
**Age Range:** 2–0 to 4–0
**Purpose:** Evaluates the developmental level of handicapped children across a broad range of skills utilizing fourteen categories of tasks. Normed for both hearing-impaired and normal children, it is administered entirely without the use of language.

**Testing Time:** 45 mintues
**Type(s) of Response:** Nonverbal

**Name:** **Southern California Sensory-Integration Tests (SCSIT)**
**Author(s):** Ayres, J.
**Publisher:** Western Psychological Services
**Copyright Date:** 1972
**Administrator:** Professional
**Age Range:** 4 to 10 years
**Purpose:** Evaluates children's visual, tactile, and kinesthetic perception, as well as motor functioning. Seventeen subtests include imitation of postures, crossing midline of body, bilateral motor coordination, right–left discrimination, and standing balance (eyes open and eyes closed).

**Testing Time:** 60–70 mintues
**Type(s) of Response:** Verbal, nonverbal

**Name:** **Stanford–Binet Intelligence Scale—4th ed.**
**Author(s):** Thorndike, R., E. Hagen, and J. Sattler
**Publisher:** Houghton–Mifflin
**Copyright Date:** 1986
**Administrator:** Professional
**Age Range:** 2 years to adult
**Purpose:** Singular test that assesses the various levels of functioning that go into the *G* factor of global intelligence.

**Testing Time:** 60–90 minutes
**Type(s) of Response:** Verbal, nonverbal

**Name:** **Test of Early Socioemotional Development (TOESD)**
**Author(s):** Hresko, W. and L. Brown
**Publisher:** Pro-Ed
**Copyright Date:** 1984
**Administrator:** Teacher, parent, and child
**Age Range:** 3–0 to 7–11
**Purpose:** Identifies young children with behavior problems, documents the degree of behavioral difficulty, identifies specific settings in which problem behaviors most often occur, and evaluates the impressions a child makes on different observers.

**Testing Time:** Varies
**Type(s) of Response:** Rater

**Name:** **Vineland Adaptive Behavior Scales**
**Author(s):** Sparrow, S., D. Balla, and D. Cicchetti
**Publisher:** American Guidance Service
**Copyright Date:** 1984
**Administrator:** Professional (teacher, diagnostician) and nonprofessional (parent)
**Age Range:** 1 month to adult
**Purpose:** Assesses individual's level of social maturity, competence, and independence. Items are designed to elicit from parent, teacher, or caregiver factual descriptions of the examinee's behavior in the following areas: daily living skills, communication, motor skills, and socialization. There are three versions (Survey, Expanded, and Classroom).
**Testing Time:** 20–90 minutes
**Type(s) of Response:** Rater

**Name:** **Wechsler Preschool and Primary Scale of Intelligence (WPPSI)**
**Author(s):** Wechsler, D.
**Publisher:** Psychological Corporation
**Copyright Date:** 1974
**Administrator:** Professional
**Age Range:** 4–0 to 6–6
**Purpose:** Assesses global levels of functioning through performance and verbal items. Yields a performance IQ, verbal IQ, and a total measure of general intelligence.
**Testing Time:** 60–90 minutes
**Type(s) of Response:** Verbal, nonverbal

**Name:** **Woodcock–Johnson Psychoeducational Battery (WJPEB)**
**Author(s):** Woodcock, R. and M. Johnson
**Publisher:** DLM Teaching Resources
**Copyright Date:** 1978
**Administrator:** Professional
**Age Range:** 3–0 to adult
**Purpose:** A comprehensive measure of cognitive ability (twelve subtests), achievement (ten subtests) and interest (five areas) normed on the same population, which permits direct comparison between aptitude and achievement to determine presence and amount of learning deficit.
**Testing Time:** 60–90 minutes
**Type(s) of Response:** Verbal, nonverbal, rater (older subjects only)

# APPENDIX C

Publishers of
Early Childhood/
Special Education
Tests and Materials

To obtain their latest catalog and price list, simply write to any of the following publishers of early childhood/special education tests and materials.

**ABC School Equipment Co.**
437 Armour Circle NE
Atlanta, GA 30324

**Academic Therapy Publications**
20 Commercial Blvd.
Novato, CA 94947

**Achievement Products, Inc.**
P.O. Box 547
Mineola, NY 11501

**Adapt Press, Inc.**
808 W. Avenue North
Sioux Falls, SD 27104

**Adaptive Therapeutic Systems, Inc.**
162 Ridge Rd.
Madison, CT 06443

**Allied Education Council**
P.O. Box 78
Galien, MI 49113

**American Guidance Service**
Publishers' Building
Circle Pines, MN 55014-1796

**American Science and Engineering, Inc.**
20 Overland St.
Boston, MA 02215

**American Speech and Hearing Association**
9030 Old Georgetown Rd. NW
Washington, DC 20014

**Ann Arbor Publishers**
P.O. Box 7249
Naples, FL 33941-7249

**ASIEP Education Co.**
3216 NE 27th
Portland, OR 97212

**Bell & Howell, A–V Products Div.**
7100 McCormick Rd.
Chicago, IL 60645

**BFA Education Media**
Division of C.B.S.
2211 Michigan Ave.
Santa Monica, CA 90404

**Bowmar**
622 Rodier Dr.
Glendale, CA 91201

**Brunner Mazel Inc.**
19 Union Sq. W
New York, NY

**C. C. Publications, Inc.**
P.O. Box 23699
Tigard, OR 97223-0108

**Charles E. Merrill Publishing Co.**
1300 Alum Creek Dr.
Columbus, OH 43216

**Child Welfare League of America**
67 Irving Pl.
New York, NY 10003

**Childcraft Education Corp.**
20 Kilmer Rd.
Edison, NJ 08818

**Cleo Learning Aids**
3957 Mayfield Rd.
Cleveland, OH 44121

**Clinical Psychology Publishing Co., Inc.**
4 Conant Sq.
Brandon, VT 05733

**Cole Supply**
9530 Hempstead Hwy
Houston, TX 77092

**Communication Skill Builders**
3130 N. Dodge Blvd.
Tucson, AZ 85733

**Community Playthings**
Rifton, NY 12471

**Council for Exceptional Children**
Publication Sales
1920 Association Dr.
Reston, VA 22091

**Creative Playthings, Inc.**
Princeton, NJ 08540

**Cuisenaire Company of America**
12 Church St.
New Rochelle, NY 10905

**Curriculum Associates, Inc.**
5 Esquire Rd.
North Bilterica, MA 01862-2589

**Delacorte Press**
1 Dag Hammerskjold Plaza
245 E. 47th St.
New York, NY 10017

**DLM Teaching Resources**
One DLM Park
Allen, TX 75002

**Dexter and Westbrook, Ltd.**
11 South Center Ave.
Rockville Centre, NY 11571

**DIAL, Inc.**
P.O. Box 911
Highland Park, IL 60035

**Didax**
P.O. Box 2258
Peabody, MA 01960

**Discovery Toys**
400 Ellinwood Way
Suite 300
Pleasant Hill, CA 94523

**Dorsey Press**
1818 Ridge Rd.
Homewood, IL 60430

**Early Recognition Intervention Systems**
P.O. Box 1635
Pawtucket, RI 02862

**Educational Activities, Inc.**
P.O. Box 392
Freeport, NY 11520

**Educational Development Laboratories**
McGraw-Hill Book Co.
1221 Avenue of the Americas
New York, NY 10020

**Educational Teaching Aids**
159 Kinzie St.
Chicago, IL 60610

**Educational Testing Service**
Box 995
Princeton, NJ 08540

**Edumate-Educational Materials**
P.O. Box 2467
Del Mar, CA 92014

**Fearon Teacher Aids**
19 Davis Dr.
Belmont, CA 94002

**Filmstrip House, Inc.**
432 Park Ave. South
New York, NY 10016

**Frank Schaffer Publications**
1028 Via Mirabel Dept. 44
Palos Verdes Estates, CA 90274

**Fred Sammons, Inc.**
Box 32
Brookfield, IL 60513

**General Electric Company**
Education Support Project
P.O. Box 43
Schnectady, NY 12301

**General Learning Corporation**
250 James Street
Morristown, NJ 07960

**Gould Athletic Supply**
3156 N. 96th St.
Milwaukee, WI 53222-3943

**Grune & Stratton, Inc.**
Orlando, FL 32887

**Gryphon House**
P.O. Box 275
Mt. Rainier, MD 20712

**Harcourt-Brace Jovanovich**
1250 6th Ave.
San Diego, CA 92101

**Headstart Bureau**
Administration of Children, Youth, and Families
400 6th Street, SW
Donohue Bldg.
Washington, DC 20013

**Holt, Rinehart & Winston**
School Department, Box 3323
Grand Central Station
New York, NY 10017

**Houghton-Mifflin Co.**
1 Beacon St.
Boston, MA 02107

**Ideal School Supply Co.**
11000 South Laverne Ave.
Oak Lawn, IL 60453

**Information Resources**
Stanford University
Stanford, CA 94035

**Instructo Corporation**
North Cedar Hollow Rd.
Paoli, PA 19301

**Instructor Publications, Inc.**
Dansville, NY 14437

**J.A. Preston Corp.**
71 5th Ave.
New York, NY 10003

**J.B. Lippincott Co.**
Educational Publishing Div.
East Washington Sq.
Philadelphia, PA 19105

**Kaplan School Supply Corp.**
600 Jonestown Rd.
Winston-Salem, NC 27103

**LADOCA Publishing Foundation**
5100 Lincoln St.
Denver, CO 80216

**Lakeshore Curriculum Materials**
2695 E. Dominguez St.
P.O. Box 6261
Carson, CA 90749

**Laureate Learning Systems**
Dept. D1
1 Mill St.
Burlington, VT 05401

**Learn-X Corporation**
1600-2400 8th Ave.
Lake City, MN 55041

**Libraries Unlimited, Inc.**
Dept. 58
Littleton, CO 80160-0263

**Lingui Systems**
716 17th St.
Moline, IL 61265

**Love Publishing Company**
1777 South Belaire St.
Denver, CO 80222

**Macmillan Co.**
Front and Brown Sts.
Riverside, NJ 08075

**Mafax Association, Inc.**
90 Cherry St.
Box 519
Johnston, PA 15902

**Markham Distributors, Inc.**
507 5th Ave.
New York, NY 10017

**McGraw-Hill, Webster Div.**
Manchester Rd.
Manchester, MO 63011

**Media Projects, Inc.**
201 East 16th St.
New York, NY 10003

**Milton Bradley Co.**
Educational Division
Springfield, MA 01101

**Minneapolis Public Schools**
Prescriptive Instruction Center
Special Education Div.
254 Upton Ave. South
Minneapolis, MN 55405

**Modern Curriculum Press**
13900 Prospect Rd.
Cleveland, OH 44136

**Modern Education Corp.**
P.O. Box 721
Tulsa, OK 74101

**Mosier Material, Inc.**
61328 Yahwahtin Ct.
Bend, OR 97702

**Nasco**
901 Janesville Ave.
Fort Atkinson, WI 53538

**National Lekotek Center**
2100 Ridge Ave.
Evanston, IL 60204

**New American Library**
Educational Division
120 Woodbine St.
Bergenfield, NJ 07621

**New Century School Department**
440 Park Ave. South
New York, NY 10016

**Nisonger Center**
Ohio State Unviersity
Columbus OH

**Northwestern University Press**
1735 Benson Ave.
Evanston, IL 60201

**Open Court Publishing Co.**
Box 599
LaSalle, IL 61301

**Opportunities for Learning**
5024 Landershim Boulevard
Dept. B7
North Hollywood, CA 91601

**Pecei Educational Publishers**
440 Davis Ct. #405
San Francisco, CA 94111

**Playworld Systems**
P.O. Box 227
New Berlin, PA 17855

**Portage Project Materials**
CESA 5-626 E. Slifer St.
P.O. Box 564
Portage, WI 53901

**Prentice-Hall International**
Englewood Cliffs, NJ 07632

**PRO-ED**
5341 Industrial Oaks Blvd.
Austin, TX 78735

**Psychological Assessment Resources**
P.O. Box 98
Odessa, FL 33556

**Psychological Corporation**
7500 Old Oak Blvd.
Cleveland, OH 44130

**Psychological Development
Publications**
P.O. Box 3198
Aspen, CO 81612

**Research Press**
2612 North Mattis Ave.
Champaign, IL 61820

**Salco Toys**
Route 1
Nerstrand, MN 55053

**Scholastic Testing Service**
480 Meyer Road
Bensenville, IL 60106

**Science Research Associates**
259 East Erie St.
Chicago, IL 60611

**S & S Arts and Crafts**
Colchester, CT 06415

**Simon & Schuster**
Rockefeller Center
630 5th Ave.
New York, NY 10020

**Slosson Educational Publications**
P.O. Box 280
East Aurora, NY 14052

**Software Reports**
Trade Service Publications, Inc.
10996 Torreyana Rd.
San Diego, CA 92121

**St. Martin's Press**
175 5th Ave.
New York, NY 10010

**Stoetling Company**
1350 South Kostner Ave.
Chicago, IL 60623

**Teachers College Press**
Columbia University
New York, NY 10027

**Technical Assistance Development
Systems (TADS)**
803 Churchill
Chapel Hill, NC 27514

**Toy Tinkers**
A.G. Spaulding & Brothers
807 Greenwood St.
Evanston, IL 60201

**Tree of Life Press**
1329 Northeast Second St.
P.O. Box 447
Gainesville, FL 32601

**Trend Enterprises, Inc.**
P.O. Box 64073
St. Paul, MN 55164

**University of Illinois Press**
Urbana, IL 61801

**University of Vermont**
Dr. T. Achenbach
Department of Psychiatry
1 South Prospect Street,
Burlington, VT 05405

**University of Washington Press**
P.O. Box 85569
Seattle, WA 98105

**Vort Corporation**
P.O. Box 11133
Palo Alto, CA 84338

**Western Psychological Services**
12031 Wilshire Blvd.
Los Angeles, CA 90025

# Author Index

# Subject Index